Outwitting Our Nerves

by Josephine A. Jackson and Helen M. Salisbury

TO

MARY PATTERSON MANLY

A LOVER OF TRUTH

"Your trouble is nervous. There is nothing we can cut out and there is nothing we can give medicine for." With these words a young college student was dismissed from one of our great diagnostic clinics.

The physician was right. In a nervous disorder there is nothing to cut out and there is nothing to give medicine for. Nevertheless there is something to be done,--something which is as definite and scientific as a prescription or a surgical operation.

Psychotherapy, which is treatment by the mental measures of psycho-analysis and re-education, is an established procedure in the scientific world to-day. Nervous disorders are now curable, as has been proved by the clinical results in scores of cases from civil life, under treatment by Freud, Janet, Prince, Sidis, DuBois, and others; and in thousands of cases of war neuroses as reported by Smith and Pear, Eder, MacCurdy, and other military observers. These army experts have shown that shell-shock in war is the same as nervousness in civil life and that both may be cured by psycho-analysis and re-education.

For more than a decade, in handling nervous cases, I have made use of the findings of recognized authorities on psychopathology. Truths have been applied in a special way, with the features of re-education so emphasized that my home has been called a psychological boarding-school. As the alumni have gone back to the game of life with no haunting memories of usual sanatorium methods, but with the equipment of a fuller self-knowledge and sense of power, they have sent back a call for some word that shall extend this helpful message to a larger circle.

There has come, too, a demand for a book which shall give accurate and up-to-date information to those physicians who are eager for light on the subject of nervous disorders, and especially for knowledge of the significant contributions of Sigmund Freud, but who are too busy to devote time to highly technical volumes outside their own specialties.

This need for a simple, comprehensive presentation of the Freudian principles I have attempted to meet in this primer of psychotherapy, providing enough of biological and psychological background to make them intelligible, and enough application and illustration to make them useful to the general practitioner or the average layman.

JOSEPHINE A. JACKSON.

Pasadena, California, 1921.

CONTENTS

OUTWITTING OUR NERVES

CHAPTER I

In Which Most of Us Plead Guilty to the Charge of "Nerves."

NERVOUS FOLK

WHO'S WHO

Whenever the subject of "nerves" is mentioned most people begin trying to prove an alibi. The man who is nervous and knows that he is nervous, realizes that he needs help, but the man who has as yet felt no lack of stability in himself is quite likely to be impatient with that whole class of people who are liable to nervous breakdown. It is therefore well to remind ourselves at once that the line between the so-called "normal" and the nervous is an exceedingly fine one. "Nervous invalids and well people are indistinguishable both in theory and in practice,"[1] and "after all we are most of us more or less neurasthenic."[2] The fact is that everybody is a possible neurotic.

[Footnote 1: Putnam: Human Motives, p. 117.]

[Footnote 2: DuBois: Physic Treatment of Nervous Disorders, p. 172.]

So, as we think about nervous folk and begin to recognize our friends and relatives in this class, it may be that some of us will unexpectedly find ourselves looking in the mirror. Some of our lifelong habits may turn out to be nervous tricks. At any rate, it behooves us to be careful about throwing stones, for most of us live in houses that are at least part glass.

THE EARMARKS

=Am I "Like Folks"?= Before we begin to talk about the real sufferer from "nerves," the nervous invalid, let us look for some of the earmarks that are often found on the supposedly well person. All of these signs are deviations from the normal and are sure indications of nervousness. The test question for each individual is this: "Am I 'like folks'?" To be normal and to be well is to be "like folks." Can the average man stand this or that? If he can, then you are not normal if you cannot. Do the people around you eat the thing that upsets you? If they do, ten chances to one your trouble is not a physical idiosyncrasy, but a nervous habit. In bodily matters, at least, it is a good thing to be one of the crowd.

Many people who would resent being called anything but normal--in general--are not at all loth to be thought "different," when it comes to particulars. Are there not many of us who are at small pains to hide the fact that we "didn't sleep a wink last night," or that we "can't stand" a ticking clock or a crowing rooster? We sometimes consider it a mark of distinction to have a delicate appetite and to have to choose our food with care. If we are frank with ourselves, some of us will have to admit that our own ailments seem interesting, while the other person's ills are "merely nervous" or imaginary or abnormal. After all, a good many of us will have to plead guilty to the charge of nervousness.

We have only to read the endless advertisements of cathartics and "internal baths," or to check up the quantity of laxatives sold at any drug store, to realize the wide-spread bondage to that great bugaboo constipation. He who is constipated can hardly prove an alibi to "nerves." Then there are the school-teachers and others who are worn out at the end of each year's work, hardly able to hold on until vacation; and the people who can't manage their tempers; and those who are upset over trifles; and those who are dissatisfied with life. To a certain degree, at least, all of these are nervous persons. The list grows.

=Half-Power Engines.= These people are all supposed to be well. They keep going--by fits and starts--and as they are used to running on three cylinders, with frequent stops for repairs, they accept this rate of living as a matter of course, never realizing that they might be sixty horse-power engines, instead of their little thirty or forty. For this large and neglected class of people psychotherapy has a stimulating message, and for them many of the following pages have been written.

=The Real Sufferers.= These so-called normal people are merely on the fringe of nervousness, on the border line between normality and disease. Beyond them there exists a great company of those whose lives have been literally wrecked by "nerves." Their work interrupted or given up for good, their minds harassed by doubts and fears, their bodies incapacitated, they crowd the sanatoria and the health resorts in a vain search for health. From New England to Florida they seek, and on to Colorado and California, and perhaps to Hawaii and the Orient, thinking by rest and change to pull themselves together and become whole again. There are thousands of these people--lawyers, preachers, teachers, mothers, social workers, business and professional folk of all sorts, the kind of persons the world needs most--laid off for months or years of treatment, on account of some kind of nervous disorder.

=Various Types of Nervousness.= The psychoneuroses are of many forms.[3] To some people "nerves" means nervous prostration, breakdown, fatigue, weakness, insomnia, the blues, upset stomach, or unsteady heart,--all signs of so-called neurasthenia or nerve-weakness. To others the word "nerves" calls up memories of strange, emotional storms that seem to rise out of nowhere, to sweep the sky clear of everything else, and to pass as they came, leaving the victim and the family equally mystified as to their meaning. These strange alterations of personality are but one manifestation of hysteria, that myriad-faced disorder which is able to mimic so successfully the symptoms of almost every known disease, from tumors and fevers to paralysis and blindness.

[Footnote 3: The technical term for nervousness is _psycho-neurosis_--disease of the psyche. There are certain "real neuroses" such as paralysis and spinal-cord disease, which involve an organic impairment of nerve-tissue. However, as this book deals only with psychic disturbance, we shall, throughout, use the term neuroses and _psycho-neuroses_ indiscriminately, to denote nervous or functional disorders.]

To still other people nervous trouble means fear,--just terrible fear without object or meaning or reason (anxiety neuroses); or a definite fear of some harmless object (phobia); or a strange, persistent, recurrent idea, quite foreign to the personality and beyond the reach of reason (obsession); or an insistent desire to perform some absurd act (compulsion); or perhaps, a deadly and pall-like depression (the blues).

As a matter of fact, the neuroses include all these varieties, and various shades and combinations of each. There are, however, certain mental characteristics which recur with surprising regularity in most of the various phases--dissatisfaction, lack of confidence, a sense of being alone and shut in to oneself, doubt, anxiety, fear, worry, self-depreciation, lack of interest in outside affairs, pessimism, fixed belief in one's powerlessness, along whatever line it may be.

Underneath all these differing forms of nervousness are the same mechanisms and the same kind of difficulty. To understand one is to understand all, and to understand normal people as well; for in the last analysis we are one and all built on the same lines and governed by the same laws. The only difference is, that, as Jung says, "the nervous person falls ill of the conflicts with which the well person battles successfully."

SUMMARY

Since at least seventy-five per cent. of all the people who apply to physicians for help are nervous patients; and since these thousands of patients are not among the mental incompetents, but are as a rule among the highly organized, conscientious folk who have most to contribute to the leadership of the world, it is obviously of vital importance to society that its citizens should be taught how to solve their inner conflicts and keep well. In this strategic period of reconstruction, the world that is being remodeled cannot afford to lose one leader because of an unnecessary breakdown.

There is greater need than ever for people who can keep at their tasks without long enforced rests; people who can think deeply and continuously without brain-fag; people who can concentrate all their powers on the work in hand without wasting time or energy on unnecessary aches and pains; people whose bodies are kept up to the top notch of vitality by well-digested food, well-slept sleep, well-forgotten fatigue, and well-used reserve energy. That such a state of affairs is no Utopian dream, but is merely a matter of knowing how, will appear more clearly in later chapters.

CHAPTER II

In which we learn what "nerves" are not, and get a hint of what they are

THE DRAMA OF NERVES

AN EXPLODED THEORY

="Nerves" not Nerves.= Pick up any newspaper, turn over a few pages, and you will be sure to come to an advertisement something like this:

Tired man, your nerves are sick! They need rest and a tonic to restore their worn-out depleted cells!

No wonder people have believed this kind of thing. It has been dinned into their ears for many years. They have read it with their breakfast coffee and gazed at it in the street cars and even heard it from their family physicians, until it has become part and parcel of their thinking; yet all the time the fundamental idea has been false, and now, at last, the theory is exploded.

So far as the modern laboratory can discover, the nerves of the most confirmed neurotic are perfectly healthy. They are not starved, nor depleted, nor exhausted; the fat-sheath is not wanting, there is no inflammation, there is nothing lacking in the cell itself, and there is no accumulation of fatigue products. Paradoxical as it may sound, there is nothing the matter with a nervous person's nerves. The faithful messengers have borne the blame for so long that their name has gotten itself woven into the very language as symbolic of disease. When we speak of nervous prostration, neurasthenia, neuroses, nervousness, and "nerves" we mean that body and mind are behaving badly because of functional disorder. These terms are good enough as figures of speech, so long as we are not fooled by them; but accepting them in their literal sense has been a costly procedure.

Thanks to the investigations of physiologist and psychologist, usually combined in the person of a physician, "nervousness" has been found to be not an organic disease but a functional one. This is a very important distinction, for an organic disease implies impairment of the tissues of the organ, while a functional disorder means only a disturbance of its action. In a purely nervous disorder there seems to be no trouble with what the nerves and organs are, but only with what they do; it is behavior and not tissue that is at fault. Of course, in real life, things are seldom as clear-cut as they are in books, and so it happens that often there is a combination of organic and functional disease that is puzzling even to a skilled diagnostician. The first essential is a diagnosis as to whether it be an organic disease, with accompanying nervous symptoms, or a functional disturbance complicated by some minor organic trouble. If the main cause is organic, only physical means can cure it, but if the trouble is functional, no amount of medicine or surgery, diet or rest, will touch it; yet the symptoms are so similar and the dividing line is so elusive, that great skill is sometimes required to determine whether a given symptom points to a disturbance of physical tissue or only to behavior.

If the physician is sometimes fooled, how much more the sufferer himself! Nausea from a healthy stomach is just as sickening as nausea from a diseased one. A fainting-spell is equally uncomfortable, whether it come from an impaired heart or simply from one that is behaving badly for the moment. It must be remembered that in functional nervousness the trouble is very real. The organs are really "acting up." Sometimes it is the brain that misbehaves instead of the stomach or heart. In that case it often reports all kinds of pains that have no origin outside of the brain. Pain, of course, is perceived only by the brain. Cut the telegraph wire, the nerve, and no amount of injury to the finger can cause pain. It is equally true that a misbehaving brain can report sensations that have no external cause, that have not come in through the regular channel along the nerve. The pain feels just the same, is every bit as uncomfortable as though its cause were external.

Sometimes, instead of reporting false pains, the brain misbehaves in other ways. It seems to lose its power to decide, to concentrate, or to remember. Then the patient is almost sure to fancy himself going insane. But insanity is a physical disease, implying changes or toxins in the brain cells. Functional disorders tell another story. Their cause is different, even though the picture they present is often a close copy of an organic disease.

=Distorted Pictures.= It should not be thought, however, that the symptoms of functional and organic troubles are identical. Hysteria and neurasthenia closely simulate every imaginable physical disease, but they do not exactly parallel any one of them. It may take a skilled eye to discover the differences, but differences there are. Functional troubles usually show a near-picture of organic disease, with just enough contradictory or inconsistent features to furnish a clue as to their real nature. For this reason it is important that the treatment of the disease be solely the province of the physician; for only the carefully trained in all the requirements of diagnosis can differentiate the pseudo from the real, the innocuous from the disastrous.

False or nervous neuritis may feel like real neuritis (the result of poisons in the blood), but it gives itself away when it localizes itself in parts of the body where there is no nerve trunk. The exhaustion of neurasthenia sometimes seems extreme enough to be the result of a dangerous physical condition; but when this exhaustion disappears as if by magic under the proper kind of treatment, we know that the trouble cannot be in the body. Let it be said, then, with all the emphasis we can command, "nerves" are not physical. Laboratory investigation, contradictory symptoms, and response to treatment all bear witness to this fact. Whatever symptoms of disturbance there may be in pure nervousness, the nerves and organs can in no way be shown to be diseased.

THE POSITIVE SIDE

="Nerves" not Imaginary.= "But," some one says, "how can healthy organs misbehave in this way? Something must be wrong. There must be some cause. If 'nerves' are not physical, what are they? They surely can't be imaginary." Most emphatically, they are real; nothing could be more maddening than to have some one suggest that our troubles are "mere imagination." No wonder such theories have been more popular with the patient's family than with the patient himself. Many years ago a physician put the whole truth into a few words: "The patient says, 'I cannot'; his friends say, 'He will not'; the doctor says, 'He cannot will.'" He tries, but in the circumstances he really cannot.

=The Man behind the Body.= The trouble is real; the organs do "act up"; the nerves do carry the wrong messages. But the nerves are merely telegraph wires. They are not responsible for the messages that are given them to carry. Behind the wires is the operator, the man higher up, and upon him the responsibility falls. In functional troubles the body is working in a perfectly normal way, considering the perverted conditions. It is doing its work well, doing just what it is told, obeying its master. The troubles are not with the bodily machine but with the master. The man behind the body is in trouble and he really has no way of showing his pain except through his body. The trouble in nervous disorders is in the personality, the soul, the realm of ideas, and that is not your body, but you. Loss of appetite may mean either that the powers of the physical organism are busily engaged in combating some poison circulating in the blood, or that the ego is "up against" conditions for which it has "no stomach." Paralysis may be due to a hemorrhage into the brain tissues from a diseased blood vessel, or it may symbolize a sense of inadequacy and defeat. Exaggerated exhaustion, halting feet, stammering tongue, may give evidence of a disturbed ego rather than of a diseased brain.

=All Body and no Mind.= At last we have begun to realize what we ought to have known all along,--that the body is not the whole man. The medical world for a long time has been in danger of forgetting or ignoring psychic suffering, while it has devoted itself to the treatment of physical disease.

By way of condoning this fault it must be recognized that the five years of medical school have been all too short to learn what is needed of physiology and anatomy, histology, bacteriology, and the various other physical sciences. But at last the medical schools are realizing that they have been sending their graduates out only half-prepared--conversant with only one half of a patient, leaving them to fend for themselves in discovering the ways of the other half. Many an M.D. has gone a long way in this exploration. Native common sense, intuition, and careful study have enabled him to go beyond what he had learned in his text-books. But in the best universities the present-day student of medicine is now being given an insight into the ways of man as a whole-- mind as well as body. The movement can hardly proceed too rapidly, and when it has had time to reach its goal, the day of the long-term sentence to nervousness will be past.

In the meanwhile most physicians, lacking such knowledge and with the eye fixed largely on the body, have been pumping out the stomach, prescribing lengthy rest-cures, trying massage, diet, electricity, and surgical operations, in a vain attempt to cure a disease of the personality. Physical measures have been given a good trial, but few would contend that they have succeeded. Sometimes the patient has recovered--in time--but often, apparently, despite the treatment rather than because of it. Sometimes, in the hands of a man like Dr. S. Weir Mitchell, results seem good, until we realize that the same measures are ineffective when tried by other men, and that, after all, what has counted most has been the personality of the physician rather than his physical treatment.

No wonder that most doctors have disliked nervous cases. To a man trained in all the exactness of the physical sciences, the apparent lawlessness and irresponsibility of the psychic side of the personality is especially repugnant. He is impatient of what he fails to comprehend.

=All Mind and no Body.= This unsympathetic attitude, often only half conscious on the part of the regular practitioners, has led many thousands of people to follow will-o'-the-wisp cults, which pay no attention to the findings of science, but which emphasize a realization of man's spiritual nature. Many of these cults, founded largely on untruth or half-falsehood, have succeeded in cases where careful science has failed. Despite fearful blunders and execrable lack of discrimination in attempting to cure all the ills that flesh is heir to by methods that apply only to functional troubles, ignorant enthusiasts and quacks have sometimes cured nervous troubles where the conscientious medical man has had to acknowledge defeat.

=The Whole Man.= But thinking people are not willing to desert science for cults that ignore the existence of these physical bodies. If they have found it unsatisfactory to be treated as if they were all body, they have also been unwilling to be treated as if they were all mind. They have been in a dilemma between two half-truths, even if they have not realized the dilemma. It has remained for modern psychotherapy to strike the balance--to treat the whole man. Solidly planted on the rock of the physical sciences, with its laboratories, physiological and psychological, and with a long record of investigation and treatment of pathological cases, it resembles the mind cure of earlier days or the assertions of Christian Science about as much as modern medicine resembles the old bloodletting, leeching practices of our forefathers.

For the last quarter-century there have been scattered groups of physicians,--brilliant, patient pioneers,--who, recognizing man as spirit inhabiting body, have explored the realm of man's mind and charted its paths. These pioneers, beginning with Charcot, have been men of acknowledged scientific training and spirit, whose word must be respected and whose success in treating functional troubles stands out in sharp contrast to the fumblings of the average practitioner in this field. The results of their work have been positive, not negative. They have not merely asserted that nervous disorders are not physical; they have discovered what the trouble is and have found it to be discoverable and removable in almost every case, provided only that the right method is used.

=Ourselves and Our Bodies.= If the statement that "nervous troubles are neither physical nor imaginary but a disease of the personality," sounds rather mystifying to the average person, it is only because the average person is not very conversant with his own inner life. We shall hope, later on, to find some definite guide-posts and landmarks which will help us feel more at home in this fascinating realm. At present, we are not attempting anything more than a suggestion of the itinerary which we shall follow. A book on physical hygiene can presuppose at least a rudimentary knowledge of heart and lungs and circulation, but a book on mental hygiene must begin at the beginning, and even before the beginning must clear away misconceptions and make clear certain fundamental principles. But the gist of the whole matter is this: in a neurosis, certain forces of the personality--instincts and their accompanying emotions--which ought to work harmoniously, having become tangled up with some erroneous ideas, have lost their power of co 鰌 eration and are working at cross purposes, leaving the individual mis-adapted to his environment, the prey of all sorts of mental and physical disturbances.

The fact that the cause is mental while the result is often physical, should cause no surprise. In the physiological realm we are used to the idea that cause and effect are often widely separated. A headache may be caused by faulty eyes, or it may result from trouble in the intestines. In the same way, we should not be too much surprised if the cause of nervous troubles is found to be even more remote, provided there is some connecting link between cause and effect. The difficulty in this case is the apparent gulf between the realm of the spirit and the realm of the body. It is hard to see how an intangible thing like a thought can produce a pain in the arm or nausea in the stomach. Philosophers are still arguing concerning the nature of the relation between mind and body, but no one denies that the closest relation does exist. Every year science is learning that ideas count and that they count physically, as well as spiritually.

=Such Stuff as "Nerves" are Made Of.= Dr. Tom A. Williams in the little composite volume "Psychotherapeutics" says that the neuroses are based not on inherently weak nervous constitutions but on ignorance and on false ideas. What, then, are some of these erroneous ideas, these misconceptions, that cause so much trouble? We shall want to examine them more carefully in later chapters, but we might glance now at a few examples of these popular bugaboos that need to be slain by the sword of cold, hard fact.

=Popular Misconceptions about the Body.=

1 "Eight hours' sleep is essential to health. All insomnia is dangerous and is incompatible with health. Nervous insomnia leads to shattered nerves and ultimately to insanity."

2 "Overwork leads to nervous breakdown. Fatigue accumulates from day to day and necessitates a long rest for recuperation."

3 "A carefully planned diet is essential to health, especially for the nervous person. A variety of food, eaten at the same time, is harmful. Acid and milk-- for example, oranges and milk--are difficult to digest. Sour stomach is a sign of indigestion."

4 "Modern life is so strenuous that our nerves cannot stand the strain."

5 "Brain work is very fatiguing. It causes brain-fag and exhaustion."

6 "Constipation is at the root of most physical ailments and Is caused by eating the wrong kind of food."

Some of these misconceptions are household words and are so all but universally believed that the thought that they can be challenged is enough to bewilder one. However, it is ideas like this that furnish the material out of which many a nervous trouble is made. Based on a half-knowledge of the human body, on logical conclusions from faulty premises, on hastily swallowed notions passed on from one person to another, they tend by the very power of an idea to work themselves out to fulfilment.

THE POWER BEHIND IDEAS

=Ideas Count.= Ideas are not the lifeless things they may appear. They are not merely intellectual property that can be locked up and ignored at will, nor are they playthings that can be taken up or discarded according to the caprice of the moment. Ideas work themselves into the very fiber of our being. They are part of us and they do things. If they are true, in line with things as they are, they do things that are for our good, but if they are false, we often discover that they have an altogether unsuspected power for harm and are capable of astonishing results, results which have no apparent relation to the ideas responsible for them and which are, therefore, laid to physical causes. Thinking straight, then, becomes a hygienic as well as a moral duty.

=Ideas and Emotions.= Ideas do not depend upon themselves for their driving-power. Life is not a cold intellectual process; it is a vivid experience, vibrant with feeling and emotion. It therefore happens that the experiences of life tend to bring ideas and emotions together and when an idea and an emotion get linked up together, they tend to stay together, especially if the emotion be intense or the experience is often repeated.

The word emotion means outgoing motion, discharging force. This force is like live steam. An emotion is the driving part of an instinct. It is the dynamic force, the electric current which supplies the power for every thought and every action of a human life.

Man is not a passive creature. The words that describe him are not passive words. Indeed, it is almost impossible to think about man at all except in terms of desire, impulse, purpose, action, energy. There are three things that may be done with energy: First, it may be frittered away, allowed to leak, to escape. Secondly, it may be locked up; this results usually in an explosion, a finding of destructive outlets. Finally, it may be harnessed, controlled, used in beneficent ways. Health and happiness depend upon which one of the three courses is taken.

CHARACTER AND HEALTH

Evidently, it is highly important to have a working knowledge of these emotions and instincts; important to know enough about them and their purpose to handle them rightly if they do not spontaneously work together for our best character and health. The problems of character and the problems of health so overlap that it is impossible to write a book about nervous disorders which does not at the same time deal with the principles of character-formation. The laws and mechanisms which govern the everyday life of the normal person are the same laws and mechanisms which make the nervous person ill. As Boris Sidis puts it, "The pathological is the normal out of place." The person who is master of himself, working together as a harmonious whole, is stronger in every way than the person whose forces are divided. Given a little self-knowledge, the nervous invalid often becomes one of the most successful members of society,--to use the word successful in the best sense.

=It Pays to Know.= To be educated is to have the right idea and the right emotion in the right place. To be sure, some people have so well learned the secret of poise that they do not have to study the why nor the how. Intuition often far outruns knowledge. It would be foolish indeed to suggest that only the person versed in psychological lore is skilled in the art of living. Psychology is not life; it can make no claim to furnish the motive nor the power for successful living, for it is not faith, nor hope, nor love; but it tries to point the way and to help us fulfil conditions. There is no more reason why the average man should be unaware of the instincts or the subconscious mind, than that he should be ignorant of germs or of the need of fresh air.

If it be argued that character and health are both inherently by-products of self-forgetful service, rather than of painstaking thought, we answer that this is true, but that there can be no self-forgetting when things have gone too far wrong. At such times it pays to look in, if we can do it intelligently, in order that we may the sooner get our eyes off ourselves and look out. The pursuit of self-knowledge is not a pleasurable pastime but simply a valuable means to an end.

KNOWING OUR MACHINE

=Counting on Ourselves.= Knowing our machine makes us better able to handle it. For, after all, each of us is, in many ways, very like a piece of marvelous and complicated machinery. For one thing, our minds, as well as our bodies, are subject to uniform laws upon which we can depend. We are not creatures of chaos; under certain conditions we can count on ourselves. Freedom does not mean freedom from the reign of law. It means that, to a certain extent, we can make use of the laws. Psychic laws are as susceptible to investigation, verification, and use as are any laws in the physical world. Each person is so much the center of his own life that it is very easy for him to fall into the way of thinking that he is different from all the rest of the world.

It is a healthful experience for him to realize that every person he meets is made on the same principles, impelled by the same forces, and fighting much the same fight. Since the laws of the mental world are uniform, we can count on them as aids toward understanding other people and understanding ourselves.

="Intelligent Scrutiny versus Morbid Introspection."= It helps wonderfully to be able to look at ourselves in an objective, impersonal way. We are likely to be overcome by emotion, or swept by vague longings which seem to have no meaning and which, just because they are bound up so closely with our own ego, are not looked at but are merely felt. Unknown forces are within us, pulling us this way and that, until sometimes we who should be masters are helpless slaves. One great help toward mastery and one long step toward serenity is a working-knowledge of the causes and an impersonal interest in the phenomena going on within. Introspection is a morbid, emotional fixation on self, until it takes on this quality of objectivity. What Cabot calls the "sin of impersonality" is a grievous sin when directed toward another person, but most of us could stand a good deal of ingrowing impersonality without any harm.

The fact that the human machine can run itself without a hitch in the majority of cases is witness to its inherent tendency toward health. People were living and living well through all the centuries before the science of psychology was formulated. But not with all people do things run so smoothly. There were demoniacs in Bible times and neurotics in the Middle Ages, as there are nervous invalids and half-well people to-day. Psychology has a real contribution to make, and in recent years its lessons have been put into language which the average man can understand.

Psychology is not merely interested in abstract terms with long names. It is no longer absorbed merely in states of consciousness taken separately and analyzed abstractly. The newer functional psychology is increasingly interested in the study of real persons, their purposes and interests, what they feel and value, and how they may learn to realize their highest aspirations. It is about ordinary people, as they think and act, in the kitchen, on the street cars, at the bargain-counter, people in crowds and alone, mothers and their babies, little children at play, young girls with their lovers, and all the rest of human life. It is the science of you, and as such it can hardly help being interesting.

While psychology deals with such topics as the subconscious mind, the instincts, the laws of habit, and association of ideas and suggestion, it is after all not so much an academic as a practical question. These forces govern the thought you are thinking at this moment, the way you will feel a half-hour from now, the mood you will be in to-morrow, the friends you will make and the profession you will choose, besides having a large share in the health or ill-health of your body in the meantime.

SUMMARY

Perhaps it would be well before going farther to summarize what we have been saying. Here in a nutshell is the kernel of the subject:

Disease may be caused by physical or by psychic forces. A "nervous" disorder is not a physical but a psychic disease. It is caused not by lack of energy but by misdirected energy; not by overwork or nerve-depletion, but by misconception, emotional conflict, repressed instincts, and buried memories. Seventy-five per cent. of all cases of ill-health are due to psychic causes, to disjointed thinking rather than to a disjointed spine. Wherefore, let us learn to think right.

In outline form, the trouble in a neurosis may be stated something like this:

Lack of adaptation to the social environment--caused by Lack of harmony within the personality--caused by Misdirected energy--caused by Inappropriate emotions--caused by Wrong ideas or ignorance.

Working backward, the cure naturally would be:

Right ideas--resulting in Appropriate emotions--resulting in Redirected energy--resulting in Harmony--resulting in Readjustment to the environment.

If the reader is beginning to feel somewhat bewildered by these general statements, let him take heart. So far we have tried merely to suggest the outline of the whole problem, but we shall in the future be more specific. Nervous troubles, which seem so simple, are really involved with the whole mechanism of mental life and can in no way be understood except as these mechanisms are understood. We have hinted at some of the causes of "nerves," but we cannot give a real explanation until we explain the forces behind them. These forces may at first seem a bit abstract, or a bit remote from the main theme, but each is essential to the story of nerves and to the understanding of the more practical chapters in Part III.

As in a Bernard Shaw play, the preface may be the most important part of this "drama of nerves." Nor is the figure too far-fetched, because, strange as it may seem, every neurosis is in essence a drama. It has its conflict, its villain, and its victim, its love-story, its practical joke, its climax, and its denouement. Sometimes the play goes on forever with no solution, but sometimes psychotherapy steps in as the fairy god-mother, to release the victim, outwit the villain, and bring about the live-happily-ever-after ending.

PART II: "HOW THE WHEELS GO ROUND"

CHAPTER III

In which we find a goodly inheritance THE STORY OF THE INSTINCTS

EACH IN HIS OWN TONGUE

A fire mist and a planet, A crystal and a cell, A jelly-fish and a saurian, And caves where cavemen dwell; Then a sense of law and beauty, And a face turned from the clod; Some call it evolution And others call it God.[4]

If we begin at the beginning, we have to go back a long way to get our start, for the roots of our family tree reach back over millions of years. "In the beginning--God." These first words of the book of Genesis must be, in spirit at least, the first words of any discussion of life. We know now, however, that when God made man, He did not complete His masterpiece at one sitting, but instead devised a plan by which the onward urge within and the environment without should act and interact until from countless adaptations a human being was made.

[Footnote 4: William Herbert Carruth.]

As the late Dr. Putnam of Harvard University says, "We stand as the representative of a Creative Energy that expressed itself first in far simpler forms of life and finally in the form of human instincts."[5] And again: "The choices and decisions of the organisms whose lives prepared the way through eons of time for ours, present themselves to us as instincts."[6]

[Footnote 5: Putnam: Human Motives, p. 32.]

[Footnote 6: Putnam: Human Motives, p. 18.]

INTRODUCING THE INSTINCTS

=Back of Our Dispositions.= What is it that makes the baby jump at a noise? What energizes a man when you tell him he is a liar? What makes a young girl blush when you look at her, or a youth begin to take pains with his necktie? What makes men go to war or build tunnels or found hospitals or make love or save for a home? What makes a woman slave for her children, or give her life for them if need be? "Instinct" you say, and rightly. Back of every one of these well-known human tendencies is a specific instinct or group of instincts. The story of the life of man and the story of the mind of man must begin with the instincts. Indeed, any intelligent approach to human life, whether it be that of the mother, the teacher, the preacher, the social worker or the neurologist, leads back inevitably to the instincts as the starting-point of understanding. But what is instinct?

We are apt to be a bit hazy on that point, as we are on any fundamental thing with which we intimately live. We reckon on these instinctive tendencies every hour of the day, but as we are not used to labeling them, it may help in the very beginning of our discussion to have a list before our eyes. Here, then, is a list of the fundamental tendencies of the human race and the emotions which drive them to fulfilment.

THE SPECIFIC INSTINCTS AND THEIR EMOTIONS (AFTER MCDOUGALL)

Instinct Emotion Nutritive Instinct Hunger Flight Fear Repulsion Disgust Curiosity Wonder Self-assertion Positive Self-feeling (Elation) Self-abasement Negative Self-feeling (Subjection) Gregariousness Emotion unnamed Acquisition Love of Possession Construction Emotion unnamed Pugnacity

Anger Reproductive Instinct Emotion unnamed Parental Instinct Tender Emotion

These are the fundamental tendencies or dispositions with which every human being is endowed as he comes into the world. Differing in degree in different individuals, they unite in varying proportions to form various kinds of dispositions, but are in greater or less degree the common property of us all.

There flows through the life of every creature a steady stream of energy. Scientists have not been able to decide on a descriptive term for this all-important life-force. It has been variously called "libido," "vital impulse" or "闹 an vital," "the spirit of life," "horm?" and "creative energy." The chief business of this life-force seems to be the preservation and development of the individual and the preservation and development of the race. In the service of these two needs have grown up these habit-reactions which we call instincts. The first ten of our list belong under the heading of self-preservation and the last two under that of race-preservation. As hunger is the most urgent representative of the self-preservative group, and as reproduction and parental care make up the race-preservative group, some scientists refer all impulses to the two great instincts of nutrition and sex, using these words in the widest sense. However, it will be useful for our purpose to follow McDougall's classification and to examine individually the various tendencies of the two groups.

=In Debt to Our Ancestors.= An instinct is the result of the experience of the race, laid in brain and nerve-cells ready for use. It is a gift from our ancestors, an inheritance from the education of the age-long line of beings who have gone before. In the struggle for existence, it has been necessary for the members of the race to feed themselves, to run away from danger, to fight, to herd together, to reproduce themselves, to care for their young, and to do various other things which make for the well-being or preservation of the race. The individuals that did these things at the right time survived and passed on to their offspring an inherited tendency to this kind of reaction. McDougall defines an instinct as "an inherited or innate psycho-physical disposition which determines its possessor to perceive or pay attention to objects of a certain class, to experience an emotional excitement of a particular quality upon perceiving such an object, and to act in regard to it in a particular manner, or at least to experience an impulse to such action." This is just what an instinct is,--an inherited disposition to notice, to feel, and to want to act in certain ways in certain situations. It is the something which makes us act when we cannot explain why, the something that goes deeper than reason, and that links us to all other human beings,--those who live to-day and those who have gone before.

It is true that East is East and West is West, but the two do meet in the common foundation of our human nature. The likeness between men and between races is far greater and far more fundamental than the differences can ever be.

=Firing Up the Engine.= Purpose is writ large across the face of an instinct, and that purpose is always toward action. Whenever a situation arises which demands instantaneous action, the instinct is the means of securing it. Planted within the creature is a tendency which makes it perceive and feel and act in the appropriate way. It will be noticed that there are three distinct parts to the process, corresponding to intellect, emotion, will. The initial intellectual part makes us sensitive to certain situations, makes us recognize an object as meaningful and significant, and waves the flag for the emotion; the emotion fires up the engine, pulls the levers all over the body that release its energy and get it ready for action, and pushes the button that calls Into the mind an intense, almost irresistible desire or impulse to act. Once aroused, the emotion and the impulse are not to be changed. In man or beast, in savage or savant, the intense feeling, the marked bodily changes, and the yearning for action are identical and unchangeable. The brakes can be put on and the action suppressed, but in that case the end of the whole process is defeated. Could anything be plainer than that an instinct and its emotion were never intended to be aroused except in situations in which their characteristic action is to be desired? An emotion is the hot part of an instinct and exists solely for securing action. If all signs of the emotion are to be suppressed, all expression denied, why the emotion?

But although the emotion and the impulse, once aroused, are beyond control, there is yet one part of the instinct that is meant to be controlled. The initial or receptive portion, that which notices a situation, recognizes it as significant, and sends in the signal for action, can be trained to discrimination. This is where reason comes in. If the situation calls for flight, fear is in order;

if it calls for fight, anger is in order; if it calls for examination, wonder is in order; but if it calls for none of these things, reason should show some discrimination and refuse to call up the emotion.

=The Right of Way.= There is a law that comes to the aid of reason in this dilemma and that is the "law of the common path."[7] By this is meant that man is capable of but one intense emotion at a time. No one can imagine himself strenuously making love while he is shaken by an agony of fear, or ravenously eating while he is in a passion of rage. The stronger emotion gets the right of way, obtains control of mental and bodily machinery, and leaves no room for opposite states. If the two emotions are not antagonistic, they may blend together to form a compound emotion, but if in the nature of the case such a blending is impossible, the weaker is for the time being forgotten in the intensity of the stronger. "The expulsive power of a new affection" is not merely a happy phrase; it is a fact in every day life. The problem, then, resolves itself into ways of making the desirable emotion the stronger, of learning how to form the habit of giving it the head start and the right of way. In our chapter on "Choosing the Emotions," we shall find that much depends on building up the right kind of sentiments, or the permanent organization of instincts around ideas. However, we must first look more closely at the separate instincts to acquaint ourselves with the purpose and the ways of each, and to discover the nature of the forces with which we have to deal.

[Footnote 7: Sherrington: Integrative Action of the Nervous System.]

I THE SELF-PRESERVATIVE INSTINCTS

=Hunger.= Hunger is the most pressing desire of the egoistic or self-preserving impulse. The yearning for food and the impulse to seek and eat it are aroused organically within the body and are behind much of the activity of every type of life. As the impulse is so familiar, and its promptings are so little subject to psychic control, it seems unnecessary to do more than mention its importance.

=Flight and Fear.= All through the ages the race has been subject to injury. Species has been pitted against species, individual against individual. He who could fight hardest or run fastest has survived and passed his abilities on to his offspring. Not all could be strongest for fight, and many species have owed their existence to their ability to run and to know when to run. Thus it is that one of the strongest and most universal tendencies is the instinct for flight, and its emotion, fear. "Fear is the representation of injury and is born of the innumerable injuries which have been inflicted in the course of evolution."[8] Some babies are frightened if they are held too loosely, even though they have never known a fall. Some persons have an instinctive fear of cats, a left-over from the time when the race needed to flee from the tiger and others of the cat family. Almost every one, no matter in what state of culture, fears the unknown because the race before him has had to be afraid of that which was not familiar.

[Footnote 8: Crile: Origin and Nature of the Emotions.]

The emotion of fear is well known, but its purpose is not so often recognized. An emotion brings about internal changes, visceral changes they are called, which enable the organism to act on the emotion,--to accomplish its object. There is only so much energy available at a given moment, stored up in the brain cells, ready for use. In such an emergency as flight every ounce of energy is needed. The large muscles used in running must have a great supply of extra energy. The heart and lungs must be speeded up in order to provide oxygen and take care of extra waste products. The special senses of sight and hearing must be sensitized. Digestion and intestinal peristalsis must be stopped in order to save energy. No person could by conscious thought accomplish all these things. How, then, are they brought about?

=Internal Laboratories.= In the wonderful internal laboratory of the body there are little glands whose business it is to secrete chemicals for just these emergencies. When an object is sighted which arouses fear, the brain cells flash instantaneous messages over the body, among others to the supra-renal glands or adrenals, just over the kidneys, and to the thyroid gland in the neck. Instantly these glands pour forth adrenalin and thyroid secretion into the blood, and the body responds. Blood pressure rises; brain cells speed up; the liver pours forth glycogen, its ready-to-burn fuel; sweat-glands send forth cold perspiration in order to regulate temperature; blood is pumped out from stomach and intestines to the external muscles. As we have seen, the body as a whole can respond to just one stimulus at a time. The response to this stimulus has the right of way. The whole body is integrated, set for this one thing. When fear holds the switchboard no other messages are allowed on the line, and the creature is ready for flight.

But after flight comes concealment with the opposite bodily need, the need for absolute silence. This is why we sometimes get the opposite result. The heart seems to stop beating, the breath ceases, the limbs refuse to move, all because our ancestors needed to hide after they had run, and because we are in a very real way a part of them.

=Old-Fashioned Fear.= There is one passage from Dr. Crile's book which so admirably sums up these points that it seems worth while to insert it at length.

We fear not in our hearts alone, not in our brains alone, not in our viscera alone--fear influences every organ and tissue. Each organ or tissue is stimulated or inhibited according to its use or hindrance in the physical struggle for existence. By thus concentrating all or most of the nerve force on the nerve-muscular mechanism for defense, a greater physical power is developed. Hence it is that under the stimulus of fear animals are able to perform preternatural feats of strength. For the same reason, the exhaustion following fear will be increased as the powerful stimulus of fear drains the cup of nervous energy even though no visible action may result.... Perhaps the most striking difference between man and animals lies in the greater control which man has gained over his primitive instinctive reactions. As compared with the entire duration of organic evolution, man came down from his arboreal abode and assumed his new role of increased domination over the physical world but a moment ago. And now, though sitting at his desk in command of the complicated machinery of civilization, when he fears a business catastrophe his fear is manifested in the terms of his ancestral physical battle in the struggle for existence. He cannot fear intellectually, he cannot fear dispassionately, he fears with all his organs, and the same organs are stimulated and inhibited as if, instead of its being a battle of credit, or position, or of honor, it were a physical battle with teeth and claws.... Nature has but one means of response to fear, and whatever its cause the phenomena are always the same--always physical.[9]

[Footnote 9: Crile: Origin and Nature of the Emotions, p. 60 ff.]

* * * * *

The moral is as plain as day: Learn to call up fear only when speedy legs are needed, not a cool head or a comfortable digestion. Fear is a costly proceeding, an emergency measure like a fire-alarm, to be used only when the occasion is urgent enough to demand it. How often it is misused and how large a part it plays in nervous symptoms, both mental and physical, will appear more clearly in later chapters.

=Repulsion and Disgust.= Akin to the instinct of flight is that of repulsion, which impels us, instead of fleeing, to thrust the object away. It leads us to reject from the mouth noxious and disgusting objects and to shrink from slimy, creepy creatures, and has of course been highly useful in protecting the race from poisons and snakes. It still operates in the tendency to put away from us those things, mental or physical, toward which we feel aversion or disgust. Recent psychological discoveries have revealed how largely a neurosis consists in putting away from us--out of consciousness,--whatever we do not wish to recognize, and so it happens that disgust plays an unexpected part in nervous disorders.

=Curiosity and Wonder.= Fortunately for the race, it has not had to wait until different features of the environment prove to be helpful or harmful. There is an instinct which urges forward to exploration and discovery and which enables the creature not only to adapt itself to the environment but to learn how to adapt the environment to itself. This is the instinct of curiosity. It is the impulse back of all advance in science, religion, and intellectual achievement of every kind, and is sometimes called "intellectual feeling."

=Self-Assertion.= It goes almost without saying that one of the strongest and most important impulses of mankind is the instinct of self-assertion; it often gets us into trouble, but it is also behind every effort toward developed character. At its lowest level self-assertion manifests itself in the strutting of the peacock, the prancing of the horse, and the "See how big I am," of the small boy. At its highest level, when combined with self-consciousness and the moral sentiments acquired from society and developed into the self-regarding sentiment, it is responsible for most of our ideas of right, our conception of what is and what is not compatible with our self-respect.

=Self-Abasement.= Self-assertion is aroused primarily by the presence of others and especially of those to whom we feel in any way superior, but when the presence of others makes us feel small, when we want to hide or keep in the background, we are being moved by the opposite instinct of self-abasement and negative self-feeling. It may be either the real or the fancied superiority of the spectators that arouses this feeling,--their wisdom or strength, beauty or good clothes. Sometimes, as in stage-fright, it is their numerical superiority. Bashfulness is the struggle between the two self-instincts, assertion and abasement. Our impulse for self-display urges us on to make a good impression, while our feeling of inferiority impels us to get away unnoticed. Hence the struggle and the painful emotion.

=Gregariousness.= Man has been called a gregarious animal. That is, like the animals, he likes to run with his kind, and feels a pronounced aversion to prolonged isolation. It is this "herd-instinct," too, which makes man so extremely sensitive to the opinions of the society in which he lives. Because of this impulse to go with the crowd, ideas received through education are accepted as imperative and are backed up by all the force of the instinct of self-regard. When the teachings of society happen to run counter to the laws of our being, the possibilities of conflict are indeed great.[10]

[Footnote 10: For a thorough discussion of the importance of this instinct, see Trotter's Instincts of the Herd in Peace and War.]

=Acquisition.= Another fundamental disposition in both animals and men is the instinct for possession, the instinct whose function it is to provide for future needs. Squirrels and birds lay up nuts for the winter; the dog hides his bone where only he can find it. Children love to have things for their "very own," and almost invariably go through the hoarding stage in which stamps or samples or bits of string are hoarded for the sake of possession, quite apart from their usefulness or value. Much of the training of children consists in learning what is "mine" and what is "thine," and respect for the property of others can develop only out of a sense of one's own property rights.

=Construction.= There is an innate satisfaction in making something,--from a doll-dress to a poem,--and this satisfaction rests on the impulse to construct, to fashion something with our own hands or our own brain. The emotion accompanying this instinct is too indefinite to have a name but it is nevertheless a real one and plays a large part in the sense of power which results from the satisfaction of good work well done. Later it will be seen how closely related is this impulse to the creative instinct of reproduction and how useful it can be in drawing off the surplus energy of that much denied instinct.

=Pugnacity and Anger.= What is it that makes us angry? A little thought will convince us that the thing which arouses our fury is not the sight of any special object, but the blocking of any one of the other instincts. Watch any animal at bay when its chance for flight has gone. The timidest one will turn and fight with every sign of fury. Watch a mother when her young are threatened,--bear, or cat or lion or human. Fear has no place then. It is entirely displaced by anger over the balking of the maternal instinct of protection. Strictly speaking, pugnacity belongs among the instincts neither of self-preservation nor of race-preservation, but is a special device for reinforcing both groups.

As fear supplies the energy for running, so anger fits us for fight,--and for nothing but fight. The mechanism is almost identical with that of fear. Brain and liver, adrenals and thyroid are the means, but the emotion presses the button and releases the energy, stopping all digestion and energizing all combat-muscles. The blood is flooded with fuel and with substances which, if not used, are harmful to the body. We were never meant to be angry without fighting. The habit of self-control has its distinct advantages, but it is hard on the body, which was patterned before self-control came into fashion. The wise man, once he is aroused, lets off steam at the woodpile or on a long, vigorous walk. He probably does not say to himself that he is a motor animal integrated for fight and that he must get rid of glycogen and adrenalin and thyroid secretion. He only knows that he feels better "on the move."

The wiser man does not let himself get angry in the first place unless the situation calls for fight. However, the fight need not be a hand-to-hand combat with one's fellow man. William James has pointed out that there is a "moral equivalent for war," and that the energy of this instinct may be used to reinforce other impulses and help overcome obstacles of all sorts. A good deal of the business man's zest, the engineer's determination, and the reformer's zeal spring from the fight-instinct used in the right way. As James, Cannon, and others have pointed out, the way to end war may be to employ man's instinct of pugnacity in fighting the universal enemies of the race--fire, flood, famine, disease, and the various social evils--rather than let it spend its force in war between nations. Even our sports may be offshoots of the fight-instinct, for McDougall holds that the play-tendency has its root in the instinct of rivalry, a modified form of pugnacity. Evidently fighting-blood is a useful inheritance, even to-day, and rightly directed is a necessary part of a complete and forceful personality.

This, then, completes the list of self-preservative instincts, those which are commonly called egoistic and which have been given us for the maintenance of our own individual personal lives. But our endowment includes another set of impulses which are no less important and which must be reckoned with if human conduct is to be understood.

CHAPTER IV

In which we learn more about ourselves THE STORY OF THE INSTINCTS (Continued)

II. THE RACE-PRESERVATIVE INSTINCTS

=Looking beyond Ourselves.= We sometimes speak of self-preservation as though it were the only law of life, while as a matter of fact it is but half the story. Nature has seen to it that there shall be planted in every living creature an innate urge toward the larger life of the race. Although the creature may never give a conscious thought to the welfare of the race, he still bears within himself a set of instincts which have as their end and aim, not the individual at all, but society as a whole, and the life of generations that are to come. He is bigger than he knows. Although he may have no notion why he feels and acts as he does, and although he may pervert the purpose for his own selfish end, he is continually being moved by the mighty impulse of the race-life, an impulse which often outrivals the desire I or his own personal existence. The craving to reproduce ourselves and the craving to cherish and protect our young are among the most dynamic forces in life. The two desires are so closely bound together that they are often spoken of as one under the name of the sex-instinct, or the family instincts. Let us look first at that part of the yearning which urges toward perpetuating our own life in offspring.

=Watching Nature Work.= It is wonderful, indeed, to watch Nature in the long process of Evolution, as she adapts her methods to the growing complexity of the organism. With a variety and ingenuity of means, but always with the same steady purpose, she works from the lowest levels,--where there is no true reproduction, only multiplication by division,--on through the beginning of reproduction proper, where a single parent produces the offspring; then on to the level where it takes two parents of different structure to produce a new organism, and sex-life begins. At first Nature does not even demand that father and mother shall come near each other. In the water, the female of this type lays an egg, and the male, guided by his instinct, swims to it and deposits his fertilizing fluid. In plant life, bird and bee, attracted by wonderfully planned perfumes and color and honey, are called in to carry the pollen from male to female cell.

But it is when we come to the highest level that we find even more subtle ways planned to accomplish the desired end. Here we enter the realm of individual initiative, for it is not now enough to leave to external forces the joining of the two life-elements. In order to make a new individual, father and mother must be drawn together, and so there enters into the situation a personal relationship with all that that implies. Because Nature has had to provide ways of drawing individuals to one another, she has put into the higher types of life the power of mutual attraction,--a power which in man, the highest of all types, is responsible for many outgrowths that seem far removed from the original purpose.

=The Love-Motif.= On the one hand, there is the persistent desire to be attractive, which manifests itself in the subtlest ways. How many of the yearnings and activities of human life have their roots in this ancient and honorable desire! The love of pretty clothes,--however it may seem to be motivated and however it may be complicated by other motives,-draws its energy, fundamentally, from the same need that provides the gay plumage and limpid song of the bird or the painted wings of the butterfly.

On the other hand, there is the capability of being attracted, with all the personal relationships which spring from the power of admiring and loving another person. The interest in others does not expend its whole force on its primary objects,--mate and children. It flows out into all human relationships, developing all the possibilities of loving which mean so much in human life; the love of man for man and woman for woman, as well as mutual love of man and woman. A force like this, once planted, especially in the higher types of life, does not spend all its energies in its main trunk. It sends out branches in many directions, bearing by-products which are rich in value for all of life.

Many of our richest relationships, our best impulses, and our most firmly fixed social habits spring from the family instincts of reproduction and parental care. The social life of our young people, so well calculated to bring young men and women together; all the beauty of family life and, as we shall later see, all the broader benevolent activities for society in general, are energized by the same love-instincts which form so large a part of human nature.

LEARNING TO LOVE

=A Four-Grade School.= It is impossible to watch the growth of the love-life of a human being, to trace its development from babyhood up to its culmination in mating and parenthood, without a sense of wonder at the steady purpose behind it all. We used to believe that the love for the young girl that suddenly blooms forth in the callow youth was an entirely new affair, something suddenly planted in him as he developed into manhood; but now we know, thanks to the uncovering of human nature by the painstaking investigations of the psycho-analytic school of psychologists, that the seeds of the love-life are planted, not in puberty, but with the beginning of life itself. Looked at in one way, all infancy and childhood are a preparation, a training of the love-instinct which is to be ready at the proper time to find its mate and play its part in the perpetuation of the race. Nature begins early. As she plants in the tiny baby all the organs that shall be needed during its lifetime, so she plants the rudiments of all the impulses and tendencies that shall later be developed into the full-grown instincts. There have been found to be four periods in the love-life of the growing child, three of them preparatory steps leading up to maturity; periods in which the main current of love is directed respectively toward self, parents, comrades, and finally toward lover or mate.

=Like Narcissus.= In the first stage, the baby's interest is in his own body. He is getting acquainted with himself, and he soon finds that his body contains possibilities of pleasurable sensations which may be repeated by the proper stimulation. Besides the hunger-satisfaction that it brings, the act of sucking is pleasurable in itself, and so the baby begins to suck his thumb or his quilts or his rattle. Later, this impulse to stimulate the nerves about the mouth finds its satisfaction in kissing, and still later it plays a definite part in the wooing process; but at first the child is self-sufficient and finds his pleasure entirely within himself. Other regions of the body yield similar pleasure. We often find a tiny child rubbing his genital organs or his thighs or taking exaggerated pleasure in riding on someone's foot in order to stimulate these nerves, which he has discovered at first merely by chance. When he begins to run around, he loves to exhibit his own body, to go about naked. None of this is naughtiness or perversion; it is only Nature's preparation of trends that she will later need to use. The child is normally and naturally in love with himself.[11] But he must not linger too long in this stage. None of the channels which his life-force is cutting must be dug too deep, else in later life they will offer lines of least resistance which may, on occasion, invite illness or perversion.

[Footnote 11: This is the stage which is technically known as auto-eroticism or self-love.]

=In Love with His Family.= Presently Nature pries the child loose from love of himself and directs part of his interests to people outside himself. Before he is a year old, part of his love is turned to others. In this stage it is natural that at first his affection should center on those who make up his home circle,--his parents and other members of the household. Even in this early choice we see a foreshadowing of his future need. The normal little boy is especially fond of his mother, and the normal little girl of her father. Not all the love goes to the parent of the opposite sex, but if the child be normal, a noticeably larger part finds its way in that direction. Observing parents can often see unmistakable signs of jealousy: toward the parent of the same sex, or the brother or sister of the same sex. The little boy who sleeps with his mother while his father is away, or who on these occasions gets all the attention and all the petting he craves, is naturally eager to perpetuate this state of affairs. Many a small boy has been heard to say that he wished his father would go away and stay all the time,--to the horror of the parents who do not understand. All this is natural enough, but it is not to be encouraged. The pattern of the father or the mother must not be stamped too deep in the impressionable child-mind. Too little love and sympathy are bad, leading to repression and a morbid turning in of the love-force; but too much petting, too many caresses are just as bad. Sentimental self-indulgence on the part of the parents has been repeatedly proved to be the cause of many a later illness for the child. As the right kind of family love and comradeship, the kind that leads to freedom and self-dependence, is among the highest forces in life, so the wrong kind is among the worst. Parents and their substitutes--nurses, sisters, and brothers--are but temporary stopping-places for the growing love, stepping-stones to later attachments which are biologically more necessary. The small boy who lets himself be coddled and petted too long by his adoring relatives, who does not shake off their caresses and run away to the other boys, is doomed to failure, and, as we shall later see, probably to illness.[12]

[Footnote 12: One of the best discussions of this theme is found in the chapter "The Only or Favorite Child," by A.A. Brill, in Psychoanalysis.]

In the later infantile period, the child, besides wanting to exhibit his own body, shows marked interest in looking at the bodies of others, and marked curiosity on sex-questions in general. He particularly wants to know "where babies come from." If his questions are unfortunately met by embarrassment or laughing evasion, or by obvious lying about the stork or the doctor or the angels, his curiosity is only whetted, and he comes to the very natural conclusion that all matters of sex are sinful, disgusting, and indecent, and to be investigated only on the sly. This conception cannot be brought into harmony with the unconscious mental processes arising from his race-instincts nor with his instinctive sense that "whatever is is right." The resulting conflict in some four-year-old children is surprisingly intense. Astonished indeed would many parents be if they knew what was going on inside the heads of their "innocent" little children; not "bad" things, but pathetic things which a little candor would have avoided.

Alongside the rudimentary impulses of showing and looking, there is developed another set of trends which Nature needs to use later on, the so-called sadistic and masochistic impulses, the desire to dominate and master and even to inflict pain, and its opposite impulse which takes pleasure in yielding and submitting to mastery. These traits, harking back to the time when the male needed to capture by force, are of course much more evident in adolescence and especially in love-making, but have their beginning in childhood, as many a mother of cruel children knows to her sorrow. In adolescence, when sex-differentiation is much more marked, the dominating impulse is stronger in the boy and the yielding impulse in the girl; but in little children the differentiation has not yet begun.

=Gang and Chum.= At about four or five years the child leaves the infantile stage of development, with its self-love and its intense devotion to parents and their substitutes. He begins to be especially interested in playmates of his own sex, to care more for the opinions of the gang--or if it be a little girl, of the chum--than for those of the parents. The life-force is leading him on to the next step in his education, freeing him little by little from a too-hampering attachment to his family. This does not mean that he does not love his father and mother. It means only that some of his love is being turned toward the rest of the world, that he may be an independent, socially useful man.

This period between infancy and puberty is known as the latency period. All interest in sex disappears, repressed by the spontaneously developing sense of shame and modesty and by the impact of education and social disapproval. The child forgets that he was ever curious on sex-matters and lets his curiosity turn into other, more acceptable channels.

=The Mating-Time.= We are familiar with the changes that take place at puberty. We laugh at the girl who, throwing off her tom-boy ways, suddenly wants her skirts let down and her hair done up. We laugh at the boy who suddenly leaves off being a rowdy, and turns into a would-be dandy. We scold because this same boy and girl who have always been so "sweet and tractable" become, almost overnight, surly and cantankerous, restive under authority and impatient of family restraint. We should neither laugh nor scold, if we understood. Nature is succeeding in her purpose. She has led the young life on from self to parents, from parents to gang or chum, and now she is trying to lead it away from all its earlier attachments, to set it free for its final adventure in loving. The process is painful, so painful that it sometimes fails of accomplishment. In any case, the strain is tremendous, needing all the wisdom and understanding which the family has to offer. It is no easy task for any person to free himself from the sense of dependence and protection, and the shielding love that have always been his; to weigh anchors that are holding him to the past and to start out on the voyage alone.

At this time of change, the chemistry of the body plays an important part in the development of the mental traits; all half-developed tendencies are given power through the maturing of the sex-glands, which bind them into an organization ready for their ultimate purpose. The current is now turned on, and the machinery, which has been furnished from the beginning, is ready for its task. After a few false starts in the shape of "puppy love," the mature instinct, if it be successful, seeks until from among the crowd it finds its mate. It has graduated from the training-school and is ready for life.

CIVILIZATION'S PROBLEM

=When Nature's Plans Fall Through.= We have been describing the normal course of affairs. We know that all too often the normal is not achieved. Inner forces or outer circumstances too often conspire to keep the young man or the young woman from the culmination toward which everything has been moving. If the life-force cannot liberate itself from the old family grooves to forge ahead into new channels, or if economic demands or other conditions make postponement necessary, then marriage is not possible. All the glandular secretions and internal stimuli have been urging on to the final consummation, developing physical and emotional life for an end that does not come; or if it does come, is not sufficient to satisfy the demands of the age-old instinct which for millions of years knew no restraint. In any case, man finds himself, and woman herself, face to face with a pressing problem, none the less pressing because it is in most cases entirely unrecognized.

=Blundering Instincts.= The older a person is, the more fixed are his habits. Now, an instinct is a race-habit and represents the crystallized reactions of a past that is old. Whatever has been done over and over again, millions of times, naturally becomes fixed, automatic, tending to conserve itself in its old ways, to resist any change and to act as it has always acted. This conserves energy and works well so long as conditions remain the same. But if for any reason there comes a change, things are likely to go wrong. By just so far as things are different, an automatic habit becomes a handicap instead of a help.

This having to act under changed conditions is exactly the trouble with the reproductive instinct. Under civilization, conditions have changed but the instinct has not. It is trying to act as it always has acted, but civilized man wills otherwise. The change that has come is not in the physical, external environment, but in man himself and in the social environment which he has created. There is in man an onward urge toward new and better things. Side by side with the desire to live as he always has lived, there is a desire to make new adaptations which are for the advancement of the whole race-life. Besides the natural wish to take his desires as he finds them, there is also the wish to modify them and use them for higher and more socially useful ends.

As the race has found through long experience that monogamy is to be preferred to promiscuous mating; that the highest interests of life are fostered by loyalty to the institution of the family; that the careful rearing of several children rather than the mere production of many is in the long run to be desired; and that a single standard of morality is practicable; so society has established for its members a standard which is in direct opposition to the immeasurable urge of the past. To make matters worse, there have at the same time grown up in many communities a standard of living and an economic competition which still further limit the size of the family and the satisfaction of the reproductive impulse.

=The Perpetual Feud.= There thus arises the strategic struggle between that which the race has found good in the past and that which the race finds good in the present. As the older race-experience is laid in they body and built into the very fiber of the individual, inherited as an innate impulse, it has become an integral part of himself, an individual need rather than a social one. On the other hand, man has, as another innate part of his being, the desire to go with the herd, to conform to the standards of his fellows, to be what he has learned society wants him to be. Hence the struggle, insistent, ever more pressing, between two sets of desires within the man himself; the feud between the past and the present, between the natural and the social, between the selfish and the ideal. On one side, there is the demand for instinctive satisfaction; on the other, for moral control; on one side the demand for pleasure; on the other, the demands of reality.[13]

[Footnote 13: "All the burdens of men or society are caused by the inadequacies in the association of primal animal emotions with those mental powers which have been so rapidly developed in man-kind."--Shaler quoted by Hinkle: Introduction to Jung's Psychology of the Unconscious.]

Two factors intensify the conflict. In the first place, the older habits have the head start. Compared with the almost limitless extent of our past history, our desire for the control of the instincts is very new indeed. It requires the long look and the right perspective to understand how very lately we have entered into our new conditions and how old a habit we are trying to break. In the second place, the larger part of the stimulus comes from within the body itself. When studying the other instincts, we saw that the best way to control was to refuse to stimulate when the situation was not suitable for discharge. But with the organically aroused sex-instinct there is no such power of choice. We may fan the flame by the thoughts we think or the environment we seek, or we may smother the flame until it is out of sight, but we cannot extinguish it by any act of ours. The issue has always been too important to be left to the individual. The stimulation comes, primarily, not by way of the mind but by way of the body. With this instinct we cannot "stop before we begin," because Nature has taken the matter out of our hands and begins for us.

THE BULWARK WE HAVE BUILT

With the competing forces so strong and the issues so great, it is not to be wondered at that society has had to build up a massive bulwark of public opinion, to establish regulations and fix penalties that are more stringent than those imposed in any other direction. Nor is it remarkable that in its effort to protect itself, society has sometimes made mistakes.

These blunders seem to lie in two directions. Assuming that it is nearly impossible for the male to control his instincts, and that, after all, it does not matter so much whether he does or not, society has blinked at license in men, and thus has fostered a demoralizing, anti-social double standard which has broken up countless homes, has been responsible for the spread of venereal diseases, and has been among the greatest curses of modern civilization. At the same time society, in its efforts to maintain its standards for woman, has taught its children, especially its girls, that anything savoring of the word "sexual" is sinful, disgusting, and impure. To be sure, very many women have modified their childish views, but an astonishingly large number conserve, even in maturity, their warped ideas about the whole subject of sex. Many a mature woman secretly believes that she, at least, is not guilty of harboring anything so "vulgar" as a reproductive instinct, not realizing that if this were so, she would be, in very truth, a freak of nature.

Of course, woman is by nature as fully endowed with sex instincts as is man. Kipling portrays the female of the species as "deadlier than the male" in that the very framework of her constitution outlines the one issue for which it was launched,--stanch against any attack which might endanger the carrying on of life. Feeling the force of this instinctive urge, she braces herself against precipitancy in response by what seems almost a negation.

Just as we lean well in when riding around a corner, in order to keep ourselves from falling out, so by an "over-compensation" for what is unconsciously felt to be danger woman increases her feeling of safety by setting up a taboo on the whole subject of sex. It is time that we freed our minds from the artificial and perverted attitude toward this dominant impulse; time to rescue the word "sex" from its implications of grossness and sensuousness, and to recognize the instinct in its true light as one of the necessary and holy forces of life, a force capable of causing great damage, but also holding infinite possibilities for good if wisely directed.

Society only gets its members into trouble when, even by implication, it attempts to deny its natural make-up, and allows little children to grow up with the false idea that one of their strongest impulses is to be shunned by them as a thing of shame. We cannot dam back the flood by building a bulwark of untruth, and then expect the bulwark to hold.

=Adaptable Energy.= We neither have to give in to our over-insistent desires nor to deny that they exist. Man has a power of adaptation. Just when we seem to run up against a dead wall, to face an irreconcilable conflict, we find a wonderful power of indirect expression that affords satisfaction to all the innate forces without doing violence to the ethical standards which have proved so necessary for the development of character.

Hunger, which, like the reproductive instinct, is stimulated by the changing chemistry of the body, can be satisfied only by achieving its primary purpose, the taking of material food; but the creative impulse to reproduce oneself possesses a unique ability to spiritualize itself and expend its energy in other lines of creative endeavor. There seems to be some sort of close connection between the especially intense energy of the reproductive instinct and the modes of expression of the instinct for construction; a connection which makes possible the utilization of threatening destructive energy by directing it toward socially valuable work. Just as we harness the mountain stream and use its wild force to light our cities, or catch the lightning to run our trolley cars, so we find man and woman--under the right conditions--easily and naturally switching over the power of their surplus sex-energy to ends which seem at first only slightly related to its original aim, but which resemble it in that they too are self-expressive and creative. If a person is able to express himself in some real way, to give himself to socially needed work; if he can reproduce himself intellectually and spiritually in artistic production, in invention, in literature, in social betterment, he is drawing on an age-old reservoir of creative energy, and by so doing is relieving himself of inner tension which would otherwise seek less beneficent ways of expression.

The world knew all this intuitively for a long time before it knew it theoretically. The novelists, who are unconsciously among the best psychologists, have thoroughly worked the vein. The average man knows it. "He was disappointed in love," we say, "and we thought he would go to pieces, but now he has found himself in his work"; or, "She will go mad if she doesn't find some one who needs her." It is only lately that science has caught up with intuition, but now the physicians and psychologists who have had the most intimate and first-hand acquaintance with the human heart are recognizing, to a man, this unique power of the love-instinct and its possibilities for creative work of every sort.[14]

[Footnote 14: Among those who have shown this connection between the love-force and creative work are Freud, Jung, Jelliffe, White, Brill, Jones, Wright, Frink, and the late Dr. Putnam of Harvard University, who writes: "Freud has never asserted it as his opinion and it certainly is not mine, that this is the only root from which artistic expression springs. On the other hand, it is probable that all artistic productions are partly referable to this source. A close examination of many of them would enable any one to justify the opinion that it is a source largely drawn upon."--Human Motives. p. 87.]

=Higher Levels.= Freud has called this spiritualization of natural forces by a term borrowed from chemistry. As a solid is "sublimated" when transformed into a gas, so a primal impulse is said to be "sublimated" when it is diverted from its original object and made to serve other ends. By this power of sublimation the little exhibitionist, who loved to show himself, may become an actor; the "cruel" boy who loved to dissect animals may become a surgeon; the sexually curious child may turn his curiosity to other things and become a scholar; the "born mother," if denied children of her own or having finished with their upbringing, may take to herself the children of the city, working for better laws and better care for needy little ones; the man or woman whose sex-instinct is too strong to find expression in legitimate, direct ways, may find it a valuable resource, an increment of energy for creative work, along whatever line his talent may lie.

There is no more marvelous provision in all life than this power of sublimation of one form of energy into another, a provision shadowing forth almost limitless possibilities for higher adaptations and for growth in character. As we think of the distance we have already traveled and the endless possibilities of ever higher excursions of the life-force, we feel like echoing Paul's words: "He who began a good work in you will perfect it unto the end." The history of the past holds great promise for the future.

=When Sublimation Fails.= But in the meantime we cannot congratulate ourselves too heartily. Sublimation too often fails. There are too many nervous wrecks by the way, too many weak indulgers of original desires, too many repressed, starved lives with no outlet for their misunderstood yearnings; and, as we shall see, too many people who, in spite of a big lifework, fail to find satisfaction because of unnecessary handicaps carried over from their childhood days. "Society's great task is, therefore, the understanding of the life-force, its manifold efforts at expression and the way of attaining this, and to provide as free and expansive ways as possible for the creative energy which is to work marvelous things for the future."

If "the understanding of the life force" is to be available for use, it must be the property of the average man and woman, the fathers and mothers of our children, the teachers and physicians who act as their advisers and friends.[15] This chapter is intended to do its bit toward such a general understanding.

[Footnote 15: "Appropriate educational processes might perhaps guide this enormous impulsive energy toward the maintenance instead of the destruction of marriage and the family. But up to the present time, education with respect to this moral issue has commonly lacked any such constructive method. The social standard and the individual impulse have simply collided, and the individual has been left to resolve the conflict, for the most part by his own resources."--G.A. Coe: Psychology of Religion, p. 150.]

PARENTAL INSTINCT AND TENDER EMOTION

=Until They Can Fly.= Only half of Nature's need is met by the reproductive instinct. Her carefulness in this direction would be largely wasted without that other impulse which she has planted, the impulse to protect the new lives until they are old enough to fend for themselves. The higher the type of life and the greater the future demands, the longer is the period of preparation and consequent period of parental care. This fact, coupled with man's power for lasting relationships through the organization of permanent sentiments, has made the, bond between parent and child an enduring one. Needless to say, this relationship is among the most beautiful on earth, the source of an incalculable amount of joy and gain. However, as we have already suggested, there lurks here, as in every beneficent force, a danger. If parents forget what they are for, and try to foster a more than ordinary tie, they make themselves a menace to those whom they most love. Any exaggeration is abnormal. If the childhood bond is over-strong, or the childhood dependence too long cultivated, then the relationship has overstepped its purpose, and, as we shall later see, has laid the foundation for a future neurosis.

=Mothering the World.= Probably no instinct has so many ways of indirect expression as this mothering impulse of protection. Aroused by the cry of a child in distress, or by the thought of the weakness, or need, or ill-treatment of any defenseless creature, this mother-father impulse is at the root of altruism, gratitude, love, pity, benevolence, and all unselfish actions.

There is still a great difference of opinion as to how man's spiritual nature came into being; still discussion as to whether it developed out of crude beginnings as the rest of his physical and mental endowment has developed, or whether it was added from the outside as something entirely new. Be that as it may, the fact remains that man has as an innate part of his being an altruistic tendency, an unselfish care for the welfare of others, a relationship to society as a whole,--a relationship which is the only foundation of health and happiness and which brings sure disaster if ignored. The egoistic tendencies are only a part of human nature. Part of us is naturally socially minded, unselfish, spiritual, capable of responding to the call to lose our lives in order that others may find theirs.

SUMMARY

Civilized man as he is to-day is a product of the past and can be understood only as that past is understood. The conflicts with which he is confronted are the direct outcome of the evolutional history of the race and of its attempt to adapt its primitive instincts to present-day ideals.

Character is what we do with our instincts. According to Freud, all of a man's traits are the result of his unchanged original impulses, or of his reactions against those impulses, or of his sublimation of them. In other words, there are three things we may do with our instincts. We may follow our primal desires, we may deny their existence, or we may use them for ends which are in harmony with our lives as we want them to be. As the first course leads to degeneracy, the second to nervous illness, and the third to happy usefulness, it is obviously important to learn the way of sublimation. Sometimes this is accomplished unconsciously by the life-force, but sometimes sublimation fails, and is reestablished only when the conscious mind gains an understanding of the great forces of life. This method of reeducation of the personality as a means of treatment in nervousness is called psycho-therapy.

=Religion's Contribution.= If it be asked why, amid all this discussion of instincts and motives we have made no mention of that great energizer religion, we answer that we have by no means forgotten it, but that we have been dealing solely with those primary tendencies out of which all of the compound emotions are made. Man has been described as instinctively and incurably religious, but there seems no doubt that religion is a compound reaction, made up of love,--sympathetic response to the parental love of God,--fear, negative self-feeling, and positive self-feeling in the shape of aspiration for the desired ideal of character; all woven into several compound emotions such as awe, gratitude, and reverence.

It goes almost without saying that religion, if it be vital, is one of the greatest sources of moral energy and spiritual dynamic, and that it is and always has been one of the greatest aids to sublimation that man has found. A force like the Christian religion, which sets the highest ideal of character and makes man want to live up to it, and which at the same time says, "You can. Here is strength to help you"; which unifies life and fills it with purpose; which furnishes the highest love-object and turns the thought outward to the good of mankind--such a force could hardly fail to be a dynamic factor in the effort toward sublimation. This book, however, deals primarily with those cases for which religion has had, to call science to her aid in order to find the cause of failure, to flood the whole subject with light, and to help cut the cords which, binding us to the past, make it impossible to utilize the great resources that are at hand for all the children of men.

=Where We Keep Our Instincts.= It must have been impossible to read through these two chapters on instinct without feeling that, after all, we are not very well acquainted with ourselves. The more we look into human nature, the more evident it becomes that there is much in each one of us of which we are only dimly aware. It is now time for us to look a little deeper,-- to find where we keep these instinctive tendencies with which it is possible to live so intimately without even suspecting their existence. We shall find that they occupy a realm of their own, and that this realm, while quite out of sight, is yet open to exploration.

CHAPTER V

In which we look below the surface and discover a veritable wonderland THE SUBCONSCIOUS MIND

STRANGERS TO OURSELVES

=Hidden Strings.= A collie dog lies on the hearthrug. A small boy with mischievous intent ties a fine thread to a bone, hides himself behind a chair, and pulls the bone slowly across the floor. The dog is thrown into a fit of terror because he does not know about the hidden string.

A Chinese in the early days of San Francisco stands spell-bound at the sight of a cable car. "No pushee. No pullee. Go allee samee like hellee!" He does not know about the hidden string.

A woman of refinement and culture thinks a thought that horrifies her sensitive soul. It is entirely out of keeping with her character as she knows it. In her misunderstanding she considers it wicked and thrusts it from her, wondering how it ever could have been hers. She does not know about the hidden string.

In the last two chapters we thought together about some of these strings, examining the fibers of which they are made and learning in what directions they pull. We found them to be more powerful than we should have supposed, more insistent and less visible. We found that instinctive desire is the string, the cable that energizes our every act, but that our desires are neither single nor simple, and are but rarely on the surface. Many of us live with them a long time, feeling the tug, but not recognizing the string.

=There's a Reason.= We take our thoughts and feelings and actions for granted, without stopping very often to wonder where they come from. But there is always a reason. When the law of cause and effect reaches the doorsill of our minds, it does not stop short to give way to the law of chance. We wake up in the morning with a certain thought on top. We say it "just happens." But nothing ever just happens. No thought that ever comes into our heads has been without its history,--its ancestors and its determining causes. But what about dreams? They, at least, you say, have no connections, no past and no future, only a weird, fantastic present. Strange to say, dreams have been found to be as closely related to our real selves, as interwoven with the warp and woof of our lives as are any of our waking thoughts. Even dreams have a reason.

We find ourselves holding certain beliefs and prejudices, interested in certain things and indifferent to others, liking some foods, some colors and disliking others. Search our minds as we will, we find no clue to many of these inner trends. Why?

The answer is simple. The cause is hidden below the surface. If we try to explain ourselves on the basis of the open-to-inspection part of our minds, we must come to the conclusion that we are queer creatures indeed. Only by assuming that there is more to us than we know, can we find any rational basis for the way we think and feel and act.

=A Real Mind.= We learn of our internal machinery by what it does. We must infer a part of our minds which introspection does not reveal, a mind within the mind, able to work for us even while we are unaware of its existence. This inner mind is usually known as the subconscious, the mind under the level of consciousness.[16] We forget a name, but we know that it will come to us if we think about something else. Presently, out of somewhere, there flashes the word we want. Where was it in the meanwhile, and what hunted it out from among all our other memories and sent it up into consciousness? The something which did that must be capable of conserving memories, of recognizing the right one and of communicating it,-- surely a real mind.

[Footnote 16: Writers of the psycho-analytic school use the word "unconscious" to denote the lower layers of this region, and "fore-conscious" to denote its upper layers. Morton Prince uses the terms "unconscious" and "conscious" to denote the different strata. As there is still a good deal of confusion in the use of terms, it has seemed to us simpler to use throughout only the general term "subconscious."]

One evening my collaborator fumbled unsuccessfully for the name of a certain well-known journalist and educator. It was on the tip of her tongue, but it simply would not come, not even the initial letter. In a whimsical mood she said to herself just as she went to sleep, "Little subconscious mind, you find that name to-night." In the middle of the night she awoke, saying, "Williams--Talcott Williams." The subconscious, which has charge of her memories, had been at work while she slept.

The history of literature abounds in stories of under-the-surface work. The man of genius usually waits until the mood is on, until the muse speaks; then all his lifeless material is lighted by new radiance. He feels that some one outside himself is dictating. Often he merely holds the pen while the finished work pours itself out spontaneously as if from a higher source.

But it is not only the man of genius who makes use of these unseen powers. He may have readier access to his subconscious than the rest of us, but he has no monopoly. The most matter-of-fact man often says that he will "sleep over" a knotty problem. He puts it into his mind and then goes about his business, or goes to sleep while this unseen judge weighs and balances, collects related facts, looks first at one side of the question and then at the other, and finally sends up into consciousness a decision full of conviction, a decision that has been formulated so far from the focus of attention that it seems to be something altogether new, a veritable inspiration.

We must infer the subconscious from what it does. Things happen,--there must be a cause. Some of the things that happen presuppose imagination, reason, intelligence, will, emotion, desire, all the elements of mind. We cannot see this mind, but we can see its products. To deny the subconscious is to deny the artist while looking at his picture, to disbelieve in the poet while reading his poem, and to doubt the existence of the explosive while listening to the report. The subconscious is an artist, a poet, and an explosive by turns. If we deny its existence, a good portion of man's doings are unintelligible. If we admit it, many of his actions and his afflictions which have seemed absurd stand out in a new light as purposeful efforts with a real and adequate cause.

=The Submerged Nine Tenths.= The more deeply psychologists and physicians have studied into these things, the more certainly have they been forced to the conclusion that the conscious mind of man, the part that he can explore at will, is by far the smaller part of his personality. Since this is to some people a rather startling proposition, we can do no better than quote the following statement from White on the relation of consciousness to the rest of the psychic life:

Consciousness includes only that of which we are aware, while outside of this somewhat restricted area there lies a much wider area in which lie the deeper motives for conduct, and which not only operates to control conduct, but also dictates what may and what may not become conscious. Stanley Hall has very forcibly put the matter by using the illustration of the iceberg. Only one-tenth of the iceberg is visible above water; nine-tenths is beneath the surface. It may appear in a given instance that the iceberg is being carried along by the prevailing winds and surface currents, but if we keep our eyes open we shall sooner or later see a berg going in the face of the wind, and, so, apparently putting to naught all the laws of aerodynamics. We can understand this only when we come to realize that much the greater portion of the berg is beneath the surface and that it is moving in response to invisible forces addressed against this submerged portion.

Consciousness only arises late in the course of evolution and only in connection with adjustments that are relatively complex. When the same or similar conditions in the environment are repeatedly presented to the organism so that it is called upon to react in a similar and almost identical way each time, there tends to be organized a mechanism of reaction which becomes more and more automatic and is accompanied by a state of mind of less and less awareness.[17]

[Footnote 17: White: Mechanisms of Character Formation.]

It is easy to see the economy of this arrangement which provides ready-made patterns of reaction for habitual situations and leaves consciousness free for new decisions. Since an automatic action, traveling along well-worn brain paths, consumes little energy and causes the minimum of fatigue, the plan not only frees consciousness from a confusing number of details, but also works for the conservation of energy. While consciousness is busy lighting up the special problems of the moment, the vast mass of life's demands are taken care of by the subconscious, which constitutes the bulk of the mind. "Properly speaking, the unconscious is the real psyche."[18]

[Footnote 18: Freud: Interpretation of Dreams, p. 486.]

=The Heart of Psychology.= In the face of all this, it is not to be wondered at that the problem of the subconscious has been called not one problem of psychology but the problem. It cannot be denied that the discoveries which have already been made as to its activities have been of immense practical importance in the understanding of normal conduct and in the treatment of the psycho-neuroses.

If some of the methods--such as hypnosis, automatic writing, and interpretation of dreams--which are used to investigate its activities seem to savor of the charlatan and the mountebank, it is because they have occasionally been appropriated by the ignorant and the unscrupulous. Their real setting is the psychological laboratory and the physician's office. In the hands of men like Sigmund Freud, Boris Sidis, and Morton Prince, they are as scientific as the apparatus of any other laboratory and their findings are as susceptible of proof. We may, then, go forward with the conviction that we are walking on solid ground and that the main paths, at least, will turn into beaten highways.

ANCESTRAL MEMORIES

=Race-Memories.= An individual as he stands at any moment is the product of his past,--the past which he has inherited and the past which he has lived. In other words, he is a bundle of memories accumulated through the experience of the race, and through his own experience as a person. Some of these memories are conscious, and these he calls his, while others fail to reach consciousness and are not recognized as part of his assets.

The instincts form the starting-point of mind, conscious and subconscious, and are the foundation upon which the rest is built. They often show themselves as part of our conscious lives, but their roots are laid deep in the subconscious from which they can never be eradicated. This deepest-laid instinctive layer of the subconscious is little subject to change. It represents the earlier adjustments of the race, crystallized into habit. It takes no account of the differences between the present and the past. It knows no culture, no reason, no lately acquired prudence. It is all energy and can only wish, or urge toward action. But since only those race-memories became instincts which had proved needful to the race in the long run, they are on the whole beneficent forces, working for the good of the race and the good of the individual, if he learns how to handle them aright and to adapt them to present conditions.

This instinctive urge toward action arouses in the individual an organic response that is felt as a tension or craving and is mainly dependent upon its own chemical constitution at the moment. Hunger is the sensation caused by the little muscular contractions in the stomach when the body is low in its food supply. Sudden fright is felt as an all-gone sensation "at the pit of the stomach." What really happens is a tightening up of the circular muscles of the blood-vessels lying in the network of the solar plexus, and a spasm of the muscles of the digestive tract. The hungry stomach impels to action until satisfied; the physical discomfort in fear impels toward measures of safety. The apparatus that is made use of by the subconscious in carrying out this instinctive urge is called the autonomic nervous system.[19] It regulates all the functions of living, not only under the stress of emotion, but during every moment of waking or sleeping.

[Footnote 19: Kempf: "The Tonus of Automatic Segments as a Cause of Abnormal Behavior," Journal of Nervous and Mental Diseases, January, 1921.]

=A Capable Manager.= The conscious mind could not possibly send messages to the numerous glands that fit the body for action, nor attend to all the delicate adjustments that enter into the process. The conscious mind in most of us does not even know of the existence of the organs and secretions involved, but something sends the messages and it is something that has a remarkable likeness to mind as we usually think of mind,-- something which takes advantage of the past and gages means to an end with a nicety that excites our wonder.

=Take no Anxious Thought.= We take food into our stomachs and forget about it, if we are wise; and this subconscious overseer who through millions of years of experience has learned how to digest food does the rest. As with digestion, so with our heart-action; we lie down at night fairly sure that there will be no break in the regular rhythm of its beat. The subconscious overseer is "on the job" and he never rests. No matter how hard we sleep, he never lets us forget to take a breath; and if we trust him, he is very likely to wake us up at the appointed time in the morning. Also, if we trust him, he carries us off to sleep as though we were babies. Has he not had long practice in the days before insomnia was invented?

=First Aid to the Injured.= In times of infection or injury, this subconscious manager is better than any doctor. The doctors say with truth that they only assist nature. If the infection is internal, antitoxins are produced within the body. If the injury is external, like a cut, the messages fly, and white blood-corpuscles are marshaled to take care of poisons and build up the tissue. If the injury is of the kind that needs rest, the subconscious doctor knows it. He therefore causes pain and rigidity, in order to induce us to hold the injured part still until it is restored.

Crile reminds us of a fact that is often noticed by surgeons. If patients under ether are handled roughly, especially in the intestinal region, respiration quickens and there are tremors and even convulsive efforts which interfere with the surgeon's work. The conscious mind cannot feel. It is asleep. But the subconscious mind, whose business it is to protect the body, is trying to get away from injury. The body uses up as much energy as though it had run for miles, and when the patient wakes up, we say that he is suffering from shock. The subconscious mind which is not affected by ether, has been exhausting itself in a vain attempt to get the body away from harm.

=A Tireless Servant.= When the conscious mind undertakes a job, it is always more or less subject to fatigue. But the subconscious after its long practice seems never to tire. We say that its activities have become automatic. With all its inherited skill, the subconscious, if left to itself, can be depended upon to run the bodily machinery without effort and without hitch. The only things that can interfere with its work are the wrong kind of emotions and the wrong kind of suggestions from the conscious mind. Barring these, it goes its way like a trusty servant, looking after details and leaving its master's mind free for other things. Having been "in the family" for generations, it knows its business and resents any interference with its duties or any infringement of its rights.

No man, then, comes into this world without inheritance: he receives from his ancestors two goodly sets of heirlooms, the instincts and the mechanism which carries on bodily functions. This is the capital with which man starts life; but immediately he begins increasing this capital, adding memories from his own experience to the accumulated race-records.

PERSONAL MEMORIES

No more startling secret has been unearthed by science than the discovery of the length and minuteness of our memories. No matter how much one may think he has forgotten, the tablets of his mind are closely written with records of infinitesimal experiences, shadowy sensations, old happenings which the conscious self has lost entirely and would scarcely recognize as its own. Many of these brain records, or neurograms, as Prince calls them, are never aroused from their dormant conditions. But others, aroused by emotion or association of ideas, may after years of inactivity, come forth again either as conscious memories or as subconscious forces, or even as physiological memories,--bodily repetitions of the pains, palpitations, and tremors of old emotional experiences.

=Irresistible Childhood.= An experience that is forgotten is not necessarily lost. Although the first few years of childhood are lost to conscious memory, these years outweigh all others in their influence on character. The Jesuit priest was right when he said, "Give me a child until he is six years old, and he will be a Catholic all his life." As Frink has so ably shown, the determining factors that enter into any adult choice, such as the choice of the Catholic or the Protestant faith, are in a large measure made up of subconscious memories from early childhood, forgotten memories of Sunday-school and church, of lessons at home or passages in books,--experiences which no voluntary effort could recall, but which still live unrecognized in our mature judgments and beliefs. Naturally we do not acknowledge these subconscious motives. We like to believe that all our decisions are based on reason, and so we invent plausible arguments for our attitudes and our actions, arguments which we ourselves implicitly believe. This process of substituting a plausible reason for a subconscious one is known as rationalization, a process which every one of us engages in many times a day.

It is indeed true that the child is father to the man. Those first impressionable years, when we believed implicitly whatever any one told us and when through ignorance we reacted emotionally to ordinary experiences, are molding us still, making us the men and women we are to-day, coloring with childish ideas many of the attitudes of our supposedly reasoning life. Bergson says:

The unconscious is our historical past. In reality the past is preserved automatically. In its entirety probably it follows us at every instant; all that we have felt, thought and willed from our earliest infancy is there, leaning over the present which is about to join it, pressing against the portals of consciousness that would fain leave it outside.

=Spontaneous Outbursts.= "How do we know all this?" some one says. "What is the evidence for these sweeping statements? If we cannot remember, how can we discover these strange memories that are so powerful but so elusive? If they are below the level of consciousness, are they not, in the very nature of the case, forever hidden from view, in the sphere of the occult rather than that of science?"

The answer to these questions is determined by one important fact; the line between the conscious and subconscious minds does not always remain in the same place; the "threshold of consciousness" is sometimes displaced, automatically allowing these buried memories to come to the surface. In sleep and delirium, in trance and hallucination, in hysteria and intoxication, the tables are turned; the restraining hand of the conscious mind is loosened and the submerged self comes forth with all its ancient memories.

It is a common experience to have a patient in delirium repeat long-forgotten verses or descriptions of events that the "real man" has lost entirely. The renowned servant-girl, quoted by Hudson, who in delirium recited passage after passage of Hebrew, Latin, and Greek, which she had heard her one-time master repeat in his study, is typical of many such instances.[20]

[Footnote 20: Hudson: The Law of Psychic Phenomena, p. 44. Quoted from _Coleridge's Biographia Literaria_, Vol. I, p. 117 (edit. 1847).]

A young girl of nineteen, a patient of mine, lapsed for several weeks into a dissociated state in which she forgot all the memories and ideas of her adult life, and returned to the period of her childhood. She used to say that she saw things inside her head and would accurately describe events that took place before she was two years of age,--scenes which she had completely forgotten in her normal life. One day when I asked her to tell me what she was seeing, she began to talk about "little sister" (herself) and "little brother." "Little sister and brother were the two little folks that lived with their mother and their daddy and they were playing on the sand-pile. You know there was only one sand-pile, not like all the ones they have down here (at the seaside), and they had a bucket that they would put sand in and they would dump it out again and they would make nice things, you know; they would play with their little dog Ponto and he was white with black and brown spots on him. Little brother had white hair and he was bigger than little sister and he had a little waist with ruffles down the front and around the collar and a black coat that came down to his knees and it had two little white bands around it. Some of the waists he wore had blue specks and some had red and black specks in it.

"Little sister had yellow curls and she had a blue coat with jiggly streaks of white in it, and she had a little white bonnet that was crocheted, and she had little blue mittens on that were tied to a string that went around her neck and down the other arm. It got pretty cold where they lived. Little sister and little brother would go out to the pile of leaves and jump on them and bounce and they would crackle. The leaves came down from the trees all of a sudden when they got tired, and they were different colors, brown and red. Little sister could walk then but she could not walk one other time before then; she could stand up by holding to a chair, but she could not go herself. One morning Big Tom said 'Run to Daddy' and she went to her daddy, and after that she always walked; they were glad and she was glad. She walked all day long. Big Tom was a man who used to help Daddy and little sister always liked him. He was a nice man."

The mother verified this scene of the first walking, saying that it had occurred on her own wedding-anniversary when the child was twenty-three months old.

One night I heard the same patient talk in her sleep in the slow and hesitating manner of a child reading phonetically from a printed page. I soon recognized the words as those of a poem of Tagore's, called "My Prayer," and remembered that a magazine containing the poem had been lying on the bed during the day. When she had finished I wakened her, saying, "Now tell me what you have been dreaming." She answered in her childish way, "I think I do not dream." She went to sleep immediately and again repeated the poem, word for word, without a single mistake. Again I awakened her with the words, "Now tell me what you have been dreaming." And again she answered, "I think I do not dream." I said: "But yes; don't you remember you were just saying, 'When the time comes for me to go'?" (the last line of the poem). "Oh, yes," she said, "I was seeing it, and I think I'll not go to sleep again. It tires me so to see it."

While she was awake she had no recollection of having seen the poem and was indeed in her dissociated state quite incapable of understanding its meaning. Asleep, she saw every word as plainly as if the page had been before her eyes.

The distorted pictures of dreams are always made of the material which past experiences have furnished and which have in many cases been dropped out of consciousness for years only to rise out of their long oblivion when the conscious mind has been put to sleep.

=Unearthing Old Experiences.= However, psychology does not have to wait for buried memories to come forth of their own free will. It has a number of successful ways of summoning them from their hiding-place and helping them across the line into consciousness. In the hands of skilled investigators and therapeutists, hypnosis, hypnoidization, automatic writing, crystal-gazing, abstraction, free association, word-association, and interpretation of dreams have all been repeatedly successful in bringing to light memories which apparently have been for many years completely blotted out of mind. As we become better acquainted with these technical devices we shall find that there are four kinds of experiences whose records are carefully stored away in our minds. Some were always so far from the center of our attention that we could swear they never had been ours; others, although once present in consciousness, were so trivial and unimportant that it seems ridiculous to suppose them conserved; others never came into our waking minds at all and entered our lives only in special states, such as sleep or delirium or dreams. All these we should expect to forget; the astonishing thing is that they ever were conserved. But there is a fourth class that is different. It is made up of experiences that were so vital, so emotional, so closely woven into the fiber of our being that it seems impossible that they ever could be forgotten. Let us look at a few examples of records of all these four kinds of experiences, examples chosen from hundreds of their kind as illustrations of the all-embracing character of buried memories.[21]

[Footnote 21: For further examples see Prince, _The Unconscious_; Prince, The Dissociation of a Personality, and Hudson, The Law of Psychic Phenomena.]

=Out of the Corners of Our Eyes.= In the first place, we are much more observing than we imagine. We may be so interested in our own thoughts that details of our environment are entirely lost on the conscious mind, but the subconscious has its eyes open, and its ears. People in hypnosis have been known to repeat verbatim whole passages from newspapers which they had never consciously read. While they were busy with one column, their wide-awake subconscious was devouring the next one, and remembering it. Prince relates the story of a young woman who unconsciously "took in" the details of a friend's appearance:

I asked B.C.A. (without warning and after having covered her eyes) to describe the dress of a friend who was present and with whom she had been conversing perhaps some twenty minutes. She was unable to do so beyond saying that he wore dark clothes. I then found that I myself was unable to give a more detailed description of his dress, although we had lunched and been together about two hours. B.C.A. was then asked to write a description automatically. Her hand wrote as follows (she was unaware that her hand was writing):

"He has on a dark greenish gray suit, a stripe in it--little rough stripe; black bow cravat; shirt with three little stripes in it; black laced shoes; false teeth; one finger gone; three buttons on his coat."

The written description was absolutely correct. The stripes in the coat were almost invisible. I had not noticed his teeth or the loss of a finger and we had to count the buttons to make sure of their number owing to their partial concealment by the folds of the unbuttoned coat. The shoe-strings I am sure under the conditions would have escaped nearly every one's notice.[22]

[Footnote 22: Prince: The Unconscious, p. 53.]

Automatic writing, the method used to uncover this subconscious perception, is a favorite method with some investigators and is often used by Morton Prince. The hand writes without the direction of the personal consciousness and usually without the person's being aware that it is writing. A dissociated person does this very easily; other people can cultivate the ability, and perhaps most of us approach it when we are at the telephone, busily writing or drawing remarkable pictures while the rest of us is engaged in conversation.

The present epidemic of the Ouija board shows how many persons there are who are able to switch off the conscious mind and let the subconscious control the muscles that are used in writing. The fact that the writer has no understanding of what he is doing and believes himself directed by some outside power, in no way interferes with the subconscious phenomenon.

=Everyday Doings.= Besides perceptions which were originally so far from the focus of attention that the conscious mind never caught them at all, there are the little experiences of everyday life, fleeting thoughts and impressions which occupy us for a minute and then disappear. Every experience is a dynamic fact and no matter how trivial the experience may be or how completely forgotten, it still exists as a part of the personality.

An amusing example of the everyday kind of forgotten experience occurred during the writing of this chapter. I wrote a sentence which pleased me very well. This is the sentence: "In the esthetic processes of evolution they [man's desires] have sunk below the surface as soon as formed, and have been covered over by an elastic and snug-fitting consciousness as the skin covers in the tissues and organs of the body." After showing this passage to my collaborator and remarking that this figure had never been used before, I was partly chagrined and partly amused to have her bring me the following sentence from White and Jelliffe: "Consciousness covered over and obscured the inner organs of the psyche just as the skin hides the inner organs of the body from vision." My originality had vanished and I was close to plagiarism. Indeed, if a history of plagiarism could be written, it would probably abound in just such stories. I had read the article containing this sentence only once, about three years before, and had never quoted it or consciously thought of it. It had lain buried for three years, only to come forth as an original idea of my own. Who knows how many times we all do just this thing without catching ourselves in the trick?

=Back-Door Memories.= There are other kinds of memories which hide in the subconscious, memories of experiences which have not come in by the front door, but have entered the mind during special states, such as sleep, delirium, intoxication, or hypnosis. What is known as post-hypnotic suggestion is the functioning of a suggestion received during hypnosis and emerging later as an impulse without being recognized as a memory. A man in a hypnotic state is told that at five o'clock he will take off his clothes and go to bed, without remembering that such a suggestion has been given him. He awakens with no recollection of the suggestion, but at five o'clock he suddenly feels impelled to go to bed, even though his unreasonable desire puts him into a highly embarrassing position. The suggestion, to be thus effective, must have been conserved somewhere in his mind outside of consciousness.

Suggestions that enter the mind during the normal sleep are also recorded,-- a fact that carries a warning to people who are in the habit of talking of all sorts of matters while in the room with sleeping children. I have sometimes suggested to sleeping patients that on waking they will remember and tell me the cause of their symptoms. The following example shows not only the conservation of impressions gained in sleep, but also the sway of forgotten ideas of childhood, still strong in mature years. This young woman, a trained nurse, with many marked symptoms of hysteria, had been asked casually to bring a book from the Public Library. She cried out in consternation, "Oh, no, I am afraid!" After a good deal of urging she finally brought the book, although at the cost of considerable effort. Later, while she was taking a nap, I said to her, "You will not remember that I have talked to you. You will stay asleep while I am talking and while you are asleep there will come to your mind the reasons why you are afraid to go to the Public Library. When you waken, you will tell me all about it." Upon awakening, she said: "Oh, do you know, I can tell you why I have always been afraid to go to the Public Library. While I was in Parochial School, Father ---- used to come in and tell us children to use the books out of the school library and never to go to the Public Library." I questioned her concerning her idea of the reason for such an injunction and what she thought was in the books which she was told not to read. She hesitatingly stated that it was her idea, even in childhood, that the books dealt with topics concerning the tabooed subject of the birth of children and kindred matters.

=Smoldering Volcanoes.= Let us now consider those emotional experiences which seem far too compelling to be forgotten, but which may live within us for years without giving any evidence of their existence. Memories like these are apt to be anything but a dead past.

Many of my own patients have uncovered emotional memories through simply talking out to me whatever came into their minds, laying aside their critical faculty and letting their minds wander on into whatever paths association led them. This is known as the free-association method, and simple as it seems, is one of the most effective in uncovering memories which have been forgotten for years. One of my patients, a refined, highly educated woman of middle age, had suffered for two years with almost constant nausea. One day, after a long talk, with no suggestion on my part, only an occasional, "What does that remind you of?" she told with great emotion an experience which she had had at eighteen years of age, in which she had for a moment been sexually attracted to a boy friend, but had recoiled as soon as she realized where her impulse was leading her. She had been so horrified at the idea of her degradation, so nauseated at what she considered her sin, that she had put it out of her mind, denied that such a thought had ever been hers, repressed the desire into the subconscious, where it had continued to function unsatisfied, unassimilated with her mature judgments. Her nausea was the symbol of a moral disgust. Physical nausea she was willing to acknowledge, but not this other thing. Upon reciting this old experience, with every sign of the original shame, she cried: "Oh, Doctor! why did you bring this up? I had forgotten it. I haven't thought of it in thirty years." I reminded her that I couldn't bring it up,--I had never known anything about it. With the emotional incoming of this memory and the saner attitude toward it which the mature woman's mind was able to take, the nausea disappeared for good. This case is typical of the psycho-neuroses and we shall have occasion to refer to it again. The present emphasis is on the fact that an emotional memory may be buried for many years while it still retains the power of reappearing in more or less disguised manifestation.

=Repressed Memories.= If we ask how so burning a memory could escape from the consciousness of a grown woman, we are driven to the conclusion that this forgetting can be the result of no mere quiet fading away, but that there must have been some active force at work which kept the memory from coming into awareness. It was not lost. It was not passive. Out of sight was not out of mind. There must have been a reason for its expulsion from the personal consciousness. In fact, we find that there is a reason. We find that whenever a vital emotional experience disappears from view, it is because it is too painful to be endured in consciousness. Nor is it ever the pain of an impersonal experience or even the thought of what some one else has done to us that drives a memory out of mind. As a matter of fact, we never expel a memory except when it bears directly on ourselves and on our own opinion of ourselves. We can stand almost anything else, but we cannot stand an idea that does not fit in with our ideal for ourselves. This is not the pious ideal that we should like to live up to and that we hope to attain some day, not the ideal that we think we ought to have--like never speaking ill of others or never being selfish--but the secret picture that each of us has, locked away within him, the specifications of ourselves reduced to their lowest terms, below which we cannot go. Energized by the instinct of positive self-feeling, and organized with the moral sentiments which we have acquired from education and the ideals of society, especially those acquired in early childhood, this ideal of ourselves becomes incorporated into our conscience and is an absolute necessity for our happiness.

We have found that when two emotions clash, one drives out the other. So in this case, the woman's positive self-feeling of self-respect, combined with disgust, drove from the field that other emotion of the reproductive instinct which was trying to get expression. Speaking technically, one repressed the other. The woman said to herself, "No, I never could have had such a thought," and promptly forgot it. Needless to say, this kind of handling did not kill the impulse. Buried in the depths of her soul, it continued to live like a live coal, until in later years, fanned by the wind of some new experience, it burst into flame.

In this case the wish had originally flashed into awareness for an instant, but very often the impulse never gets into consciousness at all. The upper layers of the subconscious, where the acquired ideals live, automatically work to keep down any desires which are thought to be out of keeping with the person as he knows himself. He then would emphatically deny that such desires had ever had any place in his life.

Freud has called this repressing force the psychic censor. To get into consciousness, any idea from the subconscious must be able to pass this censor. This force seems to be a combination of the self-regarding and herd-instincts, which dispute with the instinct for reproduction the right to "the common path" for expression.

A considerable part of any person's subconscious is made up of memories, wishes, impulses, which are repressed in this way. Of course any instinctive desire may be repressed, but it is easy to understand why the most frequently denied impulse, the instinct of reproduction, against whose urgency society has cultivated so strong a feeling, should be repressed more frequently than any other.[23]

[Footnote 23: See foot-note, p. 145, Chap. VII.]

=Past and Present.= It matters not, then, in what state experiences come to us, whether in sleep or delirium, intoxication or hypnosis, or in the normal waking condition. They are conserved and may exert great influence on our normal lives. It matters not whether the experiences be full of meaning and emotion or whether they be so slight as to pass unnoticed, they are conserved. It matters not whether these experiences be mere sense-impressions, or inner thoughts, whether they be unacknowledged hopes or fears, undesirable moods and unworthy desires or fine aspirations and lofty ideals. They are conserved and they may at a later day rise up to bless or to curse us long after we had thought them buried in the past. The present is the product of the past. It is the past plus an element of choice which keeps us from settling down in the despair of fatalism and enables us to do something toward making the present that is, a help and not a stumbling-block to the present that is to be.

SOME HABITS OF THE SUBCONSCIOUS

=The Association of Ideas.= It is only by something akin to poetic license that we can speak of lower and higher strata of mind. When we carry over the language of material things into the less easily pictured psychic realm, it is sometimes well to remind ourselves that figures of speech, if taken too literally, are more misleading than illuminating. When we speak of the deep-laid instinctive lower levels of mind and the higher acquired levels, we must not imagine that these strata are really laid in neat, mutually exclusive layers, one on top of the other in the chambers of the mind. Nor must we imagine the mental elements of instinct, idea, and memory as jumbled together in chaotic confusion, or in scattered isolated units. As a matter of fact, the best word to picture the inside of our minds is the word "group." We do not know just how ideas and instincts can group themselves together, but we do know that by some arrangement of brain paths and nerve-connections, the laws of association of ideas and of habit take our mental experiences and organize them into more or less permanent systems. Instinctive emotions tend to organize themselves around ideas to form sentiments; ideas or sentiments, which through repetition or emotion are associated together, tend to stay together in groups or complexes which act as a whole; complexes which pertain to the same interests tend to bind themselves into larger systems or constellations, forming moods, or sides to one's character. It is not highly important to differentiate in every case a sentiment from a complex, or a complex from a constellation, especially as many writers use "complex" as the generic term for all sorts of groups; but a general understanding of the much-used word "complex" is necessary for a comprehension of modern literature on psychology, psychotherapy or general education.

"=What Is a Complex=?" Reduced to its lowest terms, a complex is a group.

It may be simply a group of associated movements, like lacing one's shoes or knitting; it may be a group of movements and ideas, like typewriting or piano-playing, which through repetition have become automatic or subconscious; it may be merely a group of ideas, such as the days of the week, the alphabet or the multiplication table. In all these types it is repetition working through the law of habit that ties the ideas and movements together into an organic whole. Usually, however, the word complex is reserved for psychic elements that are bound together by emotion. In this sense, a complex is an emotional thought-habit. Frink's definition, which is one of the simplest, recognizes only this emotional type: "A complex is a system of connected ideas, having a strong emotional tone, and displaying a tendency to produce or influence conscious thought and action in a definite and predetermined direction."[24]

[Footnote 24: Frink: "What Is a Complex?" Journal American Medical Assoc., Vol. LXII, No. 12, Mar. 21, 1914.]

Emotion and repetition are the great welders of complexes. Emotion is the strongest cement in the world. A single emotional experience suffices to bind together ideas that were originally as far apart as the poles.

Sometimes a complex includes not only ideas, movements, and emotions, but physiological disturbances and sensations. Some people cannot go aboard a stationary ship without vomiting, nor see a rose, even though it prove to be a wax one, without the sneezing and watery eyes of hay-fever. This is what is known as a "conditioned reflex." Past associations plus fear have so welded together idea and bodily manifestation that one follows the other as a matter of course, long after the real cause is removed. In such ways innumerable nervous symptoms arise. The same laws which form healthy complexes, and, indeed, which make all education possible, may thus be responsible for the unhealthy mal-adaptive association-habits which lie back of a neurosis. Fortunately, a knowledge of this fact furnishes the clue to the re-education that brings recovery.

A complex may be either conscious or unconscious, but as it usually happens that either all or part of its elements are below the surface, the word is oftenest used to mean those buried systems of the subconscious mind that influence thought or behavior without themselves being open to scrutiny. It is these buried complexes, memory groups, gathered through the years of experience, that determine action in uniform and easily prophesied directions. Every individual has a definite complex about religion, about politics, about patriotism, about business, and it is the sum of these buried complexes which makes up his total personality.

=Displacement.= Association or grouping is, then, an intrinsic power of mind; but as all life seems to be built on opposites--light and darkness, heat and cold, love and hate--so mind, which is capable of association, is capable also of displacement or the splitting apart of elements which belong together. There is such a thing as the simple breaking up of complexes, when education or experience or neglect separate ideas and emotions which had been previously welded together; but displacement is another matter. Here there is still a path between idea and emotion; they still belong to the same complex, but the connection is lost sight of. The impulse or emotion attaches itself to another substitute idea which is related to the first but which is more acceptable to the personality. Sometimes the original idea is forgotten; repressed, or dissociated into the subconscious, as in anxiety neurosis; and sometimes it is merely shorn of its emotional interest and remembered as an unrelated or insignificant idea, as in compulsion neurosis.

=Transference.= Another kind of displacement which seems hard to believe possible until it is repeatedly encountered in intelligent human beings is the process called transference, by which everybody at some time or other acts toward the people he meets, not according to rational standards but according to old unconscious attitudes toward other people. Each of us carries, within, subconscious pictures of the people who surrounded us when we were children; and now when we meet a new person we are likely unconsciously to say to ourselves--not, "This person has eyebrows like my mother, or a voice like my nurse," or, "This person bosses me around as my father used to do," but, "This is my mother, this is my nurse, this is my father." Whereupon we may proceed to act toward that person very much as we did toward the original person in childhood.

Transference is subconsciously identifying one person with another and behaving toward the one as if he were that other. Analysis has discovered that many a man's hostile attitude toward the state or religion or authority in general, is nothing more than this kind of displacement of his childhood's attitude toward authority in the person of his perhaps too-domineering father. Many a woman has married a husband, not for what he was in himself, but because she unconsciously identified him with her childish image of her father.

Students of human nature have always recognized the kind of displacement which transfers the sense of guilt from some major act or attitude to a minor one which is more easily faced, just as Lady Macbeth felt that by washing her hands she might free herself from her deeper stain. This is a frequent mechanism in the psychoneuroses--not that neurotics are likely to have committed any great crime, but that they feel subconsciously that some of their wishes or thoughts are wicked.

=The Phenomena of Dissociation.= When an idea or a complex, a perception or a memory is either temporarily or permanently shoved out of consciousness into the subconscious, it is said to be dissociated. When we are asleep, the part of us that is usually conscious is dissociated and the submerged part takes the stage. When we forget our surroundings in concentration or absent-mindedness, a part of us is dissociated and our friends say that we are "not all there," or as popular slang has it, "Nobody home." When a mood or system of complexes drives out all other moods, one becomes "a different person." But if this normal dissociation is carried a step farther, we may lose the power to put ourselves together again, and then we may truly be said to be dissociated. Almost any part of us is subject to this kind of apparent loss. In neurasthenia the happy, healthy complexes which have hitherto dominated our lives may be split off and left lying dormant in the subconscious; or the power of will or concentration may seem to be gone. In hysteria we may seem to lose the ability to see or feel or walk, or we may lose for the time all recollection of certain past events, or of whole periods of our lives, or of everything but one system of ideas which monopolizes the field of attention. Sometimes great systems of memories, instincts, and complexes are alternately shifted in and out of gear, leaving first one kind of person on top and then another.[25] Stevenson's _Dr. Jekyll_ and _Mr. Hyde_ is not so fantastic a character as he seems. Any one who doubts the ability of the mind to split itself up into two or more distinct personalities, entertaining totally different conceptions of life, disliking each other, playing tricks on each other, writing notes to each other, and carrying on a perpetual feud as each tries to get the upper hand, should read Morton Prince's "Dissociation of a Personality," a fascinating account of his famous case, Miss Beauchamp.

[Footnote 25: When a memory or system of memories is suddenly lost from consciousness the person is said to be suffering from amnesia or pathological loss of memory.]

=Internal Warfare.= Conflict, often accentuated by shock or fatigue, represses or drives down certain ideas, perceptions, wishes, memories, or complexes into the subconscious, where they remain, sometimes dormant and passive but often dynamic, emotional, carrying on an over-excited, automatic activity, freed from the control of reason and the modifying influence of other ideas, and able to cause almost any kind of disturbance. So long as there is team-work between the various parts of our personality we are able to act as a unit; but just as soon as we break up into factions with no communication between the warring camps, so soon do we become quite incapable of coordination or adjustment, like a nation torn by civil war. Many of the seemingly fantastic and bizarre mental phenomena of which a human being is capable are the result of this kind of disintegration.

However, nature has a remarkable power for righting herself, and it is only under an accumulation of unfortunate circumstances that there appears a neurosis, which is nothing more than a functioning of certain parts of the personality with all the rest dissociated. We shall later inquire more fully into the causes that lead up to such a result and shall find that the mechanisms involved are these processes of organization and disorganization by which mind is wont to group together or separate the various elements within its borders.

SUMMARY

Gathering up our impressions, we find a number of outstanding qualities which we may summarize in the following way:

The Subconscious is:

1 Vast yet Explorable

The fraction that could accurately show the relation of the conscious to the unconscious part of ourselves would have such a small numerator and such a huge denominator that we might well wonder where consciousness came in at all.[26] Some one has likened the subconscious to the great far-reaching depths of the Mammoth Cave, and consciousness to the tiny, flickering lamp which we carry to light our way in the darkness. However, ever the subconscious mind is becoming explorable, and it may be that science is giving the tiny lamp the revealing power of a great searchlight.

[Footnote 26: "The entire active life of the individual may be represented by a fraction, the numerator of which is any particular moment, the denominator is the rich inheritance of the past."--Jelliffe: "The Technique of Psychoanalysis," _Psychoanalytic Review,_ Vol. III, No. 2, p. 164.]

2 Ancient yet Modern

The lowest layers of the subconscious, represented by the instincts, are as old as life itself, with their lineage reaching back in direct and unbroken line to the first living things on the ooze of the ocean floor. The higher strata are more modern, full, and accurate records of our own lifetime, beginning with our first cry and ending with to-day's thoughts.

3 Primitive yet Refined

The lowest level, representing the past of the race, is primitive like a savage, and infantile, like a child; it is instinctive, unalterable, and universal; it knows no restraint, no culture, and no prudence. The higher level, the storehouse of individual experience, bears the marks of acquired ideals, of cultivated refinement, and represents among other things the precepts and prudence of civilized society.

4 Emotional yet Intellectual

Our records of the past are not dead archives, but living forces--persistent, urging, dynamic and emotional. They give meaning to new experiences, color our judgments, shape our beliefs, determine our interests, and, if wrongly handled, make their way into consciousness as neurotic symptoms.

However, the subconscious is not all emotion. It is a mind capable of elaborate thought, able to calculate, to scheme, to answer doubts, to solve problems, to fabricate the purposeful, fantastic allegories of dreams and to create from mere knowledge the inspired works of genius.

But the subconscious has one great limitation, it cannot reason inductively. Given a premise, this mind can reason as unerringly as the most skilful logician; that is, it can reason deductively, but it cannot arrive at a general conclusion from a number of particular facts. However, except for inductive reasoning and awareness, the subconscious seems to possess all the attributes of conscious mind and is in fact an intellectual force to be reckoned with.

5 Organized yet Disorganizable

The subconscious mind is a highly organized institution, but like all such institutions it is liable to disorganization when rent by internal dissension. Ordinarily it keeps its ideas and emotions, its complexes and moods in fairly accurate order, but when upset by emotional warfare, it gets its records confused and falls into a chaotic state which makes regular business impossible.

6 Masterful yet Obedient

The subconscious, which is master of the body, is in normal life the servant of consciousness. One of its outstanding qualities is suggestibility. Since it cannot reason from particulars to a general conclusion it takes any statement given it by consciousness, believes it implicitly and acts accordingly.

The pilot wheel of the ship is, after all, the conscious mind, insignificant in size when compared with the great mass of the vessel, but all-powerful in its ability to direct the course of the voyage.

Nervous persons are people who are too much under the sway of the subconscious; so, too, are some geniuses, who narrowly escape a neurosis by finding a more useful outlet for their subconscious energies. While the poet, the inventor, and the neurotic are likely to be too largely controlled by the subconscious, the average man is to a greater extent ruled by the conscious mind; and the highest type of genius is the man whose conscious and subconscious minds work together in perfect harmony, each up to its full power.

If, as many believe, the next great strides of science are to be in this direction, it may pay some of us to be pioneers in learning how to make use of these undeveloped riches of memory, organization, and surplus energy. The subconscious, which can on occasion behave like a very devil within us, is, when rightly used, our greatest asset, the source of powers whose appearance in the occasional individual has been considered almost superhuman, but which prove to be characteristically human, the common inheritance of the race of man.

CHAPTER VI

In which we learn why it pays to be cheerful BODY AND MIND

THE MISSING LINK

=Ancient Knowledge.= People have always known that mind in some strange way carries its moods over into the body. The writer of the Book of Proverbs tells us, from that far-off day, that "A merry heart doeth good like a medicine, but a broken spirit drieth the bones." Jesus in His healing ministry always emphasized the place of faith in the cure of the body. "Thy faith hath made thee whole," is a frequent word on His lips, and ever since His day people have been rediscovering the truth that faith, even in the absence of a worthy object, does often make whole. Faith in the doctor, the medicine, the charm, the mineral waters, the shrine, and in the good God, has brought health to many thousands of sufferers. People have always reckoned on this bodily result from a mental state. They have intuitively known better than to tell a sick person that he is looking worse, but they have not always known why. They have known that a fit of anger is apt to bring on a headache, but they have not stopped to look for the reason, or if they have, they have often gotten themselves into a tangle. This is because there has always been, until recently, a missing link. Now the link has been found. After the last chapter, it will not be hard to understand that this connecting link, this go-between of body and mind, is nothing else than the subconscious mind. When we remember that it has the double power of knowing our thoughts and of controlling our bodies, it is not hard to see how an idea can translate itself into a pain, nor to realize with new vividness the truth of the statement that healthy mental states make for health, and unhealthy mental states for illness.

=Suggestion and Emotion.= There are still many gaps in our knowledge of the ways of the subconscious, but investigation has thrown a good deal of light on the problem. Two of the principles already discussed are sufficient to explain most of the phenomena. These are, first, that the subconscious is amenable to control by suggestion, and secondly, that it is greatly influenced by emotion. Tracing back the principles behind any example of the power of mind over body, one finds at the root of the matter either a suggestion or an emotion, or both. If, then, the stimulating and depressing effects of mental states are to be understood, the first Step must be a fuller understanding of the laws governing suggestion and emotion.

THE CONTAGION OF IDEAS

One of the most important points about the subconscious mind is its openness to suggestion. It likes to believe what it is told and to act accordingly. The conscious mind, too,--proud seat of reason though it may be,--shares this habit of accepting ideas without demanding too much proof of their truth. Even at his best, man is extremely susceptible to the contagion of ideas. Most of us are even less immune to this mental contagion than we are to colds or influenza; for ideas are catching. They are such subtle, insinuating things that they creep into our minds without our knowing it at all; and once there, they are as powerful as most germs.

Let a person faint in a crowded room, and a good per cent. of the women present will begin to fan themselves. The room has suddenly become insufferably close. After we have read half a hundred times that Ivory soap floats, a fair proportion of the population is likely to be seized with desire for a soap that floats,--not because they have any good reason for doing so, but simply because the suggestion has "taken." As for the harbingers of spring, they are neither the birds nor the wild flowers, but the blooming windows of the milliners, which successfully suggest in wintry February that summer is coming, and that felt and fur are out of season. It is evident that all advertising is suggestion.

The training of children, also, if it is done in the right way, is largely a matter of suggestion. The little child who falls down and bumps his head is very likely to cry if met with a sympathetic show of concern, while the same child will often take his mishaps as a joke if his elders meet them with a laugh or a diverting remark. Unlucky is the child whose mother does not know, either consciously or intuitively, that example and contagion are more powerful-- and more pleasant--than command and prohibition.

=Everything Suggestive.= Human beings are constantly communicating, one to another. Sometimes they "get over" an idea by means of words, but often they do it in more subtle ways,--by the elevation of an eyelid, the gesture of a hand, composure of manner in a crisis, or a laugh in a delicate situation. A suggestion is merely an idea passed from one person to another, an idea that is accepted with conviction and acted upon, even though there may be no logic, no reason, no proof of its truth. It is an influence that takes hold of the mind and works itself out to fulfilment, quite apart from its worth or reasonableness. Of course, logical persuasion and argument have their place in the communication of ideas; an idea may be conveyed by other ways than suggestion. But while suggestion is not everything, it is equally true that there is suggestion in everything. The doctor may give a patient a very rational explanation of his case, but the doubtful shake of the head or the encouraging look of his eye is quite likely to color the patient's general impression. The eyes of our subconscious are always open, and they are constantly getting impressions, subtle suggestions that are implied rather than expressed.

=Abnormal Suggestibility.= While everybody is suggestible, nervous people are abnormally so. It may be, as McDougall suggests, that they have so large an amount of submission or negative self-feeling in their make-up that they believe anything, just because some one else says it is true. Sometimes it is lack of knowledge that makes us gullible, and at other times the cause of our suggestibility is failure to use the knowledge that we have. Sometimes our ideas are locked away in air-tight compartments with no interaction between them. The psychologists tell us that suggestion is greatly favored by a narrowing of the attention, a "contraction of the field of consciousness," a dissociation of other ideas through concentration. This all simply means that we forget to let our common sense bring to bear counter ideas that might challenge a false one; or that worry--a veritable "spasm of the attention"--has fixed upon an idea to the exclusion of all others; or that through fatigue or the dissociation of sleep or hypnosis or hysteria, our reasoning powers have been locked out and for the time being are unable to act.

It was through experiments on hypnotized subjects that scientists first learned of the suggestibility of the subconscious mind. In hypnosis a person can be made to believe almost anything and to do almost anything compatible with the safety and the moral sense of the individual. The instinct of self-preservation will not allow the most deeply hypnotized person to do anything dangerous to himself; and the moral complexes, laid in the subconscious, never permit a person to perform in earnest an act of which the waking moral sense would disapprove. Within these limits, a person in the dissociated hypnotic state can be made to accept almost any suggestion. We found in the last chapter how open to suggestion is a person in normal sleep. Of the dissociation of hysteria we shall have occasion to speak in later chapters. Although all these special states heighten suggestibility, we must not forget how susceptible each of us is in his normal waking state.

=Living Its Faith.= All this gathers meaning only when we realize that ideas are dynamic. They always tend to work themselves out to fulfilment. The subconscious no sooner gets a conviction than it tries to act it out. Of course it can succeed only up to a certain limit. If it believes the stomach to have cancer, it cannot make cancer, but it can make the stomach misbehave. One of my patients, on hearing of a case of brain-tumor immediately imagined this to be her trouble, and developed a pain in her head. She could not manufacture a tumor, but she could manufacture what she believed to be the symptoms.

There was another patient who was supposed to have brain-tumor. This young woman seemed to have lost almost entirely the power to keep her equilibrium in walking. Her center of gravity was never over her feet, but away out in space, so that she was continually banging from one side of the room to the other, only saving herself from injury by catching at the wall or the furniture with her hands. Several physicians who had been interested in the case had found the symptoms strongly suggestive of brain-tumor. There were, however, certain unmistakable earmarks of hysteria, such as childlike bland indifference to the awkwardness of the gait which was a grotesque caricature of several brain and spinal-cord diseases, with no accurate picture of any single one. This was evidently a case, not of actual loss of power but a dissociation of the memory-picture of walking. The patient was a trained nurse and knew in a general way the symptoms of brain-tumor. When the suggestion of brain-tumor had fixed itself in her mind she was able subconsciously to manufacture what she believed to be the symptoms of that disease.

By injecting a keen sense of disapprobation and skepticism into the hitherto placidly accepted state of disability, by flashing a mirror on the physical and moral attitudes which she was assuming, I was able to rob the pathological complex of its (altogether unconscious) pleasurable feeling-tone, and to restore to its former strength and poise a personality of exceptional native worth and beauty. After a few weeks at my house she was able to walk like a normal person and went back to her work, for good.

We have already learned enough about the inner self to see in a faint way how it works out its ideas. Since the subconscious mind runs the bodily machinery, since it regulates digestion, the building up of tissue, circulation, respiration, glandular secretion, muscular tonus, and every other process pertaining to nutrition and growth, it is not difficult to see how an idea about any of these matters can work itself out into a fact. A thought can furnish the mental machinery needed to fulfil the thought. Some one catches the suggestion: "Concentration is hard on the brain. It soon brings on brain-fag and headache." Not knowing facts to the contrary, the suggestible mind accepts the proposition. Then one day, after a little concentration, the idea begins to work. Whereupon the autonomic nervous system tightens up the blood-vessels that regulate the local blood supply, too much blood stays in the head, and lo, it aches! The next time, the suggestion comes with greater force, and soon the habit is formed,--all the result of an idea. It is a good thing to remember that constant thought about any part of the body never fails to send an over-supply of blood to that part; of course that means congestion and pain.

=Hands Off!= By sending messages directly to an organ through the nerve-centers or by changing circulation, the subconscious director of our bodies can make any part of us misbehave in a number of ways. All it needs is a suggestion of an interfering thought about an organ. As we have insisted before, the subconscious cannot stand interference. Sadler well says: "Man can live at the equator or exist at the poles. He can eat almost anything and everything, but he cannot long stand self-contemplation. The human mind can accomplish wonders in the way of work, but it is soon wrecked when directed into the channels of worry."[27] In other words, hands off!--or rather, minds off! Don't get ideas that make you think about your body. The surest way to disarrange any function is to think about it. It is a stout heart that will not change its beat with a frequent finger on the pulse, and a hearty stomach that will not "act up" under attention. "Judicious neglect" is a good motto for most occasions. Take no anxious thought if you would be well. Know enough about your body to counteract false suggestions; fulfil the common-sense laws of hygiene,--eight hours in bed, plenty of exercise and fresh air, and three square meals a day. Then forget all about it. "A mental representation is already a sensation,"[28] and we have enough legitimate sensations without manufacturing others.

[Footnote 27: Sadler: Physiology of Faith and Fear.]

[Footnote 28: DuBois: Psychic Treatment of Nervous Disorders.]

=From Real Life.= Startling indeed are the tricks that we can play on ourselves by disregarding these laws. A patient who was unnecessarily concerned about his stomach once came to me in great alarm, exhibiting a distinct, well-defined swelling about the size of a match-box in the region of his stomach. I looked at it, laughed, and told him to forget it. Whereupon it promptly disappeared. The first segment of the rectus muscle had tied itself up into a knot, under the stimulus of anxious attention.

Another patient appeared at my door one day saying, "Look here!" Examination showed that her abdomen was swollen to the size of more than a six-months pregnancy. As it happened, this woman had a friend who a short time before had developed a pseudo, or hysterical pregnancy which continued for several months. My patient, accepting the suggestion, was prepared to imitate her. I gave her a punch or two and told her to go and dress for luncheon. In the afternoon she had returned to her normal size.

Another woman, suffering from chronic constipation, was firmly convinced that her bowels could not move without a cathartic, which I refused to give. However, I did give her some strychnine pills, carefully explaining that they were not for her intestines and that they would have no effect there. She did not believe me, and promptly began to have an evacuation every day. It seems that sometimes two wrong ideas are equal to a right one.

If doctors fully realized the power of suggestion, they would be more careful than they sometimes are about suggesting symptoms by the questions they ask their patients.

A patient of mine with locomotor-ataxia suffered from the usual train of symptoms incident to that disease. It turned out, however, that many of the symptoms had been suggested by the questions of former physicians who had asked him whether he had certain symptoms and certain disabilities. The patient had answered in the negative and then promptly developed the suggested symptoms. When I told him what had happened, these false symptoms disappeared leaving only those which had a real physical foundation.

Another patient, a young girl, complained of a definite localized pain in her arm, and told me that she was suffering from angina pectoris. As we do not expect to find this disease in a young person, I asked her where she got such an idea. "Dr. ---- told me so last May." "Did you feel the pain in this same place before that time?" I asked. She thought a minute and then answered: "Why no, I had a pain around my heart but I did not notice it in my arm until after that consultation." The wise physician lets his patients describe their own symptoms without suggesting others by the implication of his questions.

=Autosuggestion.= Of course we must remember that an idea cannot always work itself out immediately. Conditions are not always ripe. It often lies fallow a long time, buried in the subconscious, only to come up again as an autosuggestion, a suggestion from the self to the self. If some one tells us that nervous insomnia is disastrous, and we believe it, we shall probably store up the idea until the next time that chance conditions keep us awake. Then the autosuggestion "bobs up," common sense is side-tracked, we toss and worry--and of course stay awake. An autosuggestion often repeated becomes the strongest of suggestions, successfully opposing most outside ideas that would counteract it,--reason enough for seeing to it that our autosuggestions are of the healthful variety.

At the base of every psycho-neurosis is an unhealthful suggestion. This is never the ultimate cause. There are other forces at work. But the suggestion is the material out of which those other forces weave the neurosis. Suggestibility is one of the earmarks of nervousness. A sensible and sturdy spirit, stable enough to maintain its equilibrium, is a fairly good antidote to attack. "As a man thinketh in his heart, so is he."

WHY FEELINGS COUNT

=The Emotions Again.= It seems impossible to discuss any psychological principle without finally coming back to the subject of emotions. It truly seems that all roads lead to the instincts and to the emotions which drive them. And so, as we follow the trail of suggestion, we suddenly turn a corner and find ourselves back at our starting-point--the emotional life. Like all other ideas, suggestions get tied up with emotions to form complexes, of which the driving-power is the emotion.

If we look into our emotional life, we find, besides the true emotions, with which we have become familiar in Chapter III, a great number of feelings or feeling-tones which color either pleasurably or painfully our emotions and our ideas. On the one hand there are pleasure, joy, exaltation, courage, cheer, confidence, satisfaction; and on the other, pain, sorrow, depression, apprehension, gloom, distrust, and dissatisfaction. Every complex which is laid away in our subconscious is tinted, either slightly or intensely, with its specific feeling-tone.

=Emotions--Tonic and Poisonous.= All this is most important because of one vital fact; joyful emotions invigorate, and sorrowful emotions depress; pleasurable emotions stimulate, and painful emotions burden; satisfying emotions revitalize, and unsatisfying emotions sap the strength. In other words, our bodies are made for courage, confidence, and cheer. Any other atmosphere puts them out of their element, handicapped by abnormal conditions for which they were never fashioned. We were written in a major key, and when we try to change over into minor tones we get sadly out of tune.

There is another factor; painful emotions make us fall to pieces, while pleasant emotions bind us together. We can see why this is so when we remember that powerful emotions like fear and anger tend to dissociate all but themselves, to split up the mind into separate parts and to force out of consciousness everything but their own impulse. Morton Prince in his elaborate studies of the cases of multiple personality, Miss Beauchamp and B.C.A., found repeatedly that he had only to hypnotize the patient and replace painful, depressing complexes by healthy, happy ones to change her from a weak, worn-out person, complaining of fatigue, insomnia, and innumerable aches and pains, into a vigorous woman, for the time being completely well. On this point he says:

Exalting emotions have an intense synthesizing effect, while depressing emotions have a disintegrating effect. With the inrushing of depressive memories or ideas ... there is suddenly developed a condition of fatigue, ill-being and disintegration, followed after waking by a return or accentuation of all the neurasthenic symptoms. If on the other hand, exalting ideas and memories are introduced and brought into the limelight of attention, there is almost a magical reversal of processes. The patient feels strong and energetic, the neurasthenic symptoms disappear and he exhibits a capacity for sustained effort. He becomes re-vitalized, so to speak.[29]

[Footnote 29: Prince: _Psycho-therapeutics_, Chap. I.]

In cases like this the needed strength and energy are not lost; they are merely side-tracked, but the person feels as weak as though he were physically ill.

BODILY RESPONSE TO EMOTIONAL STATES

=Secretions.= Let us look more carefully into some of the physiological processes involved in emotional changes. Among the most apparent of bodily responses are the various external secretions. Tears, the secretion of the lachrymal glands in response to an emotion, are too common a phenomenon to arouse comment. It is common knowledge that clammy hands and a dry mouth betray emotion. Every nursing mother knows that she dares not become too disturbed lest her milk should dry up or change in character. Most people have experienced an increase in urine in times of excitement; recently physiologists have discovered the presence of sugar in the urine of students at the time of athletic contests and difficult examinations.[30] We have seen what an important role the various internal secretions, such as the adrenal and thyroid secretions play in fitting the body for flight and combat, and how large a part fear and anger have in their production. Constant over-production of these secretions through chronic states of worry is responsible for many a distressing symptom.

[Footnote 30: Cannon.]

Most graphic evidence of the disturbance of secretions by emotion is found in the response of the salivary and gastric glands to painful or pleasurable thinking. As these are the secretions which play the largest part in the digestive processes, they lead us naturally to our next heading.

=Digestion.= Everybody knows that appetizing food makes the mouth water, but not everybody realizes that it makes the stomach water also. Nor do we often realize the vital place that this watering has in taking care of our food. "Well begun is half-done," is literally true of digestion. A good flow of saliva brings the food into contact with the taste-buds in the tongue. Taste sends messages to the nerve-centers in the medulla oblongata; these centers in turn flash signals to the stomach glands, which immediately "get busy" preparing the all-important gastric juice. It takes about five minutes for this juice to be made ready, and so it happens that in five minutes after the first taste, or even in some cases after the first smell, the stomach is pouring forth its "appetite juice" which determines all the rest of the digestive process, in intestines as well as in stomach. Experiments on dogs and cats by Pawlow, Cannon, and others have shown what fear and anger and even mildly unpleasant emotions do to the whole digestive process. Cannon tells of a dog who produced 66.7 cubic centimeters of pure gastric juice in the twenty minutes following five minutes of sham feeding (feeding in which food is swallowed and then dropped out of an opening in the esophagus into a bucket instead of into the stomach). Although there was no food in the stomach, the juice was produced by the enjoyment of the taste and the thought of it. On another day, after this dog had been infuriated by a cat, and then pacified, the sham feeding was given again. This time, although the dog ate eagerly, he produced only 9 cubic centimeters of gastric juice, and this rich in mucus. Evidently a good appetite and attractively served food are not more important than a cheerful mind. Spicy table talk, well mixed with laughter, is better than all the digestive tablets in the world. What is true of stomach secretions is equally true of stomach contractions. "The pleasurable taking of food" is a necessity if the required contractions of stomach and intestines are to go forward on schedule time. A little extra dose of adrenalin from a mild case of depression or worry is enough to stop all movements for many minutes. What a revelation on many a case of nervous dyspepsia! The person who dubbed it "Emotional Dyspepsia" had facts on his side.

=Circulation.= It is not the heart only that pumps the blood through the body. The tiny muscles of the smallest blood-vessels, by their elasticity are of the greatest importance in maintaining an even flow, and this is especially influenced by fear and depression. Blushing, pallor, cold hands and feet, are circulatory disturbances based largely on emotions. Better than a hot-water bottle or electric pads are courage and optimism. A patient of mine laughingly tells of an incident which she says happened a number of years ago, but which I have forgotten. She says that she asked me one night as she carried her hot-water bottle to bed, "Doctor, what makes cold feet?" and that I lightly answered "Cowardice!" Whereupon she threw away her beloved water-bag and has never needed it since.

There is a disturbance of the circulation which results in very marked swelling and redness of the affected part. This is known as angio-neurotic edema, or nervous swelling. I do not have to go farther than my own person for an example of this phenomenon. When I was a young woman I taught school and went home every day for luncheon. One day at luncheon, some one of the family criticized me severely. I went back to school very angry. Before I entered the school-room, the principal handed me some books which she had ordered for me. They were not at all the books I wanted, and that upset me still more. As I went into the schoolroom, I found that my face was swollen until my eyes were almost shut; it was a bright red and covered with purplish blotches. My fingers were swollen so that I could not bend the joints in the slightest degree. It was a day or two before the disturbance disappeared, and the whole of it was the result of anger.

We hear much to-day about high blood pressure. They say that a man is as old as his arteries, and now it is known that the health of the arteries depends largely on blood pressure. Since this is a matter that can be definitely measured at any minute, we have an easy way of noting the remarkable effect of shifting emotions. Sadler tells of an ex-convict with a blood pressure of 190 millimeters. It seems that he was worrying over possible rearrest. On being reassured on this point, his blood pressure began to drop within a few minutes, falling 20 mm. in three hours, and 35 mm. by the following day.

=Muscular Tone.= A force that affects circulation, blood pressure, respiration, nutrition of cells, secretion, and digestion, can hardly fail to have a marked effect on the tone of the muscles, internal as well as external. When we remember that heart, stomach, and intestines are made of muscular tissue, to say nothing of the skeletal muscles, we begin to realize how important is muscular tone for bodily health. Over and over again have I demonstrated that a courageous mind is the best tonic. Perhaps an example from my "flat-footed" patients will be to the point. One woman, the young mother of a family, came to me for a nervous trouble. Besides this, she had suffered for seven or eight years from severe pains in her feet and had been compelled to wear specially made shoes prescribed by a Chicago orthopedist. The shoes, however, did not seem to lessen the pain. After an ordinary day's occupation, she could not even walk across the floor at dinner-time. A walk of two blocks would incapacitate her for many days. She was convinced that her feet could never be cured and came to me only on account of nervous trouble. On the day of her arrival she flung herself down on the couch, saying that she would like to go away from everybody, where the children would never bother her again. She was sure nobody loved her and she wanted to die. Within three weeks, in ordinary shoes, this woman tramped nine miles up Mount Wilson and the next day tramped down again. Her attitude had changed from that of irritable fretfulness to one of buoyant joy, and with the moral change had come new strength in the muscles. The death of her husband has since made it necessary for her to support the family, and she is now on her feet from eight to fourteen hours a day, a constant source of inspiration to all about her, and no more weary than the average person.

Flabbiness in the muscles often causes this trouble with the feet. "The arches of the foot are maintained by ligaments between the bones, supported by muscle tendons which prevent undue stretching of the ligaments and are a protection against flat-foot."[31] Muscle tissue has an abundant blood supply, while ligaments have very little and soon lose their resiliency if unsupported. Any lack of tone in the calf-muscles throws the weight on the less resistant ligaments and on the cartilages placed as cushions between the bony structures of the arch. This is what causes the pain.[32]

[Footnote 31: Grey's Anatomy--"The Articulations."]

[Footnote 32: Actual loss of the arch by downward displacement of the bones cannot be overcome by restoring muscle-tone. The majority of so-called cases of flatfoot are, however, in the stage amenable to psychic measures.]

Flat-footedness is only one result of weak muscles. Eye-strain is another; ptosis, or falling of the organs, is another. In a majority of cases the best treatment for any of these troubles is an understanding attempt to go to the root of the matter by bracing up the whole mental tone. The most scientific oculists do not try to correct eye trouble due to muscular insufficiency by any special prisms or glasses. They know that the eyes will right themselves when the general health and the general spirits improve. I have found by repeated experience with nervous patients that it takes only a short time for people who have been unable to read for months or years to regain their old faculty. So remarkable is the power of mind.

SUMMARY

We have found that the gap between the body and the mind is not so wide as it seems, and that it is bridged by the subconscious mind, which is at once the master of the body and the servant of consciousness. In recording the physical effects of suggestion and emotion, we have not taken time to describe the galvanometers, the weighing-machines and all the other apparatus used in the various laboratory tests; but enough has been said to show that when doctors and psychologists speak of the effect of mind on body, they are dealing with definite facts and with laws capable of scientific proof.

We have emphasized the fact that downcast and fearful moods have an immediate effect on the body; but after all, most people know this already. What they do not know is the real cause of the mood. When a nervous person finds out why he worries, he is well on the way toward recovery. An understanding of the cause is among the most vital discoveries of modern science.

The discussion, so far, has merely prepared us to plunge into the heart of the question: What is it that in the last analysis makes a person nervous, and how may he find his way out? This question the next two chapters will try to answer.

CHAPTER VII

In which we go to the root of the matter THE REAL TROUBLE

PIONEERS

=Following the Gleam.= Kipling's Elephant-child with the "'satiable curiosity" finally asked a question which seemed simple enough but which sent him on a long journey into unknown parts. In the same way man's modest and simple question, "What makes people nervous?" has sent him far-adventuring to find the answer. For centuries he has followed false trails, ending in blind alleys, and only lately does he seem to have found the road that shall lead him to his journey's end.

We may be thankful that we are following a band of pioneers whose fearless courage and passion for truth would not let them turn back even when the trail led through fields hitherto forbidden. The leader of this band of pioneers was a young doctor named Freud.

THE SEARCH FOR TRUTH

=Early Beginnings.= In 1882, when Freud was the assistant to Dr. Breuer of Vienna, there was brought to them for treatment a young woman afflicted with various hysterical pains and paralyses. This young woman's case marked an epoch in medical history; for out of the effort to cure her came some surprising discoveries of great significance to the open-minded young student.

It was found that each of this girl's symptoms was related to some forgotten experience, and that in every case the forgetting seemed to be the result of the painfulness of the experience. In other words, the symptoms were not visitations from without, but expressions from within; they were a part of the mental life of the patient; they had a history and a meaning, and the meaning seemed in some way to be connected with the patient's previous attitude of mind which made the experience too painful to be tolerated in consciousness. These previous ideas were largely subconscious and had been acquired during early childhood. When by means of hypnosis a great mass of forgotten material was brought to the surface and later made plain to her consciousness, the symptoms disappeared as if by magic.

=A Startling Discovery.= For a time Breuer and Freud worked together, finding that their investigations with other patients served to corroborate their former conclusions. When it became apparent that in every case the painful experience bore some relation to the love-life of the patient, both doctors were startled. Along with most of the rest of the world, they had been taught to look askance at the reproductive instinct and to shrink from realizing the vital place which sex holds in human life.

Breuer dropped the work, and after an interval Freud went on alone. He was resolved to know the truth, and to tell what he saw. When he reported to the world that out of all his hundreds of patients, he had been unable, after the most careful analysis, to find one whose illness did not grow from some lack of adjustment of the sex-life, he was met by a storm of protest from all quarters. No amount of evidence seemed to make any difference. People were determined that no such libel should be heaped on human nature. Sex-urge was not respectable and nervous people were to be respected.

Despite public disapproval, the scorn of other scientists, and the resistance of his own inner prejudices, Freud kept on. He was forced to acknowledge the validity of the facts which invariably presented themselves to view. Like Luther under equal duress, he cried: "Here I stand. I can do no other."

=Freudian Principles.= Gradually, as he worked, he gathered together a number of outstanding facts about man's mental life and about the psycho-neuroses. These facts he formulated into certain principles, which may be summed up in the following way.

1 There is no chance in mental life; every mental phenomenon--hence every nervous phenomenon--has a cause and meaning.

2 Infantile mental life is of tremendous importance in the direction of adult

processes.

3 Much of what is called forgetting is rather a repression into the subconscious, of impulses which were painful to the personality as a whole.

4 Mental processes are dynamic, insisting on discharge, either in reality or in phantasy.

5 An emotion may become detached from the idea to which it belongs and be displaced on other ideas.

6 Sex-interests dominate much of the mental life where their influence is unrecognized. The disturbance in a psycho-neurosis is always in this domain of sex-life. "In a normal sexual life, no neurosis." If a shock is the precipitating cause of the trouble, it is only because the ground was already prepared by the sex-disturbance.

Freud was perhaps unfortunate in his choice of the word "sex," which has so many evil connotations; but as he found no other word to cover the field, he chose the old one and stretched its meaning to include all the psychic and physical phenomena which spring directly and indirectly from the great processes of reproduction and parental care, and which ultimately include all and more than our word "love."[33]

[Footnote 33: Freud and his followers have always said that they saw no theoretical reason why any other repressed instinct should not form the basis of a neurosis, but that, as a matter of fact, they never had found this to be the case, probably because no other instinct comes into such bitter and persistent conflict with the dictates of society. Now, however, the Great War seems to have changed conditions. Under the strain and danger of life at the front there has developed a kind of nervous breakdown called shellshock or war-neurosis, which seems in some cases to be based not on the repression of the instinct of race-preservation but on the unusual necessity for repression of the instinct of self-preservation. Army surgeons report that wounded men almost never suffer from shell-shock. The wound is enough to secure the unconsciously desired removal to the rear. But in the absence of wounds, a desire for safety may at the same time be so intense and so severely repressed that it seizes upon the neurosis as the only possible means of escape from the unbearable situation. In time of peace, however, the instinct of reproduction seems to be the only impulse which is severely enough repressed to be responsible for a nervous breakdown.]

=Later Developments.= Little by little, the scientific world came to see that this wild theorizer had facts on his side; that not only had he formulated a theory, but he had discovered a cure, and that he was able to free people from obsessions, fears, and physical symptoms before which other methods were powerless. One by one the open-minded men of science were converted by the overpowering logic of the evidence, until to-day we find not only a "Freudian school," counting among its members many of the eminent scientists of the day, but we find in medical schools and universities courses based on Freudian principles, with text-books by acknowledged authorities in medicine and psychology. We find magazines devoted entirely to psycho-analytic subjects,[34] besides articles in medical journals and even numerous articles in popular magazines. Not only is the treatment of nervous disorders revolutionized by these principles but floods of light are thrown on such widely different fields of study as ancient myths and folk lore, the theory of wit, methods of child training, and the little slips of the tongue and everyday "breaks" that have until recently been considered the meaningless results of chance.

[Footnote 34: The Psychoanalytic Review and the _International Journal of Psychoanalysis._]

=A Searching Question.= We find, then, that when we ask, "What makes people nervous?" we are really asking: "What is man like, inside and out, up and down? What makes him think, feel, and act as he does every hour of every day?" We are asking for the source of human motives, the science of human behavior, the charting of the human mind. It is hard to-day to understand how so much reproach and ridicule could have been aroused by the statement that the ultimate cause of nervousness is a disturbance of the sex-life. There has already been a change in the public attitude toward things sexual.

Training-courses for mothers and teachers, elementary teaching in the schools, lectures and magazine articles have done much to show the fallacy of our old hypersensitive attitude. Since the war, some of us know, too, with what success the army has used the Freudian principles in treating war-neurosis, which was mistakenly called shell-shock by the first observers. We know, too, more about the constitution of man's mind than the public knew ten years ago. When we remember the insistent character of the instincts and the repressive method used by society in restraining the most obstreperous impulse, when we remember the pain of such conflict and the depressing physical effects of painful emotions, we cannot wonder that this most sharply repressed instinct should cause mental and physical trouble.

=What about Sublimation?= On the other hand, it has been stated in

Chapter IV

that although this universal urge cannot be repressed, it can be sublimated or diverted to useful ends which bring happiness, not disaster, to the individual. We have a right, then, to ask why this happy issue is not always attained, why sublimation ever fails. If a psycho-neurosis is caused by a failure of an insistent instinct to find adequate expression, by a blocking of the libido or the love-force, what are the conditions which bring about this blocking? The sex-instinct of every respectable person is subject to restraint. Some people are able to adjust themselves; why not all? The question, "What makes people nervous?" then turns out to mean: What keeps people from a satisfactory outlet for their love-instincts? What is it that holds them back from satisfaction in direct expression, and prevents indirect outlet in sublimation? Whatever does this must be the real cause of "nerves."

THE CAUSES OF "NERVES"

=Plural, not Singular.= The first thing to learn about the cause is that it is not a cause at all, but several causes. We are so well made that it takes a combination of circumstances to upset our equilibrium. In other words, a neurosis must be "over-determined." Heredity, faulty education, emotional shock, physical fatigue, have each at various times been blamed for a breakdown. As a matter of fact, it seems to take a number of ingredients to make a neurosis,--a little unstable inheritance plus a considerable amount of faulty upbringing, plus a later series of emotional experiences bearing just the right relationship to the earlier factors. Heredity, childhood reactions, and later experiences, are the three legs on which a neurosis usually stands. An occasional breakdown seems to stand on the single leg of childhood experiences but in the majority of cases each of the three factors contributes its quota to the final disaster.

=Born or Made?= It used to be thought that neurotics, like poets, were born, not made. Heredity was considered wholly responsible, and there seemed very little to do about it. But to-day the emphasis on heredity is steadily giving way to stress on early environment. There are, no doubt, such factors as a certain innate sensitiveness, a natural suggestibility, an intensity of emotion, a little tendency to nervous instability, which predispose a person to nerves, but unless the inborn tendency is reinforced by the reactions and training of early childhood, it is likely to die a natural death.

CHILDHOOD EXPERIENCES

=Early Reactions.= Freud found that a neurotic is made before he is six years old. When by repeated explorations into the minds of his patients, he made this important discovery, he at first believed that the disturbing factor was always some single emotional experience or shock in childhood,--usually of a sexual nature. But Freud and later investigators have since found that the trouble is not so often a single experience as a long series of exaggerated emotional reactions, a too intense emotional life, a precocity in feeling tending toward fixation of childhood habits, which are thus carried over into adult life.

=Fixation of Habits.= Fixation is the word that expresses all this,--fixation of childish habits. A neurotic is a person who made such strong habits in childhood that he cannot abandon them in maturity. He is too much ruled by the past. His unconscious emotional thought-habits are the complexes which were made in childhood and therefore lack the power of adaptation to mature life.

We saw in Chapter IV that Nature takes great pains to develop in the child the psychic and physical trends which he will need later on in his mature love-life, and that this training is accomplished in a number of well-defined periods which lead from one to the other. If, however, the child reacts too intensely, lingers too long in any one of these phases, he lays for himself action lines of least resistance which he may never leave or to which he may return during the strain and stress of adult life.

In either case, the neurotic is a grown-up child. He may be a very learned, very charming person, but he is nevertheless dragging behind him a part of his childhood which he should have outgrown long ago. Part of him is suffering from an arrest of development,--not a leg or an arm but an impulse.

=Precocious Emotions.= The habits which tend to become fixed too soon seem to be of four kinds; the habit of loving, the habit of rebelling, the habit of repressing normal instincts, and the habit of dreaming. In each case it is the excess of feeling which causes the trouble,--too much love, too much hate, too much disgust, or too much pleasure in imagination. Exaggeration is always a danger-signal. An overdeveloped child is likely to be an underdeveloped man. Especially in the emotions is precocity to be deplored. A premature alphabet or multiplication table is not nearly so serious as premature intensity of feeling, nor so likely to lead later to trouble. Of course fixation in these emotional habits does not always lead to a serious breakdown. If the fixation is not too extreme, and if later events do not happen to accentuate the trouble, the arrest of development may merely show itself in certain weaknesses of character or in isolated symptoms without developing a real neurosis.

Let us examine each of these arrested habits and the excess emotion which sets the mold before it is ready for maturity.

=Too Much Self-Love.= In the chapter on the reproductive instinct, we found that the natural way to learn to love is by successively loving oneself, one's parents and family, one's fellows, and one's mate. If the love-force gets too much pleasure in any one of these phases, it finds it hard to give up its old love and to pass on to the next phase. Thus some children take too much pleasure in their own bodies or, a little later, in their own personalities. If they are too much interested in their own physical sensations and the pleasure they get by stimulating certain zones of the body, then in later life they cannot free themselves from the desire for this kind of satisfaction. Try as they may, they cannot be satisfied with normal adult relations, but sink back into some form of so-called sex-perversion.

Perhaps it is another phase of self-love which holds the child too much. If, like Narcissus, he becomes too fond of looking at himself, is too eager to show off, too desirous of winning praise, then forever after he is likely to be self-conscious, self-centered, thinking always of the impression he is making, unable ever to be at leisure from himself. He is fixed in the Narcissistic stage of his life, and is unadapted to the world of social relations.

=Too Much Family-love.= We have already spoken of the danger of fixation in the second period, that of object-love--the period of family relationships. The danger is here again one of degree and may be avoided by a little knowledge and self-control on the part of the parents. The little girl who is permitted to lavish too much love on her father, who does not see anybody else, who cannot learn to like the boys is a misfit. The wise mother will see that her love for her boy does not express itself too much by means of hugs and kisses. The mother who shows very plainly that she loves her little boy better than she loves her husband and the mother who boasts that her adolescent boy tells her all his secrets and takes her out in preference to any girl--that deluded mother is trying to take something that is not hers, and is thereby courting trouble. When her son grows up, he may not know why, but no girl will suit him, and he will either remain a bachelor or marry some older woman who reminds him subconsciously of his mother. His love-requirements will be too strict; he will be forever trying either in phantasy or in real life to duplicate his earlier love-experiences. This, of course, cannot satisfy the demands of a mature man. He will be torn between conflicting desires, unhappy without knowing why, unable either to remain a child or to become a man, and impelled to gain self-expression in indirect and unsatisfactory ways.

Since it is not possible in this space to recite specific cases which show how often a nervous trouble points back to the father-mother complex,[35] it may help to cite the opinions of a few of our best authorities. Freud says of the family complex, "This is the root complex of the neurosis." Jelliffe: "It is the foot-rule of measurement of success in life": by which he means that just so far as we are able at the right time to free ourselves from dependence on parents are we able to adjust ourselves to the world at large. Pfister: "The attitude toward parents very often determines for a life-time the attitude toward people in general and toward life itself." Hinkle: "The entire direction of lives is determined by parental relationships."

[Footnote 35: This is technically known as the Oedipus Complex.]

=Too Much Hate.= Besides loving too hard, there is the danger of hating too hard. If it sounds strange to talk of the hatreds of childhood, we must remember that we are thinking of real life as it is when the conventions of adult life are removed and the subconscious gives up its secrets.

Several references have been made to the jealousy of the small child when he has to share his love with the parent of the same sex. For every little boy the father gets in the way. For every little girl the mother gets in the way. At one time or other there is likely to be a period when this is resented with all the violence of a child's emotions. It is likely to be very soon repressed and succeeded by a real affection which lasts through life. But underneath, unmodified by time, there may exist simultaneously the old childish image and the old unconscious reaction to it, unconscious but still active in indirect ways.

Jealousy is very often united with the natural rebellion of a child against authority. The rebellion may, of course, be directed against either parent who is final in authority in the home. In most cases this is the father. As the impulse of self-assertion is usually stronger in boys than in girls, and as the boy's impulse in this direction is reinforced by any existing jealousy toward his father, we find a strong spirit of rebellion more often playing a subconscious part in the life of men than of women. The novelist's favorite theme of the conflict between the young man and "the old man" represents the conscious, unrepressed complex. More often, however, there is true affection for the father, while the rebellion which really belongs to the childish father-image is displaced or transferred to other symbols of authority,--the state, the law, the king, the school, the teacher, the church, or perhaps to religion and authority in general. Anarchists and atheists naturally rationalize their reasons for dissent, but, for all that, they are not so much intellectual pioneers as rebellious little boys who have forgotten to grow up.

=Liking to be "Bossed."= There is a worse danger, however, than too much rebellion, and that is too little rebellion. Sometimes this yielding spirit is the result of an overdose of negative self-feeling and an under-dose of positive self-feeling; but sometimes it is over-compensation for the repressed spirit of rebellion which the child considers wicked. Consciously he becomes over-meek, because he has to summon all his powers to fight his subconscious insurrection. Whether he be meek by nature or by training, he is likely to be a failure. Everybody knows that the child who is too good never amounts to anything. He who has never disobeyed is a weakling. Naturally resenting all authority, the normal individual, if he be well trained, soon learns that some authority is necessary. He rebels, but he learns to acquiesce, to a certain degree. If he acquiesces too easily, represses too severely his rebellious spirit, swings to the other extreme of wanting to be "bossed," he is very likely to end as a nervous invalid, unfitted for the battles of life. The neurotic in the majority of cases likes authority, clings to it too long, wants the teacher to tell him what to do, wants the doctor to order him around, is generally over-conscientious, and afraid he will offend the "boss" or some one else who reminds him of the father-image. All this carries a warning to parents who cannot manage their children without dominating their lives, even when the domination is a kindly one. Perhaps the modern child is in more danger of being spoiled than bullied, but analysis of nervous patients shows that both kinds of danger still exist.

=Too Much Disgust.= The third form of excessive emotion is disgust. The love-force, besides being blocked by a fixation of childish love and of childish reactions toward authority, is very often kept from free mature self-expression by a perpetuation of a childish reaction against sex. We hardly need dwell longer on the folly of teaching children to be ashamed of so inevitable a part of their own nature. Disgust is a very strong emotion, and when it is turned against a part of ourselves, united with that other strong impulse of self-regard and incorporated into the conscience, it makes a Chinese wall of exclusion against the baffled, misunderstood reproductive instinct, which is thrust aside as alien.

=Restraint versus Denial.= Repression is not merely restraint. It is restraint plus denial. To the clamoring instinct we say not merely, "No, you may not," but "No, you are not. You do not exist. Nothing like you could belong to me." The woman with nausea (Chapter V) did not say to herself: "You are a normal, healthy woman, possessed of a normal woman's desires. But wait a while until the proper time comes." Controlled by an immature feeling of disgust, she had said: "I never thought it. It cannot be."

The difference is just this. When an ungratifiable desire is honestly faced and squarely answered, it is modified by other desires, chooses another way of discharge, and ceases to be desire. When a desire is repressed, it is still desire, unsatisfied, insistent, unmodifiable by mature points of view, untouched by time, automatic, and capable of almost any subterfuge in order to get satisfaction. A repressed desire is buried, shut away from the disintegrating effects of sunlight and air. While the rest of the personality is constantly changing under the influence of new ideas, the buried complex lives on in its immaturity, absolutely untouched by time.

=Childish Birth-theories.= When a child's questions about where babies come from are met by evasions, he is forced to manufacture his own theories. His elders would laugh if they knew some of these theories, but they would not laugh if they knew how often the childish ideas, wide of the truth, furnish the material for future neuroses. Frink tells the story of a young woman who had a compulsion for taking drugs. Although not a drug-fiend in the usual sense, she was constantly impelled to take any kind of drug she could obtain. It was finally revealed that during her childhood she had tried hard to discover how babies were made, and had at last concluded that they grew in the mother as a result of some medicine furnished by the doctor. The idea had long been forgotten, only to reappear as a compulsion. The natural desire for a child was strong in her, but was repressed as unholy in an unmarried woman. The associated childish idea of drug-taking was not repellent to her moral sense and was used as a substitute for the real desire to bear a child.

Many of my patients have suffered from the effect of some such birth-theories. One young girl, twenty years old, was greatly afflicted with myso-phobia, or the fear of contamination. She spent most of her time in washing her hands and keeping her hands and clothing free from contamination by contact with innumerable harmless objects. When cleaning her shoes on the grass, she would kneel so that the hem of her skirt would touch the grass, lest some dust should fly up under her clothes. After eating luncheon in the park with a girl who had tuberculosis, she said that she was not afraid of tuberculosis in the lungs, but asked if something like tuberculosis might not get in and begin to grow somewhere else. Her life was full to overflowing of such compulsive fears.

As opportunity offered itself from day to day, I would catch her compulsive ideas in the very act of expressing themselves, and would pin her down as to the association and the source of her fear, always taking care not to make suggestions or ask leading questions. She was finally convinced out of her own mouth that her real fear was the idea of something getting into her body and growing there. Then she told how she had questioned her mother about the reproductive life and had been put off with signs of embarrassment. For a long time she had been afraid to walk or talk with a boy, because, not knowing how conception might occur, she feared grave consequences.

Very soon after the beginning of her conversations with me, the girl realized that her fear was really a disguised desire that something might be planted within and grow. With her new understanding of herself, her compulsions promptly slipped away. She began to eat and sleep, and to live a happy, natural life.

=Chronic Repression.= It takes first-hand acquaintance with nervous patients to realize how common are stories like these. Unnecessary repressions based on false training are the cause of many a physical symptom and mental distress which a little parental frankness might have forestalled.[36]

[Footnote 36: Parents who are eager to handle this subject in the right way are often sincerely puzzled as to how to go about it. No matter how complete their education, it is very likely to fail them at this critical point. For the benefit of such parents, let it be said with all possible emphasis that the first and most important step must be a change in their own mental attitude. If there is left within them the shadow of embarrassment on the subject of sex, their children will not fail to sense the situation at once. A feeling of hesitation or a tendency to apologize for nature makes a far deeper impression on the child-mind than do the most beautiful of half-believed words on the subject. And this impression, subtle and elusive as it may seem, is a real and vital experience which is quite likely to color the whole of the child's life. If you would give your children a fair start, you must first get rid of your own inner resistances. After that, all will be clear sailing.

In the second place, take the earliest opportunity to bring up the subject in a natural way. A young father told me recently that his little daughter had asked her mother why she didn't have any lap any more. "And of course your wife took that chance to tell her about the baby that is coming," I said. "Oh, no," he answered, "she did nothing of the kind. Mary is far too young to know about such things." There are always chances if we are on the look out for them--and the earlier the better. It has been noticed that children are never repelled by the idea of any natural process unless the new idea runs counter to some notion which has already been formed. The wise parent is the one who gets in the right impression before some other child has had a chance to plant the wrong one.

Then, too, we elders are judged quite as much by what we do not say as by what we do. Happy is the child who is not left to draw his own conclusions from the silence and evasiveness of his parents. The sex-instruction which children are getting in the schools is often good, but it usually comes too late--the damage is always done before the sixth year.

When it comes to the exact words in which to explain the phenomena of generation and birth each parent must naturally find his own way. The main point is that we must tell the truth and not try to improve on nature. If we say that the baby grows under the mother's heart and later the child learns that this is not true, he inevitably gets the idea that there is something not nice about the part of the body in which the baby does grow. What could be wrong with the simple truth that the father plants a tiny seed in the mother's body and that this seed joins with another little seed already there and grows until it is a real baby ready to come into the world? The question as to how the father plants the seed need cause no alarm. If brothers and sisters are brought up together with no artificial sense of false modesty, they very early learn the difference between the male and the female body. It is simple enough to tell the little child the function of the male structure. And it is easy to explain that the seeds do not grow until the little boy and girl have grown to be man and woman and that the way to be well and to have fine strong children is to leave the generative organs alone until that time. A sense of the dignity and high purpose of these organs is far more likely to prevent perversions--to say nothing of nervousness--than is an attitude of taboo and silence.]

A certain amount of repression is inevitable and useful, but a neurotic is merely an exaggerated represser. He represses so much of himself that it will not stay down.[37] He builds up a permanent resistance which automatically acts as a dam to his normal sex instinct and forces it into undesirable outlets.

[Footnote 37: "A neurosis is a partial failure of repression." Frink: Morbid Fears and Compulsions.]

A resistance is a chronic repression, repression that has become fixed and subconscious, a habit that has lost its flexibility and outlives its usefulness. It is a fixation of repression, and is built out of an over-strong complex or emotional thought habit, acquired during childhood, incorporated into the conscience and carried over into maturity, where it warps judgment and interferes with normal development because it is fundamentally untrue and at variance with the laws of nature.

=Too Much Day-Dreaming.= The fourth habit which holds back the adult from maturity and predisposes toward "nerves" is the habit of imagination. It need hardly be said that a certain kind of imagination is a good thing and one of man's greatest assets. But the essence of day-dreaming is the exact opposite; it is the desire to see things as they are not, but as we should like them to be,--not in order that we may bring them to pass, but for the mere pleasure of dreaming. Instead of turning a microscope or a telescope on the world of reality, as positive imagination does, this negative variety refuses even to look with the naked eye. To dream is easier than to do; to build up phantasies is easier than to build up a reputation or a fortune; to think a forbidden pleasure is easier than to sublimate. "Pleasure-thinking" is not only easier than "reality-thinking,"--it is the older way.

Children gratify many of their desires simply by imagining them gratified. Much of the difficulty of later life might be avoided if the little child could be taught to work for the accomplishment of his pleasures rather than to dream of them. The normal child gradually abandons this "pleasure-thinking" for the more purposeful thinking of the actual world, but the child who loiters too long in the realm of fancy may ever after find it hard to keep away from its borders. His natural interest in sex, if artificially repressed, is especially prone to satisfy itself by way of phantasy.

=Turning back to Phantasy.= In later life, when the love-force for one reason or another becomes too strong to be handled either directly or indirectly in the real world, there comes the almost irresistible impulse to regress to the infantile way and to find expression by means of phantasy. After long experience Freud concluded that phantasy lies at the root of every neurosis. Jung says that a sex-phantasy is always at least one determiner of a nervous illness, and Jelliffe writes that the essence of the neurosis is a special activity of the imagination.

Such a statement need not shock the most sensitive conscience. The very fact that a neurosis breaks out is proof that the phantasies are repellent to the owners of them and are thrust down into the subconscious as unworthy. In fact, every neurosis is witness to the strength of the human conscience. No phantasy could cause illness. It is the phantasy plus the repression of it that makes the trouble, or rather it is the conflict between the forces back of the phantasy and the repression. The neurosis, then, turns out to be a "flight from the real," the result of a desire to run away from a difficulty. When a problem presses or a disagreeable situation is to be faced, it is easier to give up and fall ill than to see the thing through to the end. Here again, we find that nervousness is a regression to the irresponsible reactions of childhood.

=Maturity versus Immaturity.= We have been thinking of the main causes of "nerves" and have found them to be infantile habits of loving, rebelling, repressing, and dreaming. We have tried to show that these habits are able to cause trouble because of their bearing on that inevitable conflict between the ancient urge of the reproductive instinct and the later ideals which society has acquired. If this conflict be met in the light of the present, free from the backward pull, of outgrown habits, an adjustment is possible which satisfies both the individual and society. We call this adjustment sublimation. This is rather a synthesis than a compromise, a union of the opposing forces, a happy utilization of energy by displacement on more useful ideas. But if the conflict has to be met with the mind hampered by immature thinking and immature feeling; if the demands of the here-and-now are met as if it were long ago; if unhealthy and untrue complexes, old loves and hates complicate the situation; if to the necessary conflict is added an unnecessary one; then something else happens. Compromise of some kind must be made, but instead of a happy union of the two forces a poor compromise is effected, gaining a partial satisfaction for both sides, but a real one for neither. The neurosis is this compromise.

LATER EXPERIENCES

=The Last Straw.= The precipitating cause may be one of a number of things. It may be entirely within, or it may be external. Perhaps it is only a quickening of the maturing instincts at the time of adolescence, making the love-force too strong to be held by the old repressions. Perhaps the husband, wife, or lover dies, or the life-work is taken away, depriving the vital energy of its usual outlets. Perhaps the trigger is pulled by an emotional shock which bears a faint resemblance to old emotional experiences, and which stimulates both the repressing and repressed trends and makes the person at the same time say both "Yes," and "No."[38] Perhaps physical fatigue lets down the mental and moral tension and makes the conflict too strong to be controlled. Perhaps an external problem presses and arouses the old habit of fleeing from disagreeable reality. Any or all these factors may cooperate, but not one of them is anything more than a last straw on an overburdened back. No calamity, deprivation, fatigue, or emotion has been able to bring about a neurosis unless the ground was prepared for it by the earlier reactions of childhood.

[Footnote 38: "The external world can only cause repression when there was already present beforehand a strong initial tension reaching back even to childhood."--Pfister: Psychoanalytic Method, p. 94.]

THE BREAKDOWN ITSELF

="Two Persons under One Hat."= We can understand now why a neurotic can be described in so many ways. We often hear him called an especially moral, especially ethical person, with a very active conscience; an intensely social being, unable to be satisfied with anything but a social standard; a person with "finer intellectual insight and greater sensitiveness than the rest of mankind." At the same time we are told that a neurosis is a partial triumph of anti-social, non-moral factors, and that it is a cowardly flight from reality; we hear a nervous invalid called selfish, unsocial, shut in, primitive, childish, self-deceived. Both these descriptions are true to life. A neurosis is an ethical struggle between these two sets of forces. If the lower set had triumphed, the man would have been merely weak; if the higher set had been victorious, he would have been strong. As it is, he is neither one nor the other,--only nervous. The neurosis is the only solution of the struggle which he is able to find, and serves the purpose of a sort of armed armistice between the two camps.

SERVING A PURPOSE

If a neurosis is a compromise, if it is the easiest way out, if it serves a purpose, it must be that the individual himself has a hand in shaping that purpose. Can it be that a breakdown which seems such an unmitigated disaster is really welcomed by a part of our own selves? Nothing is more intensely resented by the nervous invalid than the accusation that he likes his symptoms,--and no wonder. The conscious part of him hates the pain, the inconvenience, and the disability with a real hatred. It is not pleasant to be ill. And yet, as it turns out, it is pleasanter to be ill than it is to bear the tension of unsatisfied desire or to be undeceived about oneself. Every symptom is a means of expression for repressed and forgotten impulses and is a relief to the personality. It tends to the preservation of the individual, rather than to his destruction. The nervous invalid is not short-lived, but his family may be! It has been said that a neurosis is not so much a disease as a dilemma. Rather might it be said that the neurosis is a way out of the dilemma. It is a harbor after a stormy sea, not always a quiet harbor, but at least a usable one. Unpleasant as it is, every nervous symptom is a form of compensation which has been deliberately though unconsciously chosen by its owner.

=Rationalizing Our Distress.= Among other things, a nervous symptom furnishes a seemingly reasonable excuse for the sense of distress which is behind every breakdown. Something troubles us. We are not willing to acknowledge what it is. On the other hand, we must appear reasonable to ourselves, so we manufacture a reason. Perhaps at the time when the person first feels distress, he is on a railroad train. So he says to himself, "It is the train. I must not go near the railway"; and he develops a phobia for cars. Perhaps at the onset of the fear he happens to have a slight pain in the arm. He makes use of the pain to explain his distress. He thinks about it and holds on to it. It serves a purpose, and is on the whole less painful than the feeling of unexplained impending disaster which is attached to no particular idea. Perhaps he happens to be tired when the conflict first gets beyond control. So he seizes the idea of fatigue to explain his illness. He develops chronic fatigue and talks proudly of overwork. In every case the symptom serves a real purpose, and is, despite its discomfort, a relief to the distressed personality.

A neurosis is a subconscious effort at adjustment. Like a physical symptom, it is Nature's way of trying to cure herself. It is an attempt to get equilibrium, but it is an awkward attempt and hardly the kind that we would choose when we see what we are doing.

=Securing an Audience.= Besides furnishing relief from too intense strain, a nervous breakdown brings secondary advantages that are at most only dimly recognized by the individual. One of the most intense cravings of the primitive part of the subconscious is for an audience; a nervous symptom always secures that audience. The invalid is the object of the solicitous care of the family, friends, physician, and specialist. Pomp and ceremony, so dear to the child-mind, make their appeal to the dissociated part of the personality. The repressed instincts, hungry for love and attention, delight in the petting and special care which an illness is sure to bring. Secretly and unconsciously, the neurotic takes a certain pleasure in all the various changes that are made for his benefit,--the dismantling of striking clocks, the muffling of household noises, the banishing of crowing roosters, and the changes in menu which must be carefully planned for his stomach.

This characteristic of finding pleasure in personal ministrations is plainly a regression to the infantile phase of life. The baby demands and obtains the center of the stage. Later he has to learn to give it up, but the neurotic gets the center again and is often very loth to leave it for a more inconspicuous place.

=Capitalizing an Illness.= Then, too, a neurosis provides a way of escape from all sorts of disagreeable duties. It can be capitalized in innumerable ways,--ways that would horrify the invalid if he realized the truth. Much of the resentment manifested against the suggestion that the neurosis is psychic in origin is simply a resistance against giving up the unconsciously enjoyed advantages of the illness. An honest desire to get well is a long step toward cure.

The purposive character of a nervous illness is well illustrated by two cases reported by Thaddeus Hoyt Ames.[39] A young woman, the drudge of the family, suddenly became hysterically blind, that is, she became blind despite the fact that her eyes and optic nerves proved to be unimpaired. She remained blind until it was proved to her that a part of her welcomed the blindness and had really produced it for the purpose of getting away from the monotony of her unappreciated life at home. She naturally resented the charge but finally accepted it and "turned on" her eyesight in an instant. The other patient, a man, became blind in order to avoid seeing his wife who had turned out to be not at all what he had hoped. When he realized what he was doing, he decided that there might be better ways of adjusting himself to his wife. He then switched on his seeing power, which had never been really lost, but only disconnected and dissociated from the rest of his mind.

[Footnote 39: Thaddeus Hoyt Ames: Archives of Ophthalmology, Vol. XLIII, No. 4, 1914.]

That the conscious mind has no part in the subterfuge is shown by the fact that both patients gave up their artificial haven as soon as they saw how they had been fooling themselves. The fact remains that every neurosis is the fulfilment of a wish,--a distorted, unrecognized, unsatisfactory fulfilment to be sure, but still an effort to satisfy desire. As Frink remarks, "A neurosis is a kind of behaviour." We always choose the conduct we like. It is a matter of choice. Does not this answer our question as to why some people always take unhealthy suggestions? If we take the bad one, it is because it serves the need of a part of our being.

SIGN LANGUAGE

=Talking in Symbols.= We have several times suggested that a nervous symptom is a disguised, indirect expression of subconscious impulses. It is the completeness of the disguise which makes it so hard for us to realize its true meaning. It takes a stretch of the imagination to believe that a pain in the body can mean a pain in the soul, or that a fear of contamination can signify a desire to bear a child. But in all this we must not forget the primitive, childlike nature of the instinctive life.

The savage and the child do not think as civilized man thinks. Savage or child thinks in pictures; he acts his feelings; he groups things according to superficial resemblances, he expresses an idea by its opposite; he talks in symbols. We still use these devices in poetic speech and in everyday thought. A wedding-ring stands for the marriage bond; the flag for a nation; a greyhound for fleetness; a wild beast for ferocity; sunrise for youth; and sunset for old age. "The essence of language consists in the statement of resemblance. The expression of human thought is an expression of association."[40]

[Footnote 40: Trigant Burrow: Journal of American Medical Association, Vol. LXVI, No. II, 1916.]

The association may be so accidental and superficial as to seem absurd to another person, or it may be so fundamental as to express the universal thought of man from the beginning of time. Many of the signs and symbols which crop out in neurotic symptoms and in normal dreams are the same as those which appear in myths, fairy tales and folk-lore and in the art of the earlier races.

=A Secret Code.= When the denied instincts of a man's repressed life insist on expression, and when the shocked proprieties of his repressing life demand conformity to social standards, the subconscious, held back from free speech, strikes a compromise by making use of figurative language. As Trigant Burrow says, if the moral repugnance is very strong, the disguise must be more elaborate, the symbols more far-fetched. The symbols of nervous symptoms and of dreams are a "secret code," understood by the sender but meaningless to the censoring conscience, which passes them as harmless.

=The Right Kind of Symbolism.= Sublimation itself is merely a symbolic expression of basic impulses. It follows the line of our make-up, which naturally and fundamentally is wont to let one thing stand for another and to express itself in indirect ways. Sublimation says: "If I cannot recreate myself in the person of a child, I will recreate myself in making a bridge, or a picture, or a social settlement,--or a pudding." It says: "If I cannot have my own child to love, I will adopt an orphan-asylum, or I will work for a child-labor law." It merely lets one thing stand for another and transfers all the passions that belong to the one on to the other, which is the same thing as saying that it gives vent to its original desire by means of symbolic expression.

=The Wrong Kind of Symbolism.= A nervous disorder is an unfortunate choice of symbols. Instead of spiritualizing an innate impulse, it merely disguises it. The disguise takes a number of forms. One of the commonest ways is to act out in the body what is taking place in the soul. The woman with nausea converted her moral disgust into a physical nausea, which expressed her distress while it hid its meaning. The girl who was tired of seeing her work, and the man who wanted to avoid seeing his wife chose a way out which physically symbolized their real desire. A dentist once came to me with a paralyzed right arm. He had given up his office and believed that he would never work again. It turned out that his only son had just died and that he was dramatizing his soul-pain by means of his body. His subconscious mind was saying, "My good right arm is gone," and saying it in its own way. Within a week the arm was playing tennis, and ever since it has been busy filling teeth. There were, of course, other factors leading up to the trouble, but the factor which determined its form was the sense of loss which acted itself out through the body.

Sometimes, as we have seen, the disguise takes another form. Instead of conversion into a physical symptom, it lets one idea stand for another and displaces the impulse or the emotion to the substitute idea. The girl with the impulse to take drugs fooled her conscience by letting the drug-taking idea stand for the idea of conception. The girl with the fear of contamination carried the disguise still farther by changing the desire into fear,--a very common subterfuge.

=The Case of Mrs. Y.= There came to me a short time ago a little woman whose face showed intense fright. For several months she had spent much of the time walking the floor and wringing her hands in an agony of terror. In the night she would waken from her sleep, shaking with fear; soon she would be retching and vomiting, although she herself recognized the fact that there was nothing the matter with her stomach.

Part of the time her fear was a general terror of some unknown thing, and part of the time it was a specialized fear of great intensity. She was afraid she would choke her son, to whom she was passionately devoted. During the course of the treatment, which followed the lines of psycho-analysis to be described in the next chapter, I found that this fear had arisen one evening when she was lying reading by the side of her sleeping child. Suddenly, without warning, she had a sort of mental picture of her own hands reaching out and choking the boy. Naturally she was terrified. She jumped out of bed, decided that she was losing her mind and went into a hysterical state which her husband had great trouble in dispelling. After that she was afraid to be left alone with her children lest she should kill them.

During the analysis it was discovered that what she had been reading on that first night was the thirteenth verse of the ninety-first Psalm. "Thou shalt tread upon the lion and the adder. The young lion and the dragon thou shalt trample under foot." To her the adder meant the snake, the tempter in the Garden of Eden, and hence sex. What she wanted to choke was her own insistent sex urge of which the child was the symbol and the result. On later occasions she had the same sort of hallucinations in connection with another child and on sight of a brutish kind of man who symbolized to the subconscious mind the sex-urge, of which she was afraid. Not so much by what her mother had said as by what she had avoided saying, and by her expression whenever the subject was mentioned, had she given her little daughter a fundamentally wrong idea of the reproductive instinct. Later when the girl was woman grown she still clung to the old conception, deploring the sex-part of the marriage relation and feeling herself too refined to be moved by any such sensual urge. But the strong sex-instinct within her would not be downed. It was so insistent as to be an object of terror to her repressing instinct, which could not bring itself to acknowledge its presence. The fear that came to the surface was merely a disguised and symbolic representation of this real fear which was turning her life into a nightmare.

The nausea and vomiting in this woman seemed to be symbolic of the disgust which she felt subconsciously at the thought of her own sex-desires, but sometimes the physical disturbances which accompany such phobias are the natural physical reactions to the constant fear state. Indigestion, palpitation, and tremors are not in themselves symbolic of the inner trouble but may be the result of an overdose of the adrenal and thyroid secretions and the other accompaniments of fear. In such cases the real symptom is the fear, and the physical disturbance an incidental by-product of the emotional state. In any case a nervous symptom is always the sign of something else--a hieroglyph which must be deciphered before its real meaning can be discovered.

SUMMARY

=Three Kinds of People.= Absurd as it sounds, "nerves" turn out to be a question of morals; a neurosis, an affair of conscience; a nervous symptom an unsettled ethical struggle. The ethical struggle is not unusual; it is a normal part of man's life, the natural result of his desire to change into a more civilized being. The people in the world may be divided into three classes, according to the way they decide the conflict.

=The Primitive.= The first class merely capitulate to their primitive desires. They may not be nervous, but it is safe to say that they are rarely happy. The voice of conscience is hard to drown, even when it is not strong enough to control conduct. Happily it often succeeds in making us miserable, when we desert the ways that have proved best for our kind. The "immoral" person has not yet "arrived"; he simply disregards the collective wisdom of society and gives the victory to the primitive forces which try to keep man back on his old level. We cannot break the ideals by which man lives, and still be happy.

=The Salt of the Earth.= The second class of people decide the conflict in a way that satisfies both themselves and society. They give the victory to the higher trends and at the same time make a lasting peace by winning over the energy of the undesirable impulses. By sublimation they divert the threatening force to useful work and turn it out into real life, using its steam to make the world's wheels go round. Their love-force, unhampered by childish habits, is free to give itself to adult relationships or to express itself symbolically in socially helpful ways.

=Nervous People.= To the third class belong the people who have not finished the fight. These are the folk with "nerves," the people in whom the conflict is fiercest because both sides are too strong. The victory goes to neither side; the tug of war ends in a tie. Since the energy of the nervous person is divided between the effort to repress and the effort to gain expression, there is little left for the external world. There is plenty of energy wasted on emotion, physical symptoms, phantasy, or useless acts symbolizing the struggle.

A neurotic is a normal person, "only more so." His impulses are the same impulses as those of every other person; his complexes are the same kind of complexes, only more intense. He is an exaggerated human being. He may be only slightly exaggerated, showing merely a little character-weakness or a slight physical symptom, or he may be so intensified as to make life miserable for himself and everybody near him. It is quantity, not quality, that ails him, for he differs from his steady-going neighbor not in kind but in degree. More of him is repressed and a larger part of him is fixed in a childish mold.

=Tricking Ourselves.= A neurosis is a confidence game that we play on ourselves. It is an attempt to get stolen fruit and to look pious at the same time,--not in order to fool somebody else but to fool ourselves.

No nervous symptom is what it seems to be. It is an arch pretender. It pretends to be afraid of something it does not fear at all, or to ignore something that interests it intensely. It pretends to be a physical disease, when primarily it has nothing to do with the body; and the person most deluded is the one who "owns" the symptom. Its purpose is to avoid the pain of disillusionment and to furnish relief to a distracted soul which dares not face itself.

Although the true meaning of a symptom is hidden, there is fortunately a clue by which it can be traced. Sometimes it takes the art of a psychic detective to follow the clues down, down through the different layers of the subconscious mind, until the troublesome impulses and complexes are found and dragged forth,--not to be punished for breaking the peace but to be led toward reconciliation. But "that is another story," and belongs to another chapter. We are approaching THE WAY OUT.

PART III--THE MASTERY OF "NERVES"

CHAPTER VIII

In which we pick up the clue THE WAY OUT

THE SCIENCE OF RE-EDUCATION

There is a story of an Irishman at the World's Fair in Chicago. Although his funds were getting low, he made up his mind that he would not go home without a ride on a camel. For several minutes he stood before a sign reading: "First ride 25? second ride 15? third ride 10?" Then, scratching his head, he exclaimed, "Faith, and I'll take the third ride!" Should there by any chance be a reader who, eager to find the way out without paying the price of knowledge, is tempted to say to himself "Faith, and I'll begin with

Part III," we give him fair

warning that if he does so, he will in all probability end by putting down the book in a confused and skeptical frame of mind.

It is difficult to find our way out of a maze without some faint idea of the path by which we got in. He who brings to this chapter the popular notion that nervousness is the result of worn-out nerve-cells, can hardly be expected to understand how it can be cured by a process of mental adjustment. Suggestion to that effect can scarcely fail to appear to him faddish and unpractical. But once a person has grasped the idea that "nerves" are merely a slip in the cog of hidden mental machinery, and has acquired at least a working-knowledge of "the way the wheels go round," he can scarcely fail to understand that the only logical cure must consist in some kind of readjustment of this underground machinery. If "nerves" were physical, then only physical measures could cure, but as they are psychic, the only effective measures must be psychic.

=Gross Misconceptions.= Nervousness is caused by a lack of adjustment to the world as it is; therefore the only possible cure must be some sort of readjustment between the person's inner forces and the demands of the social world. As this lack of adjustment is concerned chiefly with the repressed instinct of reproduction, it is only natural that there should be people who believe that "the way out" lies in some form of physical satisfaction of the sex-impulse--in marriage, in changing or ignoring the social code, in homo-sexual relations or in the practice of masturbation. But we have only to look about us to see that this prescription does not cure. Freud na 颲 ely asks whether he would be likely to take three years to uncover and loosen the psychic resistances of his patients, if the simple prescription of sex-license would give relief.

Since there are as many married neurotics as single, it is evident that even marriage is not a sure preventive of nervousness. License, on the other hand, can satisfy only a part of the individual's craving. Freud insists that the sex-instinct has a psychic component as well as a physical one, and that it is this psychic part which is most often repressed. He maintains that for complete satisfaction there must be psychic union between mates, and that gratification of the physical component of sex when dissociated from psychic satisfaction, results in an accumulation of tension that reacts badly on the whole organism.

The psychic tension accumulating in adult sex-relations has its inception in the mistaken attitude on the part of the wife, who remains true to her childhood training that any pleasure in sex is vulgar; or on the part of the man, who reacts to the mood of the wife, or is held by his own unbroken mother-son complex; or on the part of both the tension piles up because of society's taboo upon rearing large families. As the first two factors in this lack of adjustment grew largely out of some kind of faulty education or from faulty reaction to early experiences, the only effective way to secure a better adaptation must be through a re-education which reaches down to that part of the personality that bears the stamp of the unfortunate early factors.

=Remaking Ourselves.= As a matter of fact, the science of psychotherapy or mental treatment is simply the science of re-education,--a process designed to break up old unhealthy complexes which disrupt the forces of the individual, and to build up healthy complexes which adjust him to the social world and enable him to use his energy in useful ways.

Fortunately, minds can be changed. It is easier to make over an unhealthy complex than to make over a weak heart, to straighten out a warped idea than to straighten a bent back. Remarkable indeed have been some of the transformations in people who are supposed to have passed the plastic period in life. While it is true that some persons become "set" in middle life, and almost impervious to new ideas, it is also true that a person at fifty has more richness of experience upon which to draw, more appreciation of the value of the good, than has a person at twenty. If he really wants to change himself, he can do wonderful things by re-education.

The first step in this re-education is a grasp of the facts. If you want to pull yourself out of a nervous disorder, first of all learn as much as you can about the causes of "nerves," about the general laws of mind and body, and about your own mental quirks. If this is not sufficient, go to a specialist trained in psychotherapy and let him help you uncover those trouble-making parts of your personality which you cannot find for yourself. It is the purpose of this book to summarize the facts which most need to be known. Let us now consider those methods which the psychopathologist finds most useful in helping his patients to self-knowledge and readjustment.

=Various Methods.= As there are a number of schools of medicine, so there are a number of distinct methods of psychotherapy, each with its own theories and methods of procedure, and each with its ardent supporters. These methods may be classified into two groups. The first group includes those methods, hypnosis and psycho-analysis, which make a thorough search through the subconscious mind for the buried complexes causing the trouble, and might, therefore, be called "re-education with subconscious exploration." The other group, includes so-called explanation and suggestion, or methods of "re-education without subconscious exploration," which content themselves with making a general survey and building up new complexes without going to the trouble of uncovering the buried past. Although the theory and the technique vary greatly, the aim of all these methods is the same,--the readjustment of the individual to life.

RE-EDUCATION WITH SUBCONSCIOUS EXPLORATION

=Hypnosis.= The method by which most of the important early discoveries were made is hypnosis, or artificial sleep, a method by which the conscious mind is dissociated and the subconscious brought to the fore. It was through hypnosis that Freud, Janet, Prince, and Sidis made their first investigations into the nature of nervousness and worked their first cures. With the conscious mind asleep and its inhibitions out of the way, a hypnotized patient is often able to remember and to disclose to the physician hidden complexes of which he is unaware when awake. Hypnosis may thus be a valuable aid to diagnosis, enabling the physician to determine the cause of troublesome symptoms. He may then begin to make suggestions calculated to break up the old complexes and to build new ones, made up of more healthful ideas, desirable emotions and happy feeling-tones. As we have seen, a hypnotized subject is highly suggestible. His counter-suggestions inactivated, he believes almost anything told him and is extremely susceptible to the doctor's influence.

The dangers of hypnosis have been much exaggerated. Indeed, as an instrument in the hands of a competent physician, it is not to be feared at all.

It has, however, its limitations. Many times the very memories which need to be unearthed refuse to come to the surface. Stubborn resistances are more likely to be subconscious than conscious, and may prove too strong to be overcome in this way. Moreover, the road to superficial success is very inviting. It is easy to cure the symptom, leaving the ultimate cause untouched and ready to break out in new manifestations. The drug and drink habits may be broken up without making any attempt to discover the unsatisfied longings which were responsible for the habit. A pain may be cured without finding the mental cause of the pain or initiating any measures to guard against its return, and without giving the patient any insight into the inner forces with which he still has to deal.

Since nervousness is a state of exaggerated suggestibility and abnormal dissociation, many psychologists believe that it is unwise to employ a method which heightens the state of suggestibility and encourages the habit of dissociation. They feel that it is wiser to use less artificial methods which rest on the rational control of the conscious mind and make the patient better acquainted with his own inner forces and more permanently able to cope with new manifestations of those forces. They believe that the character of the patient is strengthened and his morale raised by methods which increase the sovereignty of reason and decrease the role of unreasoning suggestibility.

=Psycho-Analysis.= Freud's contribution has been not only a discovery of the general causes of nervousness, but a special means of locating the cause in any particular case. Abandoning hypnosis, he developed another method which he called psycho-analysis. What chemical analysis is to chemistry, psycho-analysis is to the science of the mind. It splits up the mental content into its component parts, the better to be examined and modified by the conscious mind. Psycho-analysis is merely a technical process for discovering repressed complexes and bringing them into consciousness, where they may be recognized for what they are and altered to meet the demands of real life. It is a device for finding and removing the cause of nervousness,--for bringing to light hidden desires which may be honestly faced and efficiently directed instead of being left to seethe in dangerous insurrection. In order permanently to break up a real neurosis, a man must first know himself and then change himself. He must gain insight into his own mental processes and then systematically set to work to change those processes that unfit him for life.

We shall later find that a detailed self-discovery through psycho-analysis is not always necessary, and that a more general understanding of oneself is sufficient for the milder kinds of nervousness. But because of the promise which psycho-analysis holds out to those stubborn cases before which other methods are powerless; because of the invaluable understanding of human nature which it places at the disposal of all nervous people, who may profit by its findings without undergoing an analysis; and because of the flood of light which it sheds on the motives, conduct, and character of every human being, no educated person can afford to be without a general knowledge of psycho-analysis.[41]

[Footnote 41: It is unfortunate that the records of an analysis are too voluminous for use in so brief an account as this. Since the report of one case would fill a book, and a condensed summary would require a chapter, we must refer to some of the volumes which deal exclusively with the psychoanalytic principles. For a list of these books, see Bibliography.]

=A Chain of Associations.= Psycho-analysis is not, like hypnosis, based on dissociation; it is based on the association of ideas. Its main feature is a process of uncritical thinking called "free association." To understand it, one must realize how intricately woven together are the thoughts of a human being and how trivial are the bonds of association between these ideas. One person reminds us of another because his hair is the same color or because he handles his fork in the same way. Two words are associated because they sound alike. Two ideas are connected because they once occurred to us at the same time. A subtle odor or a stray breeze serves to remind us of some old experience. Connections that seem far-fetched to other people may be quite strong enough to bind together in our minds ideas and emotions which have once been associated, even unconsciously, in past experience.

In this way, thoughts in consciousness and in the upper layers of the subconscious are connected by a series of associations, forming links in invisible chains that lead to the deepest, most repressed ideas. Even a dissociated complex has some connection with the rest of the mind, if we only have the patience to discover it. Therefore, by adopting a passive attitude, by simply letting his thoughts wander, by talking out to the physician everything that comes to his mind without criticizing or calling any thought irrelevant or far-fetched, and without rejecting any thought because of its painful character, the patient is helped to trace down and unearth the troublesome complex which may have been absolutely forgotten for many years. He is helped to relive the childhood experiences back of the over-strong habits which lasted into maturity.

=Resisting the Probe.= Naturally, it is not all fair sailing. The subconscious impulses which repressed the painful complex in the first place still shrink from uncovering it. In many cases the resistance is very strong. It, therefore, often happens that after a time the patient becomes restive; he begins to criticize the doctor and to ridicule the method. His mind goes blank and no thought will come; or he refuses to tell what does come. The nearer the probe comes to the sore spot, the greater the pain of the repressing impulses and the stronger the resistance. Usually a strange thing happens; the patient, instead of consciously remembering the forgotten experiences, begins to relive them with his original emotions transferred on to the doctor. Depending upon what person of his childhood he identifies with him, the patient develops either a strong affection or an intense antagonism to the physician, attitudes called in technical terms positive and negative transference. If the analyst is skilful, he is able to circumvent all the subterfuges of the resisting forces and to uncover and modify the troublesome complexes. Sometimes this can be accomplished at one sitting, but more often it requires long hours of conversation. Freud has spent three years on a single difficult case, and very frequently the analysis drags out through weeks or months. The amount of mental material is so great, especially in a person who is no longer young, that every analysis would probably be an interminable affair if it were not for three valuable ways of finding the clue and picking up the scent somewhere near the end of the trail. The first of these clues is nothing else than so despised a phenomenon as the patient's own night-dreams, which turn out to be not meaningless jargon, as we have supposed, but significant utterances of the inner man.

=The Message of the Dream.= When Freud rescued dreams from the mental scrap-basket and learned how to piece them together so that their message to man about himself became for the first time intelligible, he furnished the human race with what will probably be considered its most valuable key to the hidden mysteries of the mind. Freeing the dream from the superstition of olden times and from the neglect of later days, Freud was the first to discover that it is part and parcel of man's mental life, that it has a purpose and a meaning and that the meaning may be scientifically deciphered. It then invariably reveals itself to be not a prophecy for the future but an interpretation of the present and of the past, an invaluable synopsis of the drama which is being staged within the personality of the dreamer.

As modern man has swung away from the idea of the dream as a warning or a prophecy, he has accepted the even more untrue conception of dreaming as the mere sport of sleep,--the "babble of the mind," the fantastic and insignificant freak-play of undirected mental processes, or the result of physical sensations without relation to the rest of mental life. No wonder, then, that Freud's startling dictum, "A dream is a disguised fulfilment of a repressed wish," should be met with astonishment and incredulity. When a person is confronted for the first time with this statement, he invariably begins to cite dreams in which he is pursued by wild beasts, or in which his loved ones are seen lying dead. He then triumphantly asserts that no such dream could be the fulfilment of a wish.

The trouble is that he has overlooked the word "disguised." Like wit and some figures of speech, a dream says something different from what it means. It deals In symbols. Its "manifest content" may be merely a fantastic and impossible scene without apparent rhyme or reason, but the "latent content," the hidden meaning, always expresses some urgent personal problem. Although the dream may seem to be impersonal and unemotional, it nevertheless deals in every case with some matter of vital concern to the dreamer himself. It is a condensed and composite picture of some present problem and of some related childish repressed wish which the experiences of the preceding day have aroused.

As Frink says, a dream is like a cartoon with the labels omitted--absolutely unintelligible until its symbols are interpreted. Although some dreams whose symbolism is that which man has always used, can be easily understood by a person who knows, many dreams are meaningless, even to an experienced analyst, until the patient himself furnishes the labels by telling what each bit of the picture brings to his mind. The dream, as a rule, merely furnishes the starting-point for free association.

Each symbol is an arrow pointing the way to forbidden impulses which are repressed in waking life but which find partial expression during sleep. The subconscious part of the conscience is still on the job, so the repressed desires can express themselves only in distorted ways which will not arouse the censor and disturb sleep. The purpose of the dream is thus two-fold,--to relieve the tensions of unsatisfied desire, and to do this in such a subtle way as to keep the dreamer asleep. Sometimes it fails of its purpose, but when there is danger of our discovering too much about ourselves, we immediately wake up, saying that we have had a bad dream.

It is at first difficult to believe that we are capable of this elaborate mental work while we are fast asleep. However, a little investigation shows us to be more clever than we realize. The subconscious mind, in its effort to satisfy both the repressing and the repressed impulses, carries on very complicated processes, disguises material by allowing one person to stand for another, two persons to stand for one, or one person to stand for two; it shifts emotion from important to trivial matters, dramatizes, condenses, and elaborates, with a skill that is amazing. We are all of us very clever playwrights and makers of allegories--in our sleep. Also, we are all very clever at getting what we want, and the dream secures for us, in a way, something which we want very much indeed and which the world of social restraint or our own warped childish notion denies us.

Not every one can become an interpreter of dreams. It takes a skilled and patient specialist thoroughly to understand the process. But it is fortunate indeed that we possess such a valuable means of diagnosis when extraordinary conditions make it necessary to explore the subconscious in the search for trouble-making complexes.[42]

[Footnote 42: For further study of the dream, see Freud: _Interpretation of Dreams_; and _General Introduction to Psycho-Analysis_.]

=The Word-Test.= Although dreams furnish the main clues to buried complexes, they are by no means the only instrument of the psycho-analyst. Another device, called the association word-test, has been developed by Dr. Carl Jung of Switzerland. The analyst prepares a list of perhaps one hundred words, which he reads one by one to the patient, hoping in this way to strike some of the emotional reactions of which the patient himself is unaware. The latter responds with the first word that comes into his mind, no matter how absurd it may seem. The responses themselves are often significant, but the time that elapses is even more so. It usually happens that it takes very much longer for some responses than for others. If a patient's average time is one or two seconds, some responses may take five or ten or twenty seconds. Sometimes no word comes at all and the patient says that his mind is a blank. He coughs or blushes, grows pale or trembles, showing all the signs of emotion even when he himself has no notion of the cause. The significant word has hit upon a subconscious association with some emotional complex. The blocking of the mind is an effort of the resistance to keep the painful ideas out of consciousness. The telltale word then furnishes a starting point for further associations.

One of my patients blocked on the word "long." Instead of saying "short" or "pencil" or "road" or "day" or any other word which might naturally be associated with "long," she laughed and said that no word would come. Finally an emotional memory came to light. It seems that this woman had been courted by a man whom she unconsciously loved, but whom she had "turned down" because she was ambitious for a career. After the man had moved to another town, my patient heard that he was engaged to another girl. She then realized that she loved him and began to long for him with her whole heart. The meaningful word "long" thus led us to one of the emotional memories for which we were seeking.

="Chance" Signs.= There are other clues to hidden inner processes, other sign-posts pointing to the cause of a neurosis. Not only through dreams and through emotional reactions to certain words does the subconscious reveal its desires, but also through the little slips of the tongue and of the pen, the "chance" acts and unconscious mannerisms which are usually ignored as entirely insignificant. When we "make a break" and say what we secretly mean but wish to hide from ourselves or others; when we forget an appointment which part of us really wishes to avoid, or forget a name with which we are perfectly familiar; when we lose the pen so that we cannot write or the desk key so that we cannot work; when we blunder and drop things and do what we did not mean to do; then we may know--the normal as well as the nervous person--that our subconscious minds with their repressed desires are trying to get the reins and are partially succeeding.

An example from my own life may illustrate the point. In building a number of houses, I had occasion often to use the word studding, but on every occasion, I forgot the word and always had to end lamely by saying "those pieces of timber that go up and down." Each time the builder supplied the word, but the next time it was no more accessible. Finally, the reason came to me. One day when I was a little child I looked out of the window and cried, "Oh, see that great big beautiful horse." My grandmother exclaimed, "Sh! sh! that is a stud horse." Over-reaction to that impression repressed the word stud so successfully that as a grown woman I could not recall another word which happened to contain the same syllable.

During an analysis a patient of mine who had a mother-in-law situation on her hands told me a dream of the night before. "I dreamed that my mother-in-law, who has really been very ill, was taken with a sinking-spell. I rushed to the telephone to call the doctor, but found to my terror that I could not remember his number." "What is his number?" I asked, knowing that she ought to know it perfectly. "Two-eight-nine-six," she answered at once. The number really was 2876. Asleep and awake, her repressed desire for release from the mother-in-law's querulous presence was attempting to have its way. In the dream, she avoided calling the doctor by forgetting his number entirely. Awake, she evaded the issue by remembering a wrong number. In the dream she thinly disguised her desire by displacing the anxious emotion from the sense of her own guilty wishes to the idea of the mother-in-law's death. When confronted with this interpretation, the woman readily acknowledged its truth.

Even stammering, which has always been considered a physical disorder, has been proved, by psycho-analysis, to be the sign of an emotional disturbance. H. Addington Bruce reports the case of one of Dr. Brill's patients, a young man who had been stammering for several years. Observation revealed the fact that his chief difficulty was with words beginning with K and although at first he firmly denied any significance to the letter, he later confessed that his sweetheart whose name began with K had eloped with his best friend and that he had vowed never to mention her name again. Upon Dr. Brill's suggestion he tried to think of the unfaithful lover as Miss W., but soon returned, saying that he was stammering worse than ever. Investigation showed that the additional unpronounceable words contained the letter W. When he was induced to renounce his oath never to call the girl's name again, he found that he had no more difficulty with his speech.[43]

[Footnote 43: H. Addington Bruce; "Stammering and Its Cure," _McClure's_, February, 1913.]

Thus we see that even the halting tongue of a stammerer may point the way to the buried complex for which search is being made.

Since there is no accident in mental life, and since there is behind every action a force or group of forces, no smallest action is insignificant to the person trained to understand.

If this at first seems disturbing, it is only because we do not realize that there is nothing within of which we need be ashamed. People are very much alike, especially in the deeper layers of their being. What belongs to the whole human race does not need to be hidden away in darkness. There is nothing to lose and everything to gain by an increasing understanding of the chance signals which reveal the forces at work within the depths of the mind. To the analyst every little unconscious act is a valuable clue pointing toward the end of his quest.[44]

[Footnote 44: For further discussion of this subject, see Freud's _Psycho-pathology of Everyday Life_, translated by A.A. Brill.]

=The Aim of Psycho-Analysis.= As we have seen, the object of all this technique is the discovery and the removal of the resistances which have been keeping the emotional conflicts in the dark. It is a long step just to learn that there are resistances; and by reliving, bit by bit, the earlier experiences responsible for unfortunate habits, we find that the habits themselves lose much of their old power. They can be seen for what they are, and changed to suit present conditions. A wish is incomparably stronger when unconscious than when conscious; and the old stereotyped, automatic reactions tend to cease when once they have been seen for what they are. They become assimilated with the rest of the personality and modified by the mature attitudes of the conscious mind. The person then re-educates himself by the very act of discovering himself. In other cases, the uncovering is merely the first step in the process of re-education. The analyst then assumes the rôle of educator, cutting away old shackles, breaking down false standards, building up new complexes, showing the patient the naturalness of his desires, inducing him to look at them as biologic facts, and showing him how to sublimate those which may not find direct expression; in fact, leading him out into the self-expression of a free, unhampered life.[45]

[Footnote 45: "It will be readily understood that in the reconstruction of the shattered purposes, the frustrated hopes and the outraged instincts which are found to lie at the source of those human woes we call 'nervous disorders,' there takes place a gradual transposition of values, a total recasting of ideas, and that through the whole process, education in the deepest meaning of the word, enters at last into its full sovereign rights."-- Trigant Burrow.]

Among my patients at one time was a woman subject to terrible fits of despondency. She was happily married and enjoyed the marriage relationship, but could not free herself from a terrible sense of guilt and degradation, a sense which was so acute that she wanted to end her life. Although she was an active member of a church, she was starving for the real message of the church, continually bound by a feeling of aloofness which made her a stranger in the midst of friends. Psycho-analysis revealed an experience of her childhood which she had kept a secret all these years. It seems that when she was seven years of age an old minister had driven her into town and had made some sort of sex-approach on the way. Although ignorant of its significance, the child was badly frightened and overcome with a sense of guilt. She had already inferred that such subjects were not to be mentioned and she hesitated long before telling even her mother. Smoldering within her through the years had been this emotional complex about the sex-life and about people connected with a church, so that even as a grown woman the relationships of her mature years were completely ruined by her old childish reaction. With insight as to the cause of her trouble, she was able to modify her attitudes and to live a free and happy life.

Several years ago there came to me a man of exceptional intellectual ability, who for years had been totally incapacitated because of blind resistances built up in childhood. Although married to a woman whom he thoroughly liked and admired, he was absolutely miserable in his married life. He had, in fact, a deep-rooted complex against marriage, and had only allowed himself to be captured because the woman, with whom he had been good friends, had cried when he refused to marry her. During analysis it transpired that as a little boy of four he had often seen his silly young mother cry because she could not have a new dress. He had taken her side and bitterly felt that she was abused by his father. Later, at six, he had heard some coarse stories about sex to which he had over-reacted. Still later he had heard the workmen on the farm say that they could not go to the gold-fields because they had wives and were held back by marriage. "There are no idle words where children are," and this little boy had built up such a strong complex against marriage that he could not possibly be happy as a grown man. He was as much crippled by the old scar as is an arm which is bent and stunted from a deep scar in the flesh. After the analysis had broken up the adhesions, he found himself free, able to give mature expression to his repressed and dissatisfied love-instincts.

Psycho-analysis is not a process of addition, but one of subtraction. Like a surgical operation, it undoes the results of old injuries, removes foreign material, and gives nature a chance to develop freely in her own satisfactory way.

RE-EDUCATION WITHOUT SUBCONSCIOUS EXPLORATION

=Simple Explanation.- So far, "the way out" sounds rather involved. It seems to require a special kind of doctor and a complicated, lengthy process before the exact trouble can be determined. But, fortunately for the average nervous patient, this lengthy process of analysis is by no means always necessary. People with troublesome nervous symptoms, and even those who have had a serious breakdown, are constantly being cured by a kind of re-education which breaks up subconscious complexes without trying to bring them to the surface. If the dead past can be let alone, so much the better. Sometimes a bullet buried in the flesh sends up a constant stream of discomfort until it is dug out and removed; but if it has carried in no infection and the body can adjust itself, it is usually considered better to let it remain.

The subconscious makes its own deductions. If resistances are not too strong it is often possible to introduce healthy ideas by way of the conscious reason, to break up old habits, and make over the mentality without going to the trouble of uncovering some of the reactions which are responsible for the difficulty.

=Moral Hygiene.= Because this is true, there has grown up a kind of psychotherapy which is known as simple explanation, or persuasion. As usually practised, this kind of re-education pays very little attention to the ultimate cause of "nerves." It has little to say about repressed instincts or the real reasons for fearful emotions and physical symptoms. Instead, it attacks the symptom itself, contenting itself with teaching the patient that his trouble is psychic in origin; that it is based on exaggerated suggestibility and uncontrolled emotionalism; that it is made out of false ideas about the body, illogical conclusions, and unhealthy feeling-tones; and that it may be cured by a kind of moral hygiene, which breaks up these old habits and replaces them with new and better ones. It tries to inculcate the cheerful attitude of mind; to give the patient the conviction of power; to correct his false ideas about his stomach, his heart, or his head; to train him out of his emotionalism; to lead him into a state of mind more largely controlled by reason; and to make him find some useful and absorbing work.

This kind of mental and moral treatment has been sufficient to cure many neuroses of long standing. In cases that are helped by this method, the patient's love-force, robbed of the material out of which it has woven its disguise, and trained out of its bad habits by re-education, automatically makes its own readjustments and forces new channels for itself out into more useful activities. Very many nervous persons seem to need nothing more than this simple kind of help.

=When Simple Explanation Does not Explain.= For very many cases, however, this procedure, good as it is, does not go deep enough. Although it gives a sound objective education about the facts of one's body, it furnishes only the most superficial subjective knowledge of one's inner life. If the inner struggle be bitter, the competing forces will hold on to their poor refuge in the symptom, despite any number of explanations that the symptom can have no physical cause. Sometimes it is enough for a person to be shown that he is too suggestible, but often it is far more helpful for him to get an inkling as to why he likes unhealthy suggestions, and to understand something of his starved instincts which he may learn to satisfy in better ways.

PSYCHOLOGICAL EXPLANATION

Between the two extremes of the cases which need a real analysis and those which are cured by simple explanation, I have found the great bulk of nervous cases. To simple explanation with its highly useful information, I therefore add what might be called psychological explanation, a re-education which makes use of all that illuminating material unearthed by the explorations of hypnosis and especially of psycho-analysis. Along with correct ideas about such matters as digestion, sleep, and fatigue, I give, so far as the patient is able to understand, a comprehension of the rights of the denied instincts, the ways of the subconscious, the fettering hold of unfortunate childish habits, the various mental mechanisms by which we fool ourselves, and the ways by which we may make better adaptations.

=According to the Patient.= The treatment varies according to the nature of the trouble, and is somewhat dependent on the mentality of the patient. There are many people who would only be confused by being forced into a study of mental phenomena. Not being students, they would be more bewildered than helped by the details of their inner mechanisms. Others, of studious habits and inquiring minds, are encouraged to browse at will in a library of psychotherapy and to learn all that they can from the best authorities.

In any case, I give the patients as much as they are able to take of my own understanding of the subject. There are no secrets in this method. The patient is treated as a rational human being who has nothing to lose and everything to gain by the fullest knowledge that he is able to acquire. Without forcing him to plunge in over his depth, I encourage him to understand himself to the fullest possible extent. Besides individual private conferences, we have twice a day an informal gathering of all the patients in my household--"the family" as we like to call ourselves--for a reading or talk on the various ways of the body and the mind, which need to be understood for normal living and for the cure of nerves. Very often people of only average education, long without the opportunity of study, gain in a surprisingly short time enough insight to make new adaptations and cure themselves. For this, a college education is not nearly so important as an open mind. It is because of the success of this method that I have been encouraged to reach a larger number of people by means of a book, based on the same plan of re-education.

=Explanation vs. Suggestion.= Re-education through this kind of explanation is simply a matter of learning the truth and acting upon it. It is a process of real enlightenment, and is very different from suggestion which trades upon the patient's credulity, increasing his already exaggerated suggestibility.

Freud illustrates the difference between suggestion and psycho-analysis by saying that suggestion is like painting and psycho-analysis like sculpture. Painting adds something from the outside, plastering over the canvas with extraneous matter, while sculpture cuts away the unnecessary material and reveals the angel in the marble. So suggestion covers over the real trouble by crying, "Peace, peace, when there is no peace." Without attempting to remove the cause, it says to the patient: "You have no pain. You are not tired. You will sleep to-night. You will be cheerful." Sometimes the suggestion works and sometimes it does not, but at best the relief is likely to be a mere temporary makeshift. The symptom may be relieved, but the character is not changed and therefore no permanent relief is assured. It is far better for a nervous person to say to himself, "There is something wrong and I am going to find it," than to keep repeating over and over, "There is nothing wrong," and so on through a list of half-believed autosuggestions.

On the other hand, psycho-analysis, and this kind of re-education based on psycho-analytic principles, do not pay a great deal of attention to the individual symptom. Instead of adding from without they try to take away whatever has proved a hindrance to normal growth and development, and to remove unnecessary resistances which are responsible for the symptom, and which have been holding the patient back from the fullest self-expression.

=Incantation vs. Knowledge.= There came to me one day a well-known public woman who had suffered from nervous indigestion for many years. As she was able to be with me for only one night, we had time for just one conversation, but in that time she discovered what she was doing and lost her indigestion. In the course of the conversation she turned to me, saying: "Doctor, I know what a force suggestion is. I believe in its power. Will you tell me why I have not been able to cure myself of this trouble? Every night after I go to bed I repeat over and over these Bible verses," naming a number of passages relating to God's goodness and care for His children. My answer was something like this: "You are too intelligent a woman to be cured by an incantation. When you feel surging up within you the sense of God's goodness, or when you actually want to realize His loving kindness, then by all means repeat the verses. But don't prostitute those wonderful words by making them into a charm and then expect them to cure your indigestion. It is a desecration of the words and a denial of your own intelligence. Autosuggestion is a powerful force, but real psychotherapy is based not on the mechanical repetition of any set of words, but on a knowledge of the truth."

=The "Bullying Method."= Sometimes, to be sure, explanation is not enough. The brain paths between the associated ideas are so deeply worn that no amount of persuasion avails. It is easy for the doubter to say: "Well, that sounds very well, but my case is different. I have tried over and over again and I know." With people of this sort, an ounce of demonstration is worth a pound of argument.

By way of illustration we might mention the man who couldn't eat eggs. To be sure, he had tried many times but always had suffered the most intense cramps in his stomach, and no amount of talk could make him believe that an egg was not poison to him. I took the straight road of simply proving to him that he was mistaken, and had him eat an egg. After a time of apprehension and retching, he vomited the egg, thinking, of course, that he had proved his point. To his astonishment, I said, "Now, let's go and eat another." With great consternation, he finally complied, evidently expecting to die on the spot; but as I immediately prescribed a game of tennis, he scarcely had time to think of the pain, which in fact failed to appear. However, as he thereafter insisted on eating four eggs a day,--with eggs at top-notch price I decided that the joke was on the doctor!

=Enjoying the Right Things.= In substituting healthful complexes for unhealthful ones, psychotherapy not only changes ideas and emotions, but alters the feelings of pleasure or pain that are bound up with the ideas. Dr. Tom A. Williams writes: "The essence of psychotherapy and education is to associate useful activities with agreeable feeling-tones and to dissociate from injurious acts the agreeable feeling-tones that may have been acquired." Right character consists not so much in enjoying things as in enjoying the right things.

Some people enjoy being martyrs. They love to tell about the terrible strain they have been under, the amount of work they have done, or the number of times they have collapsed. One of my patients gave every evidence of satisfaction as he told about his various breakdowns. "The last time I was ill," or "That time when I was in the sanatorium," were frequent phrases on his lips. Finally, after I had asked him if he would boast about the number of times he had awkwardly fallen down in the street, and had shown him that a neurosis is not really a matter to be proud of, he saw the point and stopped taking pleasure in his mistakes.

Such signs of pleasure in the wrong things are evidence of suppressed wishes which we do not acknowledge but try to gratify in indirect ways.[46] The pleasure which ought to be associated with the idea of good work well done has somehow been switched over to the idea of being an invalid. The satisfaction which ought to go with a sense of power and ability to do things has attached itself to the idea of weakness and inability. The pleasurable feeling-tone which normally belongs to ministering to others, regresses in the nervous invalid to the infantile satisfaction of being ministered unto.

[Footnote 46: For a further elaboration of this theme, see Holt: The Freudian Wish.]

But these things are only a habit. A good look in the mirror soon makes one right about face and start in the other direction. Once started, a good habit is built up with surprising ease. It is really much more satisfying to cook a good dinner for the family's comfort than to think about one's ills; much pleasanter to enjoy a good meal than to insist on hot water and toast. Once we have satisfied our suppressed longings in more desirable ways, or by a process of self-training have initiated a new set of habits, we feel again the old zest in normal affairs, the old interest and pleasure in activities which add to the joy of life. Thus does re-education fit a man to take his place in the world's work as a socially useful being, no longer a burden, but a contributor to the sum total of human happiness.

SUMMARY

=Knowing and Doing.= Having set out to learn how to outwit our nerves, we are now ready to sum up conclusions and in the following chapters to apply them to the more common nervous symptoms. It has been shown that a nervous person is in great need of change,--not, indeed, a change in climate or in scene, in work or in diet, but a change in the hidden recesses of his own being. Outwitting nerves means first and foremost changing one's mind, an inner and spiritual process very different from the kind of change which used to be prescribed for the nervous invalid.

As Putnam says, the slogan of the suggestion-school of psychotherapy has always been, "You can do better if you try"; while that of the psycho-analytic school is, "You can do better when you know." Refuting the old adage, "Where ignorance is bliss 'tis folly to be wise," the best methods of psychotherapy insist that the first step in any thorough-going attempt to change oneself must be the great step of self-knowledge. As the conflicts which result in "nerves" are always far beyond those mental regions which are open to scrutiny, a real self-knowledge requires an examination of the half-conscious or wholly unconscious longings which are usually ignored. A real understanding of self comes only when one is willing, to analyze his motives until he sees the connection between them and his nervous symptoms, which are but the symbolic gratification of desires he dares not acknowledge.

Although these deeply buried complexes are the real force behind a nervous illness, the material out of which the symptoms are manufactured is taken largely from superficial misconceptions concerning the bodily functions. It is therefore a great help, also, to possess a fund of information,--not technical nor detailed but accurate as far as it goes,--about the more important workings of the bodily machinery. A little knowledge about the actual chemistry of fatigue and the way it is automatically cared for by the body is likely to do away with the idea of nervous exhaustion as resulting from accumulation of fatigue. A simple understanding of the biological and physiological facts concerning the assimilation of food and the elimination of waste material leaves the intelligent person less ready to convert his psychic discomfort into indigestion and constipation.

Chapters

IX to XIII in this book, which at first glance may seem to belong to a work on physiology rather than on psychology are designed to give just such needed insight.

But knowing the truth is only the first half of the way out. Every neurosis is a deliberate choice by a part of the personality. Self-discovery is helpful only when it leads to better ways of self-expression. The final aim of psychotherapy is the happy adjustment of the individual to the demands of society and the establishment of useful outlets for his energy. This phase of the subject will be discussed more fully in Chapter XVI.

=The Future Hope.= Much has been said about the cure of a neurosis. There are enough people already in the maze of nervousness to warrant the setting up of numerous signs reading, "This way out." But after all, is not a blocking of the way in of vastly more importance? As it is always easier to prevent than to cure, so it is easier to train than to reform. If re-education is the cure, why is not education the ounce of prevention which shall settle the problem for all time?

If the general public understood what "nerves" are, it is hardly conceivable that there could be so many breakdowns as there are at present. If a man's family and friends, to say nothing of himself, understood what he is doing when he suddenly collapses and has to quit work, it is not likely that he would choose that way out of his difficulties.

Most important of all, when parents know that the foundation of nervousness is laid in childhood, they will see to it that their children are started right on the road to health. When fathers and mothers realize that an over-strong bond between parents and children is responsible for a large proportion of nervous troubles, most of them will make sure that such exaggeration is not allowed to develop.

And, finally, when parents are freed from their "conspiracy of silence" by a reverent attitude toward the whole of life, their very saneness will impart to their children a wholesome respect for the reproductive instinct. There will then be found in the next generation fewer half-starved men and women carrying the burden of unnecessary repressions and the pain of unsatisfied yearnings.

Not that such a day will usher in the millennium. We are not suggesting a panacea for all the social ills. There is an inevitable conflict between the instinctive urge of the life-force and the demands of society, a conflict which makes men and women either finer or baser, according to the way they handle it. What is claimed is that the right kind of education--using the word in its largest, deepest sense--will remove the most fruitful cause of nervousness by taking away the extra burden of misconception and making it easier for people to be "content with being moral."[47]

[Footnote 47: Frink: _Morbid Fears and Compulsions._]

CHAPTER IX

In which we discover new stores of energy and learn the truth about fatigue
THAT TIRED FEELING

UNFAILING RESOURCES

"They that wait upon the Lord shall renew their strength. They shall mount up with wings as eagles. They shall run and not be weary. They shall walk and not faint."

It is safe to say that many a person loves this promise of the prophet Isaiah without taking it in anything like a literal sense. The words are considered to be so figurative and so highly spiritualized that they seem scarcely to relate at all to this earthly life, much less to the possibilities of these physical bodies.

Besides the nervous folk who feel themselves so weary that they scarcely have strength to live, there are thousands upon thousands of men and women who are called normal but who have lost much of the joy of life because they feel their bodies inadequate to meet the demands of everyday living.

To such men and women the Biblical promise, "As thy day, so shall thy strength be," comes now as the message of modern science. Nature is not stingy. She has not given the human race a meager inheritance. She did not blunder when she made the human body, nor did she allow the spirit of man to develop a civilization to whose demand his body is not equal. After its long process of development through the survival of the fittest, the human body, unless definitely diseased, is a perfectly adequate instrument, as abundantly able to cope with the complex demands of modern society as with the simpler but more strenuous life of the stone age. The body has stored within its cells enough energy in the shape of protein, carbohydrate and fat to meet and more than meet any drains that are likely to be made upon it, either through the monotony of the daily grind or the excitement of sudden emergency. Nature never runs on a narrow margin. Her motto seems everywhere to be, "Provide for the emergency, enough and to spare, good measure, pressed down, running over." She does not start her engines out with insufficient steam to complete the journey. On the contrary, she has in most instances reserve boilers which are almost never touched. As a rule the trouble is not so much a lack of steam as the ignorance of the engineer who is unacquainted with his engine and afraid to "let her out."

="The Energies of Men."= Perhaps nothing has done so much to reveal the hidden powers of mankind as that remarkable essay of Professor William James, "The Energies of Men."[48] Listen to his introductory paragraph as he opens up to us new "levels of energy" which are usually "untapped":

[Footnote 48: James: On Vital Reserves.]

Every one knows what it is to start a piece of work, either intellectual or muscular, feeling stale--or cold, as an Adirondack guide once put it to me. And everybody knows what it is to "warm up to his job." The process of warming up gets particularly striking in the phenomenon known as the "second wind." On usual occasions we make a practice of stopping an occupation as soon as we meet the first effective layer (so to call it) of fatigue. We have then walked, played or worked "enough," so we desist. That amount of fatigue is an efficacious obstruction on this side of which our usual life is cast. But if an unusual necessity forces us to press onward, a surprising thing occurs. The fatigue gets worse up to a certain critical point, when gradually or suddenly it passes away, and we are fresher than before. We have evidently tapped a level of new energy, masked until then by the fatigue-obstacle usually obeyed. There may be layer after layer of this experience. A third and fourth "wind" may supervene. Mental activity shows the phenomenon as well as physical, and in exceptional cases we may find, beyond the very extremity of fatigue-distress, amounts of ease and power that we never dreamed ourselves to own, sources of strength habitually not taxed at all, because habitually we never push through the obstruction, never pass those early critical points.

Again Professor James says:

Of course there are limits; the trees don't grow into the sky. But the plain fact remains that men the world over possess amounts of resource which only very exceptional individuals push to their extremes of use. But the very same individual, pushing his energies to their extreme, may in a vast number of cases keep the pace up day after day, and find no "reaction" of a bad sort, so long as decent hygienic conditions are preserved. His more active rate of energizing does not wreck him; for the organism adapts itself, and as the rate of waste augments, augments correspondingly the rate of repair.[49]

[Footnote 49: Ibid., pp. 6-7.]

Another psychologist, Boris Sidis, writes: "But a very small fraction of the total amount of energy possessed by the organism is used in its relation with the ordinary stimuli of its environment."[50] These men--Professor James and Dr. Sidis--represent not young enthusiasts who ignorantly fancy that every one shares their own abundant strength, but careful men of science who have repeatedly been able to unearth unsuspected supplies of energy in "worn out" men and women, supposed to be at the end of their resources. Every successful physician and every leader of men knows the truth of these statements. What would have happened in the great war if Marshal Foch had not known that his men possessed powers far beyond their ken, and had not had sublime faith in the "second wind"?

[Footnote 50: Sidis: P. 112 of the composite volume Pychotherapeutics.]

=What about Being Tired?= If all these things are true, why do people need to be told? If man's equipment is so adequate and his reserves are so ample, why after all these centuries of living does the human race need to learn from science the truth about its own powers? The average man is very likely to say that it is all very well for a scientist sitting in his laboratory to tell him about hidden resources, but that he knows what it is to be tired. Is not the crux of the whole question summed up in that word "tired"? If we do not need to rest, why should fatigue exist? If the purpose of fatigue seems to be to slow down our efforts, why should we disregard it or seek to evade its warnings? The whole question resolves itself into this: What is fatigue? In view of the hampering effect of misconception on this point, it is evident that the question is not academic, but intensely practical. We shall find that fatigue is of two kinds,--true and false, or physical and moral, or physiological and nervous,--and that while the two kinds feel very much alike, their origin and behavior are quite different.

PHYSIOLOGICAL FATIGUE

=Fatigue, not Exhaustion.= In the first place, then, fatigue very seldom means a lack of strength or an exhaustion of energy. The average man in the course of a lifetime probably never knows what it is to be truly exhausted. If he should become so tired that he could in no circumstances run for his life, no matter how many wild beasts were after him, then it might seem that he had drained himself of all his store of energy. But even in that case, a large part of his fatigue would be the result of another cause.

=A Matter of Chemistry.= True fatigue is a chemical affair. It is the result of recent effort,--physical, mental, or emotional,--and is the sum of sensations arising from the presence of waste material in the muscles and the blood. The whole picture becomes clear if we think of the body as a factory whose fires continuously burn, yielding heat and energy, together with certain waste material,--carbon dioxide and ash. Within man's body the fuel, instead of being the carbon of coal is the carbon of glycogen or animal starch, taken in as food and stored away within the cells of the muscles and the liver. The oxygen for combustion is continuously supplied by the lungs. So far the factory is well equipped to maintain its fires. Nor does it fail when it comes to carrying away waste products. Like all factories, the body has its endless chain arrangement, the blood stream, which automatically picks up the debris in its tiny buckets--the blood-cells and serum--and carries it away to the several dumping-grounds in lungs, kidneys, intestines, and skin.

Besides the products of combustion, there are always to be washed away some broken-down particles from the tissues themselves, which, like all machinery, are being continuously worn out and repaired. By chemical tests in the laboratory, the physiologist finds that a muscle which has recently been in violent exercise contains among other things carbon dioxid, urea, creatin, and sarco-lactic acid, none of which are found in a rested muscle. Since all this debris is acid in reaction and since we are "marine animals," at home only in salt water or alkaline solution, the cells must be quickly washed of the fatigue products, which, if allowed to accumulate, would very soon poison the body and put out the fires.

=No Back Debts.= The human machine is regulated to carry away its fatigue products as fast as they are made, with but slight lagging behind that is made good in the hours of sleep, when bodily activities are lessened and time is allowed for repair. Unless the body is definitely diseased, it virtually never carries over its fatigue from one day to another. In the matter of fatigue, there are no old debts to pay. Nature renews herself in cycles, and her cycle is twenty-four hours,--not nine or ten months as many school-teachers seem to imagine, or eleven months as some business men suppose. In order to make assurance doubly sure, many set apart every seventh day for a rest day, for change of occupation and thought, and for catching up any slight arrears which might exist. But the point is that a healthy body never gets far behind.

If through some flaw in the machine, waste products do pile up, they destroy the machine. If the heart leaks or the blood-cells fail in their carrying-power, or if lungs, kidneys or skin are out of repair, there is sometimes an accumulation of fatigue products which poisons the whole system and ends in death. But the person with tuberculosis or heart trouble does not usually allow this to happen. The body incapacitated by disease limits its activities as closely as possible within the range of its power to take care of waste matter. Even the sick body does not carry about its old toxins. The man who had not eliminated the poisons of a month-old effort would not be a tired man. He would be a dead man.

=A Sliding Scale.= If all this be true, real fatigue can only be the result of recent effort. If one is still alive, the results of earlier effort must long since have disappeared. The tissue-cells retain not the slightest trace of its effects. Fatigue cannot possibly last, because it either kills us or cures itself. Up to a certain point, far beyond our usual high-water mark, the more a person does the more he can do. As Professor James has pointed out, the rate of repair increases with the rate of combustion. Under unusual stress, the rate of the whole machine is increased: the heart-pump speeds up, respirations deepen and quicken, the blood flows faster, the endless chain of filling and emptying buckets hurries the interchange of oxygen and carbon dioxid, until the extreme capacity is reached and the organism refuses to do more without a period of rest.

The whole arrangement illustrates the wonderful provisions of Nature. Although each individual is continuously manufacturing enough carbonic-acid gas to kill himself in a very few minutes, he need not be alarmed for fear that he may forget to expel his own poisons. Nobody can hold his breath for more than a few minutes. The naughty baby sometimes tries, but when he begins to get black in the face, he takes a breath in spite of himself. The presence of carbonic-acid gas in the circulation automatically regulates breathing, and the greater the amount of gas the deeper the breath. The faster we burn the faster we blow. As with breathing, so with all the rest of elimination and repair. The body dares not get behind.

="Second Wind."= A city man frequently sets out on a mountain tramp without any muscular preparation for the trip. He walks ten or fifteen miles when his average is not over one or two. Sometimes after a few hours he feels himself exhausted, but a glorious view opens out before him and he goes on with new zest. He has merely increased his rate of repair and drawn on a new stock of energy. That night he is tired, and the next day he is likely to be stiff and sore. There is a little fatigue left in him, but it takes only a day or two for the body to be wholly refreshed, especially if he hastens the process by another good walk. Up to a certain point, far beyond our usual limit, the more we do, the more we can do.

One day after a long walk my little daughter said that she could go no farther and waited to be carried. But she soon spied a dog on ahead and ran off after him with new zest. She followed the dog back and forth, running more than a mile before she reached home, and then in the exuberance of her spirits, ran around the house three times.

=The Emotions Again.= What is the key that unlocks new stores of energy and drives away fatigue? What is it in the amateur mountain-climbers that helps the body maintain its new standard? What keeps indefatigable workers on the job long after the ordinary man has tired? Is it not always an invigorating emotion,--the zest of pursuit, the joy of battle, intense interest in work, or a new enthusiasm? All great military commanders know the importance of morale. They know that troops can stand more while they are going forward than while running away, that the more contented and hopeful they are, the better fighters they make; discouragement, lack of interest, the fighting of a losing game, dearth of appreciation, futility of effort, monotony of task, all conspire in soldier or civilian to use up and to lock up energy which might have been available for real work. Approaching the matter from a new angle, we find once more that the difference between strength and weakness is in many cases merely a difference in the emotions and feeling-tones which habitually control.

Fatigue is a safety-device of nature to keep us within safe limits, but it is a device toward which we must not become too sensitive. As a rule it makes us stop long before the danger point is reached. If we fall into the habit of watching its first signals, they may easily become so insistent that they monopolize attention. Attention increases any sensation, especially if colored by fear. Fear adds to the waste matter of fatigue little driblets of adrenalin and other secretions which must somehow be eliminated before equilibrium is reestablished. This creates a vicious circle. We are tired, hence we are discouraged. We are discouraged, hence we are more tired. This kind of "tire" is a chemical condition, but it is produced not by work but by an emotion. He who learns to take his fatigue philosophically, as a natural and harmless phenomenon which will soon disappear if ignored, is likely to find himself possessed of exceptional strength. We can stand almost any amount of work, provided we do not multiply it by worry. We can even stand a good deal of real anxiety provided it is not turned in on ourselves and directed toward our own health.

="Decent Hygienic Conditions."= If fatigue products cannot pile up, why is extra rest ever needed? Because there is a limit to the supply of fuel. If the fat-supply stored away for such emergencies finally becomes low, we may need an extra dose of sleeping and eating in order to let the reservoirs fill again. But this never takes very long. The body soon fills in its reserves if it has anything like common-sense care. The doctrine of reserve energy does not warrant a careless burning of the candle at both ends. It presupposes "decent hygienic conditions,"--eight hours in bed, three square meals a day, and a fair amount of fresh air and exercise.

="Over There."= On the other hand, the stories that floated back to us from the war zone illustrate in the most powerful way what the human body can do when necessity forbids the slightest attention to its needs. One of the best of these stories is Dorothy Canfield's account of Dr. Girard-Mangin, "France's Fighting Woman Doctor." Better than any abstract discussion of human endurance is this vibrant narrative of that little woman, "not very strong, slightly built, with some serious constitutional weakness," who lived through hardships and accomplished feats of daring which would have been considered beyond the range of possibility--before the war.

Think of her out there in her leaky makeshift hospital with her twenty crude helpers and her hundreds of mortally sick typhoid patients; four hundred and seventy days of continuous service with no place to sleep--when there was a chance--except a freezing, wind-swept attic in a deserted village. Think of her in the midst of that terrible Battle of Verdun, during four black nights without a light, among those delirious men, and then during the long, long ride with her dying patients over the shell-swept roads. Listen to her as she speaks of herself at the end of that ride, without a place to lay her head: "Oh, then I did feel tired! That morning for the first time I knew how tired I was, as I went dragging myself from door to door begging for a room and a bed. It was because I was no longer working, you see. As long as you have work to do you can go on." Then listen to her as she receives her orders to rush to a new post, before she has had time to lay herself on the bed she has finally found. "Then at once my tiredness went away. It only lasted while I thought of getting to bed. When I knew we were going into action once more, I was myself again." Watch her as she rides on through the afternoon and the long dangerous night; as she swallows her coffee and plum-cake, and operates for five hours without stopping; as she sleeps in the only place there is--a "quite comfortable chair" in a corner; and as she keeps up this life for twenty days before she is sent--not on a vacation, mind you, but to another strenuous post.[51]

[Footnote 51: Dorothy Canfield: _The Day of Glory._]

This brave little woman is not an isolated example of extraordinary powers. The human race in the great war tapped new reservoirs of power and discovered itself to be greater than it knew. Professor James's assertions are completely proved,--that "as a rule men habitually use only a small part of the powers which they actually possess," and that "most of us may learn to push the barrier (of fatigue) further off, and to live in perfect comfort on much higher levels of power."

=How?= The practical question is: how may we--the men and women of ordinary powers, away from the extraordinary stimulus of a crisis like the great war--attain our maximum and drop off the dreary mantle of fatigue which so often holds us back from our best efforts? It may be that the first step is simply getting a true conception of physical fatigue as something which needs to be feared only in case of a diseased body, and which is quite likely to disappear under a little judicious neglect.

In the second place, fatigue shows itself to be closely bound up with emotions and instincts. The great releasers of energy are the instincts. What but the mothering instinct and the love of country could uncover all those unsuspected reserves of Dr. Girard-Mangin and others of her kind? What is it but the enthusiasm for work which explains the indefatigable energy of Edison and Roosevelt? If the wrong kind of emotion locks up energy, the right kind just as surely unlocks great stores which have hitherto lain dormant. If most people live below their possibilities, it is either because they have not learned how to utilize the energy of their instinctive emotions in the work they find to do, or because some of their strongest instincts which are meant to supply motive power to the rest of life are locked away by false ideas and unnecessary repressions, and so fail to feed in the energy which they control. In such a case, the "spring tonic" that is needed is a self-knowledge which shall release us from hampering inhibitions and set us free for enthusiastic self-expression.

NERVOUS FATIGUE

What of the Nervous Invalid? If the normal man lives constantly below his maximum, what shall we say of the nervous invalid? Fatigability is the very earmark of his condition. In many instances he seems scarcely able to raise his hand to his head. Sometimes he can scarcely speak for weariness. Frequently to walk a block sends him to bed for a week. I once had a patient who felt that she had to raise her eyelids very slowly for fear of over-exertion. She could speak only about two or three words a day, the rest of the time talking in whispers. She could not raise a glass to her lips if it were full of water, but could manage it if only half full. A person nearly dead with some fatal disease does not appear more powerless than a typical neurasthenic.

If it he true that accumulation of fatigue is promptly fatal, what shall we say of the woman who says that she is still exhausted from the labor of a year ago,--or of ten years ago? What of the business man who travels from sanatorium to sanatorium because five years ago he went through a strenuous year? What of the college student who is broken down because he studied too hard, or the teacher who is worn out because of ten hard years of teaching? There can be but one answer. No matter what their feelings, they can be suffering from no true physiological fatigue. Something very real has happened to them, but only through ignorance and the power of suggestion can it be called fatigue and attributed to overwork.

=Stories of Real People.= Perhaps if we look over the stories of a few people who have been members of my household, we may work our way to an understanding of the truth. We give only the barest outline of the facts, thinking that the cumulative effect of a number of cases will outweigh a more detailed description of one or two. The most casual survey shows that whatever it was that burdened these fine men and women, it was not lack of energy. No matter how extreme had been their exhaustion, they were able at once, without rest or any other physical treatment, to summon strength for exertions quite up to those of a normal person.

The second point that stands out clearly to any one acquainted with these inner histories is the conviction that in each case the trouble was related in some way to the unsatisfied love-life, to the insistent and thwarted instinct of reproduction. In some cases no search was made for the cause. The simple explanation that there was no lack of power was sufficient to release inhibited energy. But in every case where the cause was sought, it was found to be some outer lack of satisfaction, or some inner repression of the love-force.

=From Prostration to Tennis.= One young woman, Miss A., had suffered for ten years from the extremest kind of fatigue. She could not walk a block without support and without the feeling of great exhaustion. Before her illness she had had a sweetheart. Not understanding her normal physical sensations when he was near, she had felt them extremely wicked and had repressed them with all her strength. Later, she broke off the engagement, and a little while after developed the neurosis. Within a week after coming to my house, she was playing tennis, walking three miles to church, and generally living the life of a normal person.

=Making Her Own Discoveries.= Then there was Miss B. who for four years had been "exhausted." She had such severe pains in her legs that she was almost helpless. If she sewed for half an hour on the sewing machine, she would be in bed for two weeks. Although she was engaged to be married, she could not possibly shop for her trousseau. Two years before, a very able surgeon had been of the opinion that the pain in the legs was caused by an ovarian tumor. He removed the tumor, assuring the patient that she would be cured. However, despite the operation and the force of the suggestion, the pains persisted.

After she had been with me for a few days, she sewed for an hour on the machine. In a day or so she took a four-mile walk in a ca 駉 n near the house and, on returning in the afternoon, walked two and a half miles down town to do some shopping. I did not make an analysis in her case because she recovered so quickly,--going home well within two weeks. But she declared that she had found the cause while reading in one of the books on psychology. I had my suspicions that the long-drawn-out engagement had something to do with the trouble, but I did not confirm my opinion. A long engagement, by continually stimulating desire without satisfying it, only too often leads to nervous illness.

=Afraid of Heat.= Professor X., of a large Eastern college, had been incapacitated for four years with a severe fatigue neurosis and an intense fear of heat. Constantly watching the weather reports, he was in the habit of fleeing to the Maine coast whenever the weather-prophet predicted warm weather. After a short re 雑 ucation, he discovered that his fatigue was symbolic of an inner feeling of inadequacy, and that it bore no relation to his body. Discarding his weariness and throwing all his energies into the Liberty Loan Campaign, he found himself speaking almost continuously throughout one of the hottest days in the history of California, with the thermometer standing at 107 degrees. After that he had no doubt as to his cure.

=In Bed from Fear.= Miss C. was carried into my house rolled in a blanket. She had been confined to her bed except for fifteen minutes a day, during which time she was able to lie in a hammock! It seems that her illness was the result of fear, an over-reaction to early teaching about self-abuse. Her mother had frightened her terribly by giving her the false idea that this practice often leads to insanity. Having indulged in self-abuse, she believed herself going insane, and very naturally succumbed to the effects of such a fear. After a few days of re-education, she was as strong as any average person. Having no clothing but for a sick-room, she borrowed hat, skirt, and shoes, and walked to church, a three-mile walk.

=Empty Hands.= Miss Y., a fine woman of middle age, suffering from extreme fatigue could neither sleep nor eat. She could only weep. She had spent her life taking care of an invalid girl who had recently died. Now her hands were empty. Like many a mother whose family has grown up, she had no outlet for her mothering instinct, and her sense of impotency expressed itself in the only way it knew how,--through her body. As there is never any lack of unselfish work to be done, or of people who need mothering, she soon found herself and learned how to sublimate her energy in useful activities.

=Defying Nature.= One young man from Wyoming had felt himself obliged to give up his business because he could neither work nor eat. It soon cropped out that he and his wife had decided that they must not have any children. With a better understanding of the great forces which they were defying, his strength and his appetite came back and he went back to work, rejoicing.

=Left-over Habits.= Often a state of fatigue is the result of a carried-over habit. One of my patients, a young girl, had several years before been operated on for exophthalmic goiter. This is a disease of the thyroid gland, and is characterized by rapid heart, extreme fatigue, and numerous other symptoms. Although this girl's goiter had been removed, the symptoms still persisted. She could not walk nor do even a little work, like wiping a few dishes. I took her down on the beach, let her feel her own pulse and mine and then ran with her on the sand. Again I let her feel our pulses and discover for herself that hers had quickened no more than was normal and had slowed down as soon as mine. After a few such lessons, she was convinced that her symptoms were reverberations for which there was no longer any physical cause.

Another young girl, Miss L., had had a similar operation for goiter six years before. Since that time she had been virtually bedridden. During the first meal she had at my house her sister sat by her couch because she must not be left alone. By the second meal the sister had gone, and Miss L. ate at the table with the other guests. That night she managed to crawl upstairs, with a good deal of assistance and with great terror at the probable results of such an effort. After that, she walked up-stairs alone whenever she had occasion to go to her room. Her heart will always be a little rapid and her body will never be very strong, but she now lives a helpful happy life at home and among her friends.

In cases like this the exaggeration proves the counterfeit. Nobody could have been so down and out physically without dying. The exaggeration secures attention and gives the little satisfaction to the natural desires which are denied expression, and which gain an outlet through habit along the lines previously worn by the real disease. Many a person is still suffering from an old pain or an old disability whose cause has long since disappeared, but which is stamped on the mind and believed in as a present reality. Since the sensation is as real as ever, it is sometimes very hard to believe that it is not legitimate, but if the person is intelligent, a little explanation and re-education usually suffices.

=Twenty Years an Invalid.= Mr. S., from Ohio, had spent much of his time for twenty years going from one sanatorium to another. There was scarcely a health resort in the country with which he was not familiar. The day he came to me he felt himself completely exhausted by the two-block walk from the car. He explained that he could scarcely listen to what I was saying because his brain was so fagged that concentration was impossible. When asked to read a book, he dramatically exclaimed, "Books and I have parted company!" I set him to work reading "Dear Enemy" but it was not a week before he was devouring the deeper books on psychology, in complete forgetfulness of the pains in his head. Playing golf and walking at least six miles every day, he rejoiced in a new sense of strength in his body, which for twenty years he had considered "used up." He is now doing a man-sized job in the business and philanthropic life of his home city.

=Brain-fag.= This feeling of brain-fag is one of the commonest nervous symptoms; and almost always it is supposed to be the result of intellectual overwork. Some people who easily accept the idea that physical work cannot cause nervous breakdown can scarcely give up the deep-rooted notion that intense mental work is harmful. Intellectual effort does give rise to fatigue in exactly the same way as does physical exertion, but the body takes care of the waste products of the one just as it does those of the other. Du Bois says that out of all his nervous cases he has not found one which can be traced to intellectual overwork. I can say the same thing, and I know no case in all the literature of the subject whose symptoms I can believe to be the result of mental labor.

The college students who break down are not wrecked by intellectual work. In some cases, one strong factor in their undoing is the strain and readjustment necessary because of the discrepancies between some of their deepest religious beliefs and the truth as they learn it in the class-room. The other factors are merely those which play their part in any neurosis.

=Re-educating the Teacher.= School-teachers are prone to believe themselves worn out from the mental work and the strain of the strenuous life of teaching. Many a fine, conscientious teacher has come to me with this story of overwork. But the school-teacher is as easily re-educated as is any one else. I usually begin the process by stating that I taught school myself for ten years and can speak from experience. After I explain that there is no physical reason why the teachers of some cities are fagged out at the end of nine months while those in other cities whose session is longer can hold on for ten months, and stenographers who lead just as strenuous a life manage to exist with only a two-weeks' vacation, they begin to see that perhaps after all they have been fooling themselves by a suggestion, "setting" themselves for just so long and expecting to be done up at the end of the term. Many of these same teachers have gone back to their work with a new sense of "enough and to spare" and some of them have written back that they have passed triumphantly through especially trying years with no sense of depletion.

In any work, it is the feeling of strain which tells, the emotionalism and feeling sorry for oneself because one has a hard job. It is wonderful what a sense of power comes from the simple idea that we are equal to our tasks.

=Sudden Relief.= The story of Mr. V. illustrates Professor James's statement that often the fatigue gets worse up to a certain critical point, and then suddenly passes away. Mr. V. was another patient who was "physically exhausted." When the rest of "the family" went clamming on the beach, he felt himself too weak for such exertions, so I left him on the sand to hold the bag while the rest of us dug for clams. The minute I turned my back he disappeared. I found him lying flat on his back, resting, behind the bulk-head. I decided that he needed the two-mile walk home and we all set out to walk. "Doctor, this is cruel. It is dangerous. My knees can never stand this. I shall be ill!" ran the constant refrain for the first mile. Then things went a bit better. Toward the last he found, to his absolute astonishment, that the fatigue had entirely rolled away. The last half-mile he accomplished with perfect ease. Needless to say, he never again complained of physical exhaustion.

=False Neuritis.= Miss T. was suffering from fatigue and very severe pains in her arms, pains which were supposed to be the result of real neuritis, but which did not correspond to the physiological picture of that disease. A consultation revealed the fact that her love-instinct had been repeatedly stimulated, and then at the last, when it had expected satisfaction, had been disappointed. A discussion of her life, its inner forces, and her future aims helped to pull her together again and give her instinct new outlets. The pains and the fatigue disappeared at once.

=Something Wrong.= These cases are chosen at random and are typical of scores of others. In no single case was the trouble feigned or imaginary or unreal. But in every case it was a mistake. _The sense of loss of muscular power was really a sense of loss of power on the part of the soul._ Some inner force was reaching out, reaching out after something which it could never quite attain. As it happened, in every case that I analyzed, the force which felt itself defeated and inadequate was the thwarted instinct of reproduction. Like a man pinned to the ground by a stronger force, it felt itself most helpless while struggling the hardest. Just as we feel a thrill of fright when we step up in the dark and find no step there, so this instinct had gotten itself ready for a step which was not there. Inner repressions or outer circumstances had denied satisfaction and left only an undefined sense that something was wrong. The life-force, feeling itself helpless, limp, tired, had no way of expressing itself except in terms of the body. Since expression is itself a relief and an outlet for feeling, the denied desire had seized on suggestions of overwork to explain its sense of weariness, and had symbolized its soul-pain by converting it into a physical pain. The feeling of inadequacy was very real, but it was simply displaced from one part of the personality to another,--from an unknown, inarticulate part to one which was more familiar and which had its own means of expression.

=Locked-up Energy.= We do not know just how the soul can make its pain so intensely real to the body, but we do know that any conviction on the part of the subconscious mind is quickly expressed in the physical machine. A conviction of pain or of powerlessness is very soon converted into a feeling which can scarcely be denied. The mere suggestion that the body is overworked is enough to make it tired.

We know, too, that the instincts are the great releasers of energy. So it happens that when our most dynamic instinct--that for the reproduction of the race--is repressed, we lack one of the greatest sources of usable energy. The energy is there, but it is not accessible. Inhibited and locked away, it is not fed into the engine, and we feel exactly as though it were nil. Despite its name, the disease neurasthenia does not signify a real asthenia or weakness. Rather, it is a disorder in which there is plenty of energy that has somehow been temporarily misplaced. Then, too, we must remember that under the depressing influence of chronic fear, not quite so much energy is stored away as would otherwise be. All the bodily functions are slowed down; food is not so completely assimilated, the heart-beat is weakened, the breathing is more shallow, and fatigue products are more slowly eliminated. As Du Bois says, "An emotion tires the organism more than the most intense physical or intellectual work."

=Avoid the Rest-Cure.= It is a healthful sign that the rest-cure is fast going out of style. Wherever it has helped a nervous patient, the real curative agent has been the personality of the doctor and the patient's faith in him. The whole theory was based on ignorance of the cause of nerves. People suffering from "nervous exhaustion" are likely to be just as "tired" after a month in bed as they were before. Why not? Physical fatigue is quickly remedied, and what can rest do after that? What possible effect can rest have on the fatigue of a discouraged instinct? Since the best releaser of energy is enthusiasm, don't try to get that by lying around in bed or playing checkers at a health resort.

SUMMARY

If you are chronically and perpetually fatigued, or if you tire more easily than the other people you know, consult a competent physician and let him look you over. If he tells you that you have neither tuberculosis, heart trouble, Bright's disease, nor any other demonstrable disease, that you are physically fit and "merely nervous," give yourself a good shake and commit the following paragraphs to memory.

A CATECHISM FOR THE WEARY ONE

WHAT?

Q. What is fatigue?

A. It is a chemical condition resulting from effort that is very recent.

Q. What else creates fatigue?

A. Worry, fear, resentment, discontent, and other depressing emotions.

Q. What magnifies fatigue?

A. Attention to the feeling.

Q. What makes us weary long after the cause is removed?

A. Habit.

WHY?

Q. Why do many people believe themselves over-worked?

A. Because of the power of suggestion.

Q. Why do they take the suggestion?

A. Because it serves their need and expresses their inner feelings.

Q. Why are they willing to choose such an uncomfortable mode of expression?

A. Because they don't know what they are doing, and the subconscious is very insistent.

WHO?

Q. Who gets up tired every morning?

A. The neurotic.

Q. Who fancies his brain so exhausted that a little concentration is impossible?

A. The neurotic.

Q. Who still believes himself exhausted as the result of work that is now ancient history?

A. The neurotic.

Q. Who lays all his woes to overwork?

A. The neurotic.

Q. Who complains of fatigue before he has well begun?

A. The neurotic.

Q. Who may drop his fatigue as soon as he "gets the idea?"

A. The neurotic.

HOW?

Q. How can he get the idea?

A. By understanding himself.

Q. How may he express his inner feelings?

A. By choosing a better way.

Q. How can he forget his fatigue?

A. By ignoring it.

Q. How can he ignore it?

A. By finding a good stiff job.

If he wants advice in a nutshell, here it is: Get understanding! Get courage! Get busy!

CHAPTER X

In which the ban is lifted DIETARY TABOOS

MISUNDERSTOOD STOMACHS

=Modern Improvements.= Most people have heard the story of the little girl who wanted to know what made her hair snap. After she had been informed that there was probably electricity in her hair, she sat quiet for a few minutes and then exclaimed: "Our family has all the modern improvements! I have electricity in my hair and Grandma has gas on her stomach!" Judged by this standard many American families are well abreast of the times; and if we include among the modern improvements not only gas on the stomach but also nervous dyspepsia, acid stomach, indigestion, sick-headache, and biliousness, we must conclude that a good proportion of the population is both modern and improved.

Despite all this the stomach is one of the best-equipped mechanisms in the world. It, at least, is not modern. After their age-long development the organs of the body are remarkably standardized and adapted to the work required of them. It is safe to say that ninety per cent. of all so-called "stomach trouble" is due not to any inherent weakness of the organ itself but to a misunderstanding between the stomach and its owner.

=Organic Trouble.= Unfortunately, there are a few real organic causes for trouble. There are a few cancers of the stomach and a certain number of ulcers. But if the patients whom I have seen are in any way typical, the ulcers that really are cannot compare in number with the ulcers that are supposed to be. Patients go to physicians with so many tales of digestive distress that even the best doctors are fooled unless they are especially alert to the ways of "nerves." They must find some explanation for all the various functional disturbances which the patients report, and as they are in the habit of taking only the body into account, they find the diagnosis of stomach ulcer as satisfactory as any.

There is, of course, such a thing as an enlarged or sagging stomach. But it is only in the rarest of cases that such a condition leads to any functional disturbances unless complicated by suggestion. In most cases a person can go about his business as happily as ever unless he gets the idea that ptosis must inevitably lead to pain and discomfort.

Confusion sometimes arises when the stomach is blamed for disturbances which originate elsewhere. One day a very sick-looking girl came to me with eager expectation written all over her face. Her stomach was misbehaving and she had heard that I could cure nervous indigestion. It needed little more than a glance to know that she was suffering from organic heart trouble. A boy of sixteen had been taking a stomach-tonic for three months, but the thin, wiry pulse pointed to a different ailment. His digestive disturbances were merely the echo of an organic disease of the kidneys. When the body is burdened by disease, it may have little energy left for digesting food, but in that case the trouble must be sought in other quarters than the stomach.

Aside from a few organic difficulties, there is almost no real disease of the stomach. Its misdoings are not matters of food and chemistry, muscle-power and nerve supply, but are the end results of slips in the mental and emotional life of its owner.

=Fads Dynamogenic.= What is it that gives the impetus to fads about eating, or about religious belief? Are they advocated by the individual whose libido is finding abundant expression in the natural channels of business and family life, or by his less fortunate brother who can gain a sense of power only by means of some unaccustomed idea? William James says:

This leads me to say a word about ideas considered as dynamogenic agents or stimuli for unlocking what would otherwise be unused reservoirs of individual power.... In general, whether a given idea shall be a live idea depends more on the person into whose mind it is injected than on the idea itself. Which is the suggestive idea for this person and which for that one? Mr. Fletcher's disciples regenerate themselves by the idea (and the fact) that they are chewing and re-chewing and super-chewing their food. Dr. Dewey's pupils regenerate themselves by going without their breakfast--a fact, but also an ascetic idea. Not every one can use these ideas with the same success.

Because it is so adaptable and sturdy, the stomach lends itself readily to these devices for gaining self-expression; but the danger lies in bringing the process of digestion into conscious attention which interferes with automatic functioning. Still further, the disregard of physiological chemistry is likely to deprive the body of food-stuffs which it requires.

The average person is too sensible to be carried off his feet by the enthusiasm of the health-crank, but as most of us are likely to pick up a few false notions, it may be well to be armed with the simple principles of food chemistry in order to combat the fads which so easily beset us and to know why we are right when we insist on eating three regular meals of the mixed and varied diet which has proved best for the race through so many years of trial and experience.

WHAT WE NEED TO EAT

=The Essence of Dietetics.= To the layman the average discussion of food principles is, to say the least, confusing. Dealing largely, as it does, with unfamiliar terms like carbohydrate and hydrocarbon and calories, it is hard to translate into the terms of the potatoes left over from dinner and the vegetables we can afford to buy. But the practical deductions are not at all difficult to understand. Boiled down to their simplest terms, the essential principles may be stated in a few sentences. The body must secure from the food that we eat, tissue for its cells, energy for immediate use or to be stored for emergency, mineral salts, vitamins, water and a certain bulk from fruits and vegetables,--this latter to aid in the elimination of waste matter.

Food for repairing bodily tissue is called protein and is secured from meat, eggs, milk, and certain vegetables, notably peas. Fuel for heat and energy is in two forms--carbohydrate (starch and sugar) and fat. We get sugar from sugar-cane and beets, and from syrups, fruit, and honey. Starch is furnished from flour products--mainly bread--from rice, potatoes, macaroni, tapioca, and many vegetables. Fats come from milk and butter, from nuts, from meat-fat--bacon, lard and suet--and from vegetable oils. The mineral salts are obtained mainly from fruit and vegetables, which also provide certain mysterious vitamins necessary for health, but as yet not well understood.

=What the Market Affords.= The moral from all this is plain. The human body needs all the foods which are ordinarily served on the table. Whenever, through fad or through fear, we leave out of our diet any standard food, we are running a risk of cutting the body down on some element which it needs. They say that variety is the spice of life. In the matter of food it is more than that, it is the essence of life. Eat everything that the market affords and you will be sure to be well nourished. If you leave out meat you will make your body work overtime to secure enough tissue material from other foods. If you leave out white bread, you will lose one of the greatest sources of energy. If you leave out tomatoes and cucumbers and strawberries, you deprive your body of the salts and vitamins which are essential.

=A Simple Rule.= There is one point that is good to remember. The average person needs twice as much starch as he needs of protein and fat together. That is, if he needs four parts of protein and three of fat, he ought to eat about fourteen parts of starch. This does not mean that we need to bother ourselves with troublesome tables of what to eat, but only to keep in mind in a general way that we need more bread and potatoes than we do meat and eggs. The body does not have to rebuild itself every day. It is probable that a good many people eat too much protein food. If a man is doing hearty work he must have a good supply of meat, but the average person needs only a moderate amount. Here again, the habits of the more intelligent families are likely to come pretty near the dictates of science.

=For the Children.= The mother of a family ought to know that the children need plenty of bread, butter, and milk. Despite all the notions to the contrary, good well-baked white bread is neither indigestible nor constipating. It is indeed the staff of life. Two large slices should form the background of every meal, unless there is an extraordinary amount of other starchy food or unless the person is too fat. Milk-fat (from whole milk, cream, and butter) is by far the best fat for children. Besides fat, it furnishes a certain growth-principle necessary for development. As the dairyman cannot raise good calves on skimmed milk, so we cannot raise robust children without plenty of butter and milk. The pity of it is that poor people are forced to try! Milk is also the best protein for children, whose kidneys may be overstrained by trying to care for the waste matter from an excessive quantity of eggs and meat. Bread and butter, milk, fruit, vegetables, and sugar in ample quantities and meat and eggs in moderate quantities are pretty sure to make the kind of children we want. Above all things, let us train them not to be afraid of normal amounts of any regular food or of any combination of foods.

=The Fear of Mixtures.= There are many people who can without flinching face almost any single food, but who quail before mixtures. Perhaps there is no notion which is more firmly entrenched in the popular mind than this fear of certain food-combinations, acquired largely from the advertisements of certain so-called "food specialists."

The most persistent idea is the fear of acid and milk. It is interesting to watch the new people when they first come to my table. Confronted with grape-fruit and cream at the same meal, or oranges and milk, or cucumbers and milk, they eat under protest, in consternation over the disastrous results that are sure to follow. Out of all these scores of people, many of whom are supposed to have weak stomachs, I have never had one case of indigestion from such a combination. When a person knows that the stomach juices themselves include hydrochloric acid which is far more acid than any orange or grapefruit, that the milk curdles as soon as it reaches the stomach, and that it must curdle if it is to be digested, he has to be very "set" indeed if he is to cling to any remnant of fear.

Of course to say that the stomach is well prepared chemically, muscularly, and by its nerve supply to handle any combination of ordinary food in ordinary amounts is not the same thing as saying that we may devour with impunity any amount of anything. It is a good thing for every one to know when he has reached his limit, and a person with organic heart disease should avoid eating large quantities at one time, or when he is extraordinarily fatigued or emotionally disturbed, lest at such a time he may put a fatal strain on the pneumogastric nerve that controls both stomach and heart.

THE FEAR OF CERTAIN FOODS

=Physical Idiosyncrasies.= Most of our false fears on food subjects come from some tradition--either a social tradition or a little private, pet tradition of one's own. Some one once was ill after eating strawberries and cream. What more natural than to look back to those little curdles in the dish and to start the tradition that such mixtures are dangerous? The worst of it is that the taboo habit is very likely to grow. One after another, innocent foods are thrown out until one wonders what is left A patient of mine, Mr. G., told me that he had a short time before gone to a physician with a tale of woe about his sour stomach. "What are you eating?" asked the doctor. "Bran crackers and prunes." "Then," said the learned doctor, "you will have to cut out the prunes!" Needless to say, this man ate everything at my table, and flourished accordingly.

There may be such a thing as physical idiosyncrasies for certain foods. I have often heard of them, but I have never seen one. I have often challenged my patients to show me some of the "spells" which they say invariably follow the eating of certain foods, but I have almost never been given an exhibition. The man who couldn't eat eggs did throw up once, but he couldn't do it a second time. Many people have threatened to break out with hives after strawberries. One woman triumphantly brought me what looked like a nice eruption, but which proved to be the after-results of a hungry flea! After that she ate strawberries,--without the flea and without the hives.

=Not Miracles but Ideas.= Conversions on food subjects are so common at my table that I should have difficulty in remembering the individual stories. Scores of them run together in my mind and make a sort of composite narrative something like this: "Oh, no, thank you, I don't eat this. You really must excuse me. I have tried many times and it is invariably disastrous." Then a reluctant yielding and a day or two later some talk about miracles. "It really is wonderful. I don't understand," etc. Experiences like these only go to show the power of the subconscious mind, both in building up wrong habit-reactions and in quickly substituting healthy ones, once the false idea is removed.

Among my stomach-patients there were two men, brothers-in-law, immigrants from the Austrian Tyrol, and now resident in one of the cow-boy states. Leonardo spoke little English, and though Giovanni understood a very little, he spoke only Italian.

Several years before I knew them, Giovanni had developed a severe case of stomach trouble and had finally gone to a medical center for operation. The disturbance, however, was not relieved by the operation and before long his brother-in-law fell into the same kind of trouble. For several years the two had spent much of their time dieting, vomiting, and worrying over their sour stomachs. Giovanni finally became so ill that his sick-benefit society had actually assessed its members to pay for his funeral expenses. About this time a business man of their town, impressed by the cure of a former patient who had made a quick recovery after seven years of invalidism, persuaded the two men to take their little savings and come to California to be under my care. The evening meal and breakfast went smoothly enough, although the menu included articles which they had been taught to avoid. However, as I left the house on a necessary absence soon after breakfast, I saw Leonardo weeping in the garden and Giovanni spitting up his breakfast, out at the entrance gate. On my return, I found one of "the family" literally sitting on the coat-tails of Leonardo, while Giovanni hovered at a distance, safe from capture. Leonardo upbraided me bitterly for having undone all the gain they had made in the long months of rigid dieting, for now the vomiting had returned, because they had eaten sugar on their oatmeal at breakfast! I made Leonardo drink an egg-nog, took him into the consultation-room and held my hand on his knee to keep him in his chair, while explaining to him as best I could the physiologic action of the hydrochloric acid on the digestive juice, which he feared as a sour stomach, the sign of indigestion.

During the conversation I said, "I suppose Giovanni imitated you in this mistaken fear about your health." The reply was, "No, I got it off him!" Nearly two hours later he exclaimed in astonishment: "Why, that milk hasn't come up! Maybe I am cured!" "Of course you are cured," I answered; "there never was anything really the matter with your stomach, so you are cured as soon as you think you are."

Later Giovanni was inveigled into the house by the promise that he would have to eat nothing more than milk soup. All was smooth sailing after this. For my own part I feared for the permanency of the cure, for they were returning to the old environment. But more than three years have passed, and grateful letters still come telling of their continued health.

Another patient, a teacher of domestic science in a big Eastern university, had lived on skimmed milk and lime-water from Easter to Thanksgiving. Several attempts to enlarge the dietary by adding cream or white of egg had only served to increase the sense of discomfort. Finding nothing in the history of the case to warrant a diagnosis of organic disease of the stomach, I served her plate with the regular dinner, bidding her have no hesitancy even over the pork chops and potato chips. She gained nine pounds in weight the first week, and in two and a half months was forty pounds to the good.

=When Re-education Failed.= But there is one patient who has had to have his lesson repeated at intervals. This man laughingly calls himself a disgrace to his doctor because he is a "repeater." His story illustrates the power of an autosuggestion and the disastrous effect of attention to a physiological function. When Mr. T. came first to me he weighed only 120 pounds, although he is over six feet tall and of large frame. From the age of sixteen he had followed fads in eating and thought he had a weak stomach. I treated his "weak stomach" to everything there was in the market, including mince-pies, cabbage, cheese, and all the other so-called indigestibles. He gained 16-1/2 pounds the first week and 31 pounds in five weeks. One would think that the idea about the weak stomach would have died a natural death, but it did not. Again and again he came back to me like a living skeleton, the last time weighing only 105 pounds, and again and again he has gone back to his home in the Middle West plump and well. Twice while he was at home he underwent unnecessary operations, once for an ulcer that was not there and once for supposed chronic spasm of the pylorus. Needless to say, the operations did not help. You cannot cut out an idea with a knife. Neither can you wash it out with a stomach-pump; else would Mr. T. long ago have been cured! This particular idea of his seems to be proof against all my best efforts at re-education. Psycho-analysis is impracticable, partly because of the duration of the habit of repression, but the history, and certain symbolic symptoms, indicate the Freudian mechanisms at work. All I can do is to feed him up, bully him along, and keep him from starving to death. Just now he is doing very well at home, although he has moved to California so as not to be too far away from "the miracle-worker."

If Mr. T.'s case had been typical, I should long ago have lost my faith in psychotherapy. Keeping people from starving is worth while, but is less satisfactory than curing them of what ails them. The nervous patient who has a relapse is no credit to his doctor. It is only when the origin of his trouble is not removed that the bond of transference tends to become permanent. The neurotic who is well only while under the influence of his physician is still a neurotic. However, as most people's complexes are neither so deeply buried nor so obstinate as this, a simple explanation or a single demonstration is usually enough to loose the fettering hold of old misconceptions.

COMMON AILMENTS

="Gas on the Stomach."= We all know people who suffer from "gas." Indeed, very few of us escape an occasional desire to belch after a hearty meal. But the person with nervous indigestion rolls out the "gas" with such force that the noise can sometimes be heard all over the house. He may keep this up for hours at a time, under the conviction that he is freeing himself from the products of fermenting food. He may exhibit a well-bloated stomach as proof of the disastrous effect of certain articles of diet. The gas and the bloating are supposed to be the sign and the seal of indigestion, a positive evidence that undigested food is fermenting in the stomach.

But what is fermentation? It is, necessarily, a question of the growth of bacteria and is a process which we may easily watch in our own kitchens. Bread rises when the yeast-cells have multiplied and acted on the starch of the flour, producing enough gas to raise the whole mass. Potatoes ferment because bacteria have multiplied within them. Canned fruit blows up because enough bacteria have developed inside to produce sufficient gas to blow open the can. Every housewife knows that it takes time for each of these processes. Bread has to stand several hours before it will rise; potatoes do not ferment under twelve hours, and canned fruit is not considered safe from the fermenting process under three days. Evidently there is some mistake when a person begins to belch forth "gas" within an hour or two after a meal. As a matter of fact, it is not gas at all but merely air that is swallowed with the food or that was present in the empty stomach.

When the food enters the stomach it necessarily displaces air, which normally comes out automatically and noiselessly. But if, through fear or attention, a certain set of muscles contract, the pent-up air may come forth awkwardly and noisily or it may stay imprisoned until we take measures to let it out. A hearty laugh is as good as anything, but if that cannot be managed, we may have to resort to a cup of hot water which gives the stomach a slap and makes it let go. Two belches are enough to relieve the pressure. After that we merely go on swallowing air and letting it out again, a habit both awkward and useless.

If the emotion which ties the muscle-knot is very intense, and the stomach refuses to let go under ordinary measures, the pain may be severe. But a quantity of hot water or a dose of ipecac is sure to relieve the situation. If the person is able to give himself a good moral slap and relax his unruly muscles, he reaches the same end by a much pleasanter road.

Some people are fond of the popular remedy of hot water and soda. Their faith in its efficacy is likely to be increased by the good display of gas which is sure to follow. As any cook knows, soda and acid always fizz. The soda is broken up by the hydrochloric acid of the stomach and forms salt and carbon dioxid, a gas. However, as the avowed aim of the remedy is the relief of gas rather than its manufacture, and as the soda uses up the hydrochloric acid needed in digestion, the practice cannot be recommended as reasonable.

=Gastritis.= I once knew a woman who went to a big city to consult a fashionable doctor. When she returned she told with great satisfaction that the doctor had pronounced her case gastritis. "It must be true," she added, "because I have so much gas on my stomach!" The diagnosis of gastritis used to be very common. The ending itis means inflammation,--gastritis, enteritis, colitis, each meaning inflammation of the corresponding organ. An inflammation implies an irritant. There can be no kind of itis without the presence of something which irritates the membrane of the affected part. If we get unusual and irritating bacteria in some spoiled food, we are likely to have an acute inflammation until the offending bacteria are expelled. But an inflammation of this kind never lasts. People who have had ptomaine poisoning sometimes assert that they are afterwards susceptible to poisoning by the kind of food which first made them ill. Such a susceptibility is not so much a hold-over effect from the poison as a hold-over fear which tends to repeat the physical reaction whenever that food is eaten. I, myself, have had ptomaine poisoning from canned salmon, but I have never since had any trouble about eating salmon.

=Sour Stomach.= Sometimes when a person lies down an hour or so after a meal, some of the contents of his stomach comes up in his throat. Then if he be ignorant of physiology, he may be very much alarmed because his stomach is "sour." Not knowing that he would have far greater cause for alarm if his stomach were not sour, he may, if the idea is interesting to him, begin to restrict his diet, to take digestive tablets, and to develop a regular case of nervous dyspepsia. Sometimes when the specialists measure the amount of hydrochloric acid in the stomach, they do find too much or too little acid; but this merely means that an emotion has made the glands work overtime or has stopped their action for a little while. The functions of the body are so very, very old that there is little likelihood of permanent disturbance.

=Biliousness.= The stomach is not the only part of the body concerning which we lack proper confidence. Next to it the liver is the most maligned organ in the whole body. Although the liver is about as likely to be upset in its process of secreting bile as the ocean is likely to be lacking in salt, many an intelligent person labels every little disturbance "biliousness" and lays it at the door of his faithful, dependable liver.

As a matter of fact, the liver is liable to injury from virtually but three sources--alcohol, bacterial infection, and cancer--and even a liver hardened by alcohol goes on secreting bile as usual. The patient dies of dropsy but not of "liver complaint."

Some people act as if they thought bile were a poison. On the contrary, it is a very useful digestant; it aids in keeping down the number of harmful bacteria and helps to carry the food from intestines to blood. Every day the liver manufactures at least a pint of this important fluid. The body uses what it needs and stores the surplus for reserve in the gall-bladder. The flow is continuous and, despite all appearances to the contrary, there is no such thing as a torpid or an over-active liver.

It is true that after a "bilious" person has vomited for a few minutes he is likely to throw up a certain amount of bile, which is supposed to have been lying in his stomach and causing the nausea. In fact, however, this bile is merely a part of the usual supply stored away in the gall-bladder. By the very act of retching, the bile is forced out of the bile channels into the stomach and thence up into the mouth. Anybody can throw up bile at any time if he only tries hard enough.

One of the favorite habits of certain people is the taking of calomel and salts. After such a dose they view with satisfaction the green character of the stools and conclude that they have rid themselves of a great amount of harmful matter. As a matter of fact, the greater part of the coloring in the stools is from the calomel itself, changed in the intestines from one salt of mercury to another. Any excess bile is the result of the irritating action of the calomel on the intestinal wall, an irritation which makes the bowel hurry to cast out this foreign substance without waiting for the bile to be absorbed as usual.

A patient once told me that he had bought medicine from a street fakir and by his direction had followed it with a dose of salts. He saved the bowel movement, washed it in a sieve, and discovered a great number of "gall-stones," which the medicine had so effectively washed from his system. He was much astonished when I told him that his gall-stones were merely pieces of soap. He did not know that everybody manufactures soap in his body every day, and that by taking an extra quantity of oil in the shape of the fakir's medicine and an extra quantity of potash in the salts, he had merely augmented a normal physiological process. The supposed action of calomel belongs to the same class of phenomena, and has no slightest effect on the liver or on real gall-stones, which are the precipitate of bile-salts in the gall-bladder, and which cannot be reached by any medicine.

If the popular notions about biliousness are ill founded, what then causes the disturbances which undoubtedly do occur and which show themselves in attacks of nausea or sick headache? The answer can be given in a word of four letters; a coated tongue, a bilious attack and a sick headache are all the outcome of a mood. Stocks have gone down or the wife is cranky or the neighbors are hateful. Adrenalin and thyroid secretions are poured out as the result of emotion; digestion is stopped, circulation disturbed, and the whole apparatus thrown out of gear.

=Sick-Headache.= Sick-headache is primarily a circulatory disturbance; and although the disturbance may have been inaugurated by some chemical unbalance, the sum total of the force that makes a sick-headache is emotional. The emotion, of course, need not be conscious in order to be effective. If we picture the arteries all over the body as being supplied with, among other things, a wall of circular muscles, and then imagine messages of emotion being flashed to the nerves controlling this muscle wall, we may get an idea of what happens just before a sick-headache. Some parts of the arteries contract too much and other parts relax. The arteries to the head tighten up at the extremities and become loose lower down. The force of the blood-stream against the constricted portion can hardly fail to cause pain. The sick part of the headache is merely a sympathetic strike of the nerves which control circulation and stomach.

The moral of all this is plain. If a sick-headache is the result of an emotional spasm of the blood-vessels, the obvious cure is a change of the emotion. Some people manage it by going to a party or a picnic, others by ignoring the symptoms and keeping on with their work. A woman physician whom I know was in the midst of a violent headache when called out on an obstetrical case. She felt sorry for herself, but went on the case. In the strenuous work which followed, she quite forgot the headache, which disappeared as if by magic.

Sometimes it happens that a headache recurs periodically or at regular intervals. It is easy to see that in such cases the exciting cause is fear and expectation. At some time in the past, headaches have occurred at an interval of, say, fourteen days; as the next fourteenth day approaches the sufferer says to himself: "It is about time for another headache. I am afraid it will come to-morrow," and of course it comes. One man told me that if he ate Sunday-night supper he inevitably had a headache on Monday morning. We were about to sit down to a simple Sunday supper and he refused very positively to join us. I told him he could stay all night and that I would take care of him if the Monday sickness appeared. He accepted my challenge but was unable to produce a headache. In fact, he felt so unusually flourishing the next morning that he insisted on frying the bacon for my entire family. That was the end of the Monday headaches.

=A Few Examples.= As sick-headache has always been considered a rather stubborn difficulty, not amenable to most forms of treatment, it may be well to cite a few cases which were helped by educational methods. A patient came home from a walk one day and announced that he was going to bed. When questioned, be said: "I am tired and I have a sick-headache. Isn't it logical to go to bed?" To which I answered that it would be far more logical to put some food into his stomach and change the circulation than to lie in bed and think about his pain. This man was completely cured. I have had patients throw up one meal, and very rarely two, but I have never had to supply more than three meals at a time. The waste of food I consider amply justified by the benefit to the patient.

There once came to me an elderly woman, the wife of a poor minister. She was suffering from attacks of nausea, which recurred every five to ten days with intense pain through the eyes, and with photo-phobia or fear of light. I found that she had by dint of heroic efforts raised a large and promising family on the salary of an itinerant minister--from four hundred to six hundred a year! All the time she had been feeling sorry for herself because her husband did not appreciate her. One day, after reading one of his letters which seemed to show an utter lack of appreciation of all that she was doing, she fell down in the field beside her plow, paralyzed. From that time on she had been more or less of an invalid, continually nursing her grudge and complaining that she ought not to have been made to bear so many children.

After I had heard this plaint over and over for about a week, I said: "Perhaps you ought not to have had that little daughter, the little ewe-lamb. Maybe she was one too many." "Oh, no," came the quick response. "I couldn't have spared her." Then I went down the line of the fine stalwart sons. Perhaps she could have spared John or Tom or Fred? Finally she saw the whole matter in a different light,--saw herself as a queen among women, the mother of such a family.

As to the husband, I tried to show her that she was not very clever to live with a man all those years without discovering that he was not likely to change. "You can't change him but you can change your reaction to him. If something keeps hurting your hand, you don't keep on being sore. You grow callous. Isn't it about time you grew a moral callous, too?"

I put her on the roof to sleep, on account of her fear of light. Only once did she start a headache, which I quickly nipped in the bud by making her get up and dress. She had come to stay "three months or four,--if I get along well." At the end of four weeks she left, an apparently well woman. The last I heard of her she was stumping the state for temperance, the oldest of an automobile party of speakers, and the sturdiest physically. With the emotional grievance, disappeared also the physical effects in stomach and head.

Miss S., a very brilliant woman, ambitious to make the most of her life, had been shelved for twenty-five years because of violent sick-headaches which made it impossible for her to undertake any kind of work. She had not been able to read a half-hour a day without bringing on a terrible headache. I insisted on her reading, and very soon she was so deep in psychological literature that I had difficulty in making her go to bed at all. After learning the cause of her headaches and gaining greater emotional control, she succeeded so well in freeing herself from the old habit, that she now leads the busiest kind of useful life with only an occasional headache, perhaps once in six months.

A certain minister suffered constantly from a dull pain in his head, besides having violent headaches every few days. He started in to have a bad spell the day after his arrival at my house. As I was going out of the door, he caught my sleeve. "Doctor," he said, "would It be bad manners to run away?" "Manners?" I answered. "They don't count, but morals, yes." He stayed--and that was his last bad headache. Both chronic and periodic pains disappeared for good.

One woman who had suffered from bad headaches for eighteen years lost them completely under a process of re-education. On the other hand, I have had patients who were not helped at all. The principles held good in their cases, but they were simply not able to lose the old habit of tightening up the body under emotion.

=Hysterical Nausea.= Sometimes nausea is merely the physical symbol of a subconscious moral disgust. We have already told the stories of "the woman with the nausea" (Chapter V) and of Mrs. Y. (Chapter VII). These cases are typical of many others. Their bodies were perfectly normal, and when, through psycho-analysis and re-education, they were helped to make over their childish attitudes toward the sex-life, the nausea disappeared.

=Loss of Appetite.= A nervous patient with a good appetite is "the exception that proves the rule." The neurotic is usually under weight and often complains that he feels satiated almost as soon as he begins to eat. Loss of appetite may, of course, mean that the body is busy combating toxins in the blood, but in a nervous person it usually means a symbolic loss of appetite for something in life, a struggle of the personality against something for which he has "no stomach." Psycho-analysis often reveals the source of the trouble, and a little bullying helps along the good work. By simply taking away a harmful means of expression, we may often force the subconscious mind to find a better language.

SUMMARY

Since the stomach seems to be an organ which is much better fitted to care for food than to care for a depressing emotion or a false idea, it seems far more sensible to change our minds than to keep enlarging our list of eatables which are taboo.

And since most indigestion is in very truth nothing more nor less than an emotional disturbance, worked up by fear, anger, discontent, worry, ignorance, suggestion, attention to bodily functions which are meant to be ignored, love of notice and the conversion of moral distress into physical distress, the best diet list which can be furnished to Mr. Everyman in search of health must read something like this:

MENU

Monday, Tuesday, Wednesday, Thursday, Friday, Saturday, Sunday

A Calm Spirit Plenty of Good Cheer A Varied Diet Commonsense Good Cooking Judicious Neglect of Symptoms Forgetfulness of the Digestive Process A Little Accurate Knowledge A Determination to BE LIKE FOLKS

CHAPTER XI

In which we relearn an old trick THE BUGABOO OF CONSTIPATION

POPULAR SUPERSTITIONS

In line with the taboos connected with the taking of food are the ceremonials attendant upon its elimination. Taking anxious thought about functions well established by nature is a feature of conversion-hysteria, the displacement of emotional desire from its psychic realm into symbolic physical expression. Whatever other symptoms nervous people may manifest, they are almost sure to be troubled with chronic constipation. It is true that there are many constipated people who do not seem to be nervous and who resent being classed among the neurotics. Everybody knows that the occasional individual who has difficulty in swallowing his food is nervous and that the, trouble lies not in the muscles of his throat but in the ideas of his mind. But very few people seem to realize that the more common individual who makes hard work of that other simple process--elimination of his intestinal waste matter--is suffering from the same kind of disturbance and giving way to a nervous trick. When all the facts are in, the constipated person will have hard work to clear himself of at least one count on the charge of nerves.

=An Oft-told Tale.= Sooner or later, then, the neurotic, whether he calls himself a neurotic or not, is very likely to begin worrying over his diet or his sedentary occupation. He imagines himself the victim of autointoxication, afflicted with paralysis of the colon or dearth of intestinal secretions. He leaves off eating white bread, berries, cheese, chocolate, and many another innocent food, and insists on a diet of bran-biscuit, flaxseed breakfast-foods, prunes, spinach, cream, and olive-oil with doses of mineral oil between meals. In all probability, he begins a course of massage or he starts to take extra long walks and to exercise night and morning, pulling his knees up to his chin and touching his fingers to his toes. When all these measures fail, he gives in to the morning enema or the nightly pill, in imminent danger of succumbing to a life-long habit.

THE TRUTH ABOUT CONSTIPATION

=What the Colon Is For.= It is well, then to have a fair understanding of the structure and purpose of our intestinal machinery. Contrary to general opinion, the intestines are not a dumping-ground but a digestive organ. After the food is partly digested in the stomach, it passes through a twenty-two foot tube (the small intestine) into a five-foot tube (the large intestine or colon) where digestion is completed, the nutriment is absorbed, and the waste matter is passed on and out through the rectum. As the food passes along the colon, pushed slowly ahead by the peristaltic wave, or rhythmic muscular contractions of the intestinal wall, it is seized upon by the four hundred varieties of friendly bacteria which inhabit the intestines of every healthy person, and is changed into a form which the body can assimilate. Digestion in the stomach and small intestine is carried on by means of certain digestive juices, but in the large intestine it is the bacteria which do the work. Without them we could not live.

Around the colon is a thick network of little blood vessels, all of which lead straight to the liver, the storehouse of the body. After the food is fully digested, it is passed through the thin intestinal wall into these tiny vessels and carried away to liver and muscles for storage or for immediate use.

This process of absorption is carried on throughout the whole length of the colon. Not until the very end of the intestine is reached is all the nutrition abstracted. The bowel-content can properly be called waste matter only after it has reached the rectum or pouch at the lower end of the colon. Even then, this waste matter is not poison, but merely indigestible material which the body cannot handle.

=Food, not Poison.= The colon is not a cesspool but a digestive and assimilating organ. Its content is not poison but food. Active elimination is important not so much because delay causes autointoxication or poisoning as because too large a mass is hard to manage and irritates the intestinal wall. The problem is not so much one of toxicology as of simple mechanics. If Nature had put within the body five feet of tubing which could easily become a cesspool and a breeder of poison, it is not at all likely that she would have laid alongside an elaborate system of blood vessels leading not out to the kidneys but into the storehouse of the liver; and if civilized man's changed manner of living had so upset Nature's plans as easily to transform his internal machinery into a chronic source of danger, we may be sure that he would long ago have gone the way of the unfit and succumbed to his own poisons.

=Possible Invasions.= It is true that the intestinal tract, like the rest of the body, is open to attack by harmful bacteria. But in a great majority of cases, these enemy bacteria are either quickly destroyed by the beneficent microbes within or are immediately cast out as unfit. Any germs irritating to the intestinal wall cause the mucous membrane to produce an unusual flow of mucus which washes away the offending bacteria in what we call a diarrhea.[52]

[Footnote 52: If the invading army proves obstinate and the diarrhea continues a day or so, it is wise to assist Nature by a dose of castor-oil, which gives an additional insult to the intestinal wall, spurs it on to a desperate effort, and hastens the cleansing process. In severe cases the more promptly the castor-oil is administered the better. Such emergency measures are very different from the habitual use of insulting drugs.]

Sometimes the wrong kind of bacteria do persist, causing anemia, rheumatism, sciatica, or neuritis. When these disorders are not the result of infection from teeth, tonsils, or other sources of poison, but are really caused by intestinal bacteria, I have found that a diet of buttermilk (lactic acid bacteria), with turnip-tops or spinach to supply the necessary mineral salts, often succeeds in planting the right bacteria and driving out the disturbing ones. These disorders are invasions from without, like tuberculosis or malaria, and are as likely to attack the person with easy bowel movements as the one with the most chronic constipation.

=Autointoxication.= A good deal of the talk about autointoxication is just talk. It sounds well and affords an easy explanation for all sorts of ills, but in a large majority of cases the diagnosis can hardly be substantiated. Uninformed writers of newspaper articles on the care of the body, or purveyors of purgatives or apparatus for internal baths are fond of dilating on the "foulness of the colon" as a leading cause of disease. As a rule, they advise either a strict diet, some kind of cathartic, or an elaborate process of washing out the colon to clear the body of its terrible accumulation of poisons.

=Cathartics and Enemas.= He who makes a practice of flushing out his intestinal tract with high enemas and internal baths is like a person who eats a good dinner and then proceeds to wash out his stomach. In the mistaken idea that he is making himself clean, he is washing what was never intended to be washed and robbing the body of the nutrition which it needs. And the man who persists in the pill habit is making a worse mistake, adding insult to injury and forcing the mucous membrane to toughen itself against such malicious attacks.

=Cathartics and Operations.= Even in emergencies, the use of purgatives as a routine measure is happily decreasing year by year. For many years I have deplored the use of purgatives before and after operations. That other practitioners are coming to the same conclusion is witnessed by a number of papers recently read in medical societies condemning purgation at the time of operation.

Among the most favorably received papers of the California Medical Societies have been one by Emmet L. Rixford, surgeon of the Stanford University Medical College, read before the Southern California Medical Society at Los Angeles December 8, 1916, and one by W.D. Alvarez at the California Medical Society, Del Monte, 1918,--both condemning the use of purgatives as a routine measure before operations. An article entitled the "Use and Abuse of Cathartics" in the "Journal of the American Medical Association" admirably summarizes the disadvantages of purgation at such a time.[53]

[Footnote 53: "1 Danger of dissemination of infection throughout the peritoneal cavity, in case localized infection exists.

"2 Increased absorption of toxins and greater bacterial activity by reason of the fact that undigested food has been carried down into the colon to serve as pabulum for bacteria, and that liquid feces form a better culture medium than solid feces.

"3 Increased distention of the intestine with gas and fluid, when it should be empty....

"4 Psychic and physical weakness produced by dehydration of the body, disturbance in the salt balance of the system, and the loss of sleep occasioned by the frequent purging during the night preceding the operation. As Oliver Wendell Holmes says: 'If it were known that a prize fighter were to have a drastic purgative administered two or three days before a contest, no one will question that it would affect the betting on his side unfavorably. If this be true for a powerful man in perfect health, how much more true must it be of the sick man battling for life.'

"5 Increase in postoperative distress and danger: thirst, gas pains, and even ileus...."--Journal of American Medical Association, Vol. 73, No. 17, p. 1285, Oct. 25. 1919.]

Four years ago I was called to a near-by city to see a former patient who two days before had had a minor operation,--removal of a cyst of the breast. She was dazed, almost in a state of surgical shock and very near collapse. I found that she had been put through the usual course of purgation before operation and starvation afterward, and I diagnosed her condition as a state bordering on acidosis, or lowering of the alkaline salts of the body. I ordered food at once. She rallied and recovered.

A few months later this same woman had to undergo a much more serious operation for multiple fibroids of the uterus and removal of the appendix. This time I advised the surgeon against the use of any purgative, and he took my remarks so seriously that he did not even allow an enema to be given. This time the patient showed no signs of exhaustion and had very few gas pains. I firmly believe that the day will soon come when a patient under operation, or a patient after childbirth, will no longer be depleted by a weakening and dehydrating cathartic and by a period of starvation, at a time when he needs all the energy he can summon.

=Cathartics and Childbirth.= The article referred to in the "Journal of the American Medical Association" cites the experiences of Dr. R. McPherson of the Lying-in Hospital of New York, "who showed that the routine purgation after confinement is not only useless but harmful. Of 322 women who were not purged, only three had fever (and one of them a mammary abscess); most of them had normal bowel movements and those who did not were given an enema every third day. Of 322 women who were delivered by the same technique and the same operators but were purged in the usual routine manner, twenty-eight had some fever." This experience of one physician is corroborated by that of others who find that the more we tamper with the natural functions in time of stress the harder do we make the recuperative process. There are certainly times when catharsis is necessary but "one thing is certain, the day for routine purgation is past."[54] Even in emergencies we need to know why we administer cathartics and in chronic cases we may be sure that they are always a mistake.

[Footnote 54: Ibid, p. 1286.]

="An Old Trick."= Before we make a practice of interfering with Nature's processes, it is well to remember how old and stable those processes are. As long as there has been the taking in of food, there has been also the casting out of waste matter. The sea-anemone closes in on the little mollusk that floats against its waving petals, assimilates what it can and rejects the rest. In the long line from sea-anemone to man, this automatic process of elimination has gone on without a hitch, adapting itself with perfect success to the changing habits of the varying types of life. So old a process is not easily upset. And, be it noted, in the human body this automatic, involuntary process still goes on with very little trouble until it reaches a point in the body where man, the thinking animal, tries to control it by conscious thought.

=A Question of Evacuation.= Much of the misconception about constipation arises from the mistaken idea that this is a disorder of the whole intestine or at least of the whole colon. As a matter of fact, the trouble is almost wholly in the rectum. There is no trouble with the general traffic movement, but only with the unloading at the terminus. In my experience, the patient reports that he feels the fecal mass in the lower part of the rectum, but that he is unable to expel it. Examination by finger or by X-ray reveals a mass in the rectal pouch. If there is a piling up of freight further back on the line, it is only because the unloading process has been delayed at the terminus.

So long as the bowel-content is in the region of automatic control, there is very little likelihood of trouble. An occasional case of organic trouble-- appendicitis, lead-colic, mechanical obstruction, new growths or spinal-cord disease--may cause a real blockade, but in ninety-nine cases out of every hundred there is little trouble so long as the involuntary muscles, working automatically under the direction of the subconscious mind, are in control. By slow or rapid stages, on time or behind time, the bowel-content reaches the upper part of the rectum and passes through a little valve into the lower pouch. Here is where the trouble begins.

=Meddlesome Interference.= In the natural state the little human, like the other animals, empties his bowel whenever the fecal mass enters the lower portion of the rectum. The presence of the mass in the rectum constitutes a call to stool which is responded to as unthinkingly as is the desire for air in the taking of a breath. But the tiny child soon has to learn to control some of his natural functions. At the lower end of the rectum there is a purse-string muscle called the _Sphincter-ani_, an involuntary muscle which may with training be brought partly under voluntary control. Under the demands of civilization, the baby learns to tighten up this muscle until the proper time for evacuation. Then, if he be normal, he lets go, the muscles higher up contract and the bowel empties itself automatically, as it always did before civilization began.

There is, however, a possibility of trouble whenever the conscious mind tries to assume control of functions which are meant to be automatic. Under certain conditions necessary control becomes meddlesome interference. If the child for one reason or another takes too much interest in the function of elimination; if he likes too much the sense-gratification from stimulation of the rectal nerves and learns to increase this gratification by holding back the fecal mass; if he gets the idea that the function is "not nice" and takes the interest that one naturally feels in subjects that are taboo; or if he catches from his elders the suggestion that the bowel movement is a highly important process and that something disastrous is likely to happen unless it is successfully performed every day; then his very interest in the matter tends to interfere with automatic regulation, and to cause trouble.

Just as people often find it hard to let go the bladder muscle and urinate when in a hurry or under observation, and just as an apprehensive woman in childbirth tightens up the purse-string muscle of the womb, so the little child, or the grown up who catches the suggestion of difficulty in the bowel movement, loses the trick of letting go. Instead of merely exercising control by temporarily inhibiting the function, he tries to carry through the process itself by voluntary control--and fails. Constipation is a perfect example of the power of suggestion, and of the troublesome effect of a fear-idea in the realm of automatic functions.

FOOD AND CONSTIPATION

Since the waste matter from all foods finally reaches the rectum, and since constipation is merely a difficulty in the forces of expulsion, it is hard to see how any normal food in the quantities usually eaten could have the slightest effect on the problem. When we remember that it takes food from twelve to twenty-four hours to reach the rectum, and that it has during all that time been subjected to the action of the powerful chemicals of the digestive tract, it is hard to imagine a piece of cheese, of whatever variety, strong enough to stop the contraction of the muscles of the upper rectum or to tie the sphincter-muscle into a knot. It would be difficult to find a food which could pass without effect through twenty-seven feet of intestinal tubing only to become suddenly effective on the wall of the rectum. If the wrong kind of food is the cause of constipation, why does the rectum prove to be the most refractory portion of the tube? On what principle could a piece of chocolate inhibit the call to stool or contract the sphincter muscle? On the other hand, even if it should be conceded that constipation were the result of lack of lubricating secretions in the colon, how could two tablespoonfuls of mineral oil be a sufficient lubricant after being mixed with liquid and solid food through many feet of the intestinal tract?

=An Adaptable Apparatus.= The lining of the intestines has plenty of secretions to take care of its function. It is as well adapted to the vicissitudes of life as are the other parts of the body. The muscular coat is no more liable to paralysis or spasm than are the voluntary muscles. As the skin adapts itself to all waters and all weathers, and as the lungs adjust themselves to varying air-pressures, so the intestinal wall makes ready adaptation to any common-sense demands, adjusting itself with ease to an athletic or a sedentary life, and to the normal variations of diet. What man has eaten throughout the centuries man may eat to-day. If you will but believe it, your intestines will make no more objection to white bread, blackberries, and cheese, along with all other ordinary articles of food, than the skin makes to varying kinds of water. Naturally, the suggested idea that a food will constipate tends to carry itself out to fulfilment and to prevent the call to stool from rising to the level of consciousness; but the real force lies not in the food but in the suggestion.

=The Bran Fad.= It is when we try to improve on the normal human diet that we really insult the body. He who leaves off eating nourishing white bread and takes to bran muffins is simply cheating his body. Bran has a small food value, but the human body is not made to extract it. Not only does bran fail to give us any nourishment itself, but it lessens the power of the intestines to care for other food.[55] The fad for bran is based on the well-known fact that we need a certain quantity of bulk in order to stimulate the intestinal wall to normal peristalsis. We do need bulk, but not more than we naturally get from a normal and varied diet including a reasonable amount of fruit and vegetables.

[Footnote 55: See an article entitled "Bread and Bran," Journal of American Medical Association, July 5, 1919, p. 36.]

It is true that the suggestion of the efficacy of bran, dates, spinach, or any other food is frequently quite sufficient to give relief, temporarily, just as massage, manipulation of the vertebrae, the surgeon's knife, or mineral oil may be enough to carry the conviction of power to a suggestible individual. But who wants to take his suggestions in such inconvenient forms as these?

=Change of Water.= Another popular superstition centers around drinking-waters. There are people who cannot move from one town to another, much less take an extensive trip, without a fit of constipation--or a box of pills. If they only knew it, there is no water on earth which could make a person constipated. A new water, full of unusual minerals, might hasten the bowel movement, but on what possible principle could it retard it? Constipation has nothing to do with food or with water, but solicitous care about either can hardly fail to create the trouble which it tries to avoid.

THE CURE

=Taking off the Brakes.= Since constipation is wholly due to the acceptance of a false suggestion, the only logical cure must be release from the power of that suggestion. "He is able as soon as he thinks he is able"; not that thought gives the power, but that the right thought releases the inhibition of the mistaken thought. As soon as the brakes are taken off, the internal machinery is quite able to make the wheels go round. The bowel will empty itself if we let it. The function of elimination is not a new trick learned with difficulty by the aged, but a trick as old and as elemental as life itself. Like balancing on a bicycle, it may not be done by any voluntary muscular effort, but it just does itself when one learns how.

Once the sense of power comes, once the mind forgets to be doubtful or afraid, then the old automatic habit invariably reasserts itself. Meddlesome interference may throw the mechanism out of gear, but fortunately it cannot strip the gears. Constipation is an inhibition or restraint of function, but is never a loss of function. No one is too old, no one is too fixed in the bad habit to relearn the old trick. I have had a good many patients with chronic constipation, but I have never had one who failed to learn. Real conviction speedily brings success, and in many cases success seems to outrun conviction. So efficient is Nature if she has only half a chance!

=Some People Who Learned.= Unless you are over ninety-two, do not despair. One old lady of that age, a sort of patient by proxy, was able to cure herself without even one consultation. Her daughter had been a patient of mine and had been cured of the constipation with which she had been busy for many years. The mother, who believed her own bowel paralyzed, had been in the habit of lying on the bed and taking a copious enema every second day of her life. When, however, she heard of her daughter's cure, the bright old woman gave up her enemas and let her bowels do their own functioning. She stayed cured until her death at ninety-five.

=A Fifty-year Habit.= Another old lady was not quite so easily convinced. She ridiculed the idea that her son of fifty, who had been "constipated in his cradle" could be cured of his lifelong habit, but he was cured. As long as there is life and the light of reason, so long may Nature's functions be re 雜 tablished.

=The Whole Family.= Nor is any one too young to learn. A tiny baby is easily taught. There came to me for two consultations a mother and her two babies, all three constipated. The four-year-old child, mentally deficient, had been fed on milk of magnesia from his infancy, and the four-months-old baby had been started on the same path. I explained to the mother the mechanism of elimination, told her to give up cathartics, and to set a regular time for herself and the baby, but was a little dubious about the mentally deficient four-year-old. However she soon reported that they had all three promptly acquired the new habit. Four years later she told me that they had never had any more trouble.

=A Record History.= When Miss H. first came to my house, she told a story that was almost incredible. She said that for many months she had been taking eight tablespoonfuls of mineral oil three times a day besides a cathartic at night, and an enema in the morning. No wonder she was a little dubious over such mild treatment as mine seemed to be!

Constipation was only one of this young woman's troubles. She could not sleep and was so fatigued that she believed herself at the end of her physical capital. When she first came to me she had tears in her eyes most of the time and used to confide to various people that she was sure she was a patient that I could not cure,--a very common belief among nervous invalids! She was sure that I did not understand her case, and that she could not get anything out of this kind of treatment.

It was only a very short time, however, before her bowels were functioning like those of a normal person. She lost her insomnia and her fatigue and went away as well as ever. When she got back to her office, she found that her old position, which she had believed secure to her, had been given to another. She had to go out and hunt a new job and face conditions harder than she had had before, but she came through with flying colors. A short time ago Miss H. came back to see me,--a happy, robust young woman, very different from the person I had first known. She assured me that she had never had any return of her old symptoms and that she was as well as a person could be.

=Living up to a Suggestion.= Mrs. T. had not had a natural movement of the bowels in twenty-five years. After the birth of a child, twenty-five years before, her physician had told her that her muscles had been so badly torn in labor that they could not carry through a natural movement. After that she had never gone a day without a pill or an enema. I explained to her that when any muscle of the rectum is injured in childbirth, it is the sphincter-ani, and that since this is the muscle whose contraction holds back the bowel content, its injury would tend to over-free evacuation rather than to constipation. She saw the point and within two or three days regained her old power of spontaneous evacuation.

=Practical Steps.= The first step, then, in acquiring normal habits is the conviction of the integrity of our physical machines and a determination not to interfere by thought, or by physical meddling, with the elemental functions of our bodies. After this all-important step, there are a few practical suggestions which it is well to follow. Most of them are nothing more than the common-sense habits of personal hygiene which are so obvious as to be almost axiomatic, but which are nevertheless often neglected:

1 Eat three square meals a day.

2 Drink when thirsty, having conveniently at hand the facilities for drinking.

3 Heed the call to stool as you heed the call of hunger. When the stool passes the little valve between the upper and lower portions of the rectum, it gives the signal that the time for evacuation has come. If this signal is always heeded, it will automatically start the machinery that leads to evacuation. If it is persistently ignored because one is too busy, or because the mind is filled with the idea of disability, the call very soon fails to rise to the level of consciousness. The feces remain in the rectum, and the bad habit is begun.

4 Choose a regular time and keep that appointment with yourself as regularly as possible. In all the activities of Nature, there is a rhythm which it is well to observe.

5 Take time to acquire the habit. Do not be in a hurry. Do not strain. No amount of effort will start the movement. Just let it come of itself.

6 Finally, should the unconscious suggestion of lack of power stubbornly remain in force, take a small enema on the third day. If the waste matter accumulates for three or more days, the bulk becomes so great that the circular muscles of the rectum are unable to handle it, just as the fingers cannot squeeze down to expel water from too large a mass of wet blankets. Take only a small enema--never over a quart at a time--and expel the water immediately. One or two such measures will bring away the mass in the rectum. The material farther up still contains food elements and is not yet ready for expulsion. Lessen the amount of water each time until no outside help is needed. Once you get the right idea, all enemas will be superfluous.

SUMMARY

If you would have in a nutshell an epitome of the truth about constipation, indigestion, insomnia, and the other functional disturbances common to nervous folk, you can do, no better than to commit to memory and store away for future reference that choice limerick of the centipede, which so admirably sums up the whole matter of meddlesome interference:

A centipede was happy quite Until a frog in fun Said, "Pray, which leg comes after which?" This raised her mind to such a pitch, She lay distracted in the ditch, Considering how to run.

Whoever tries to consider "which leg comes after which" in any line of physiological activity, is pretty sure to find himself in the ditch considering how to run. Wherefore, remember the centipede!

CHAPTER XII

In which handicaps are dropped A WOMAN'S ILLS

"THE FEMALE OF THE SPECIES"

If ever there was a man who wished himself a woman, he has hidden away the desire within the recesses of his own heart. But one does not have to wait long to hear a member of the female sex exclaim with evident emotion, "Oh, dear, I wish I had been born a man!" It is probable that if these same women were given the chance to transform themselves overnight, they would hesitate long when it actually came to the point. The joys of being a woman are real joys. However, in too many cases these joys seem hardly to compensate for the discomforts of the feminine organism. It is the body that drags. Painful menstrual periods, the dreaded "change of life," various "female troubles" with a number of pregnancies scattered along between, make some of the daughters of Eve feel that they spend a good deal of their lives paying a penalty merely for being women. Brought up to believe themselves heirs to a curse laid on the first woman, they accept their discomforts with resignation and try to make the best of a bad business.

="Since the War."= Nothing is quite the same since the war. Among other things we have learned that many of our so-called handicaps were nothing but illusions,--base libels on the female body. Under the stern necessity of war the women of the world discovered that they could stand up under jobs which have until now been considered quite beyond their powers. Society girls, who were used to coddling themselves, found a new joy in hard and continuous work; middle-aged women, who were supposed to be at the time of life when little could be expected of them, quite forgot themselves in service. Ambulance drivers, nurses, welfare workers, farmerettes, Red-Cross workers, street-car conductors and "bell-boys," revealed to themselves and to the world unsuspected powers of endurance in a woman's body. Although some of the heavier occupations still seem to be "man's work," better fitted for a man's sturdier body, we know now that many of these disabilities were merely a matter of tradition and of faulty training.

There still remains, however, a goodly number of women who are continuously or periodically below par because of some form of feminine disability. Some of these women are suffering from real physical handicaps, but many of them need to be told that they are disabled not by reason of being women but by reason of being nervous women.

="Nerves" Again.= Despite the organic disturbances which may beset the reproductive organs, and despite the havoc wrought by venereal diseases, it may be said with absolute assurance that the majority of feminine ills are the result neither of the natural frailty of the female body, nor even of man's infringement of the social law, but are the direct result of false suggestion and of false attitudes toward the facts of the reproductive life. The trouble is less a difficulty with the reproductive organs than a difficulty with the reproductive instinct. "Something wrong" with the instinct is translated by the subconscious mind into "something wrong" with the related generative organs, and converted into a physical pain.

That this relation has always been dimly felt is shown by the fact that the early Greeks called nervous disorders hysteria, from the Greek word for womb. It is only lately, however, that the blame has been put in the right place and the trouble traced to the instinct rather than to the organs of reproduction.

=Why Women Are Nervous.= Although women hold no monopoly, it must be conceded that they are particularly prone to "nerves." The reason is not hard to find. Since the leading factor in a neurosis is a disturbance of the insistent instinct of reproduction, a disturbance usually based on repression, then any class of persons in whom the instinct is particularly repressed would, in the very nature of the case, be particularly liable to nervousness.

No one who thoroughly knows human nature would attempt to deny that woman is as strongly endowed as man with the great urge toward the perpetuation of the race, or that she has had to repress the instinct more severely than has man. The man insists on knowing that the children he provides for are his own children. Whatever the degree of his own fidelity, he must be sure that his wife is true to him. Thus has grown up the insistence that, no matter what man does, woman, if she is to be counted respectable, shall control the urge of the instinct and live up to the requirements of continence set for her by society.

Unfortunately, however, there is more often blind repression than rational control. The measures taken to prevent a girl's becoming a tom-boy are measures of sex-repression quite as much as of sex-differentiation. Over-reaction of sensitive little souls to lessons in modesty often causes distortion of normal sex-development. Ignorance concerning the phenomena of life is commended as innocence, while it really implies a sex-curiosity which has been too severely repressed. The young woman blushes at thoughts of love, while the young man is filled with a sense of dignity. We smile at the picture of "Miss Philura's" confusion as she hesitatingly sends up to her Creator a petition for the much-desired boon of a husband. But really, why shouldn't she want one? Many a young woman, in order to deaden her senses to the unsuspected lure of the reproductive instinct by what is really an awkward attempt at sublimation, makes a fetish of dress and social position and considers only the marriage of convenience; or, on the other hand, she scorns men altogether and throws herself into a "career."

Young men are not so often taught to repress, but neither are they taught to swing their vital energies into altruistic channels through sublimation. Since the woman of his class will not marry him until he has money, the young man too often satisfies his undirected instincts in a commercial way. The statistics of venereal diseases prove that here, as elsewhere, goods subject to barter are subject to contamination. In a late marriage, too often a contaminated body accompanies the material possessions which the standards of society have demanded of a husband.

But the woman pays in still other coin for the repressions arising from faulty childhood training. Unable to find expression for herself either in marriage or in devotion to work, because some old childish repression is still denying all outlet to her legitimate desire, she frequently falls into a neurosis; or if she escapes a real breakdown, she gives expression to unsatisfied longings in some isolated nervous symptoms which in many cases center about the organs of generation. There then results any one of the various functional disturbances which are only too often mistaken for organic disease. What is needed in cases like this is not a gynecologist nor a surgeon, but a psycho-pathologist--or perhaps only a grasp of the facts. Let us look at the more common of these disturbances in order to gain an understanding of the situation.

THE MENSTRUAL PERIOD

=Potential Motherhood.= Among the normal phenomena of a woman's life is the recurring cycle of potential motherhood. Every three or four weeks a new ovum or egg matures in the ovary and undergoes certain chemical changes, which send into the blood a substance called a hormone. This hormone is a messenger, stimulating the mucous membrane of the womb into making its velvet pile longer and softer, and its nutrient juices more abundant in readiness for the ovum.

The same stimulus causes the whole organism to make ready for a new life. As in hunger, the chemistry of the body produces the muscle-tension that is felt as a craving for food, so this recurring chemical stimulus produces a definite craving in body and mind. This craving brings about an increased irritability or sensitiveness to stimuli which may result either in a joyous or a fretful mood.

During sleep the social inhibitions are felt less distinctly and the sleeper dreams love-dreams woven from messages coming up from all the minute nerve-endings in the expectant reproductive organs. But if no germ-cell travels up the womb-canal and tube to meet and impregnate the ovum, the womb-lining rejects the egg as chemically unfit. All the furbishings are loosened from the walls and slowly cast out, constituting the menstrual flow. The phenomenon as a whole is a physiological function and should be accompanied by a sense of well-being and comfort as is the exercise of any other function, such as digestion or muscular activity. Only too often, however, it is dreaded as an unmitigated disaster, a time for giving up work or fun and going to bed with a hot-water bottle until "the worst is over." Let us see how this perversion comes about.

=Why Menstruation Is Painful.= What sort of atmosphere is created for the young girl as she attains puberty? Most girls get their first inkling of the menstrual period from the periodic "sick spells" of mother or sister. This knowledge comes without conscious thought and is a direct observation of the subconscious mind, which records impressions with the accuracy and completeness of a photographic plate. Hearing the talk about a "sick-time" and observing the signs of "cramps" among older friends, the young girl's subconscious mind plays up to the suggestion and recoils with fear from the newly experienced sensations in the maturing organs of reproduction.

This recoil of fear interferes with the circulation in the functioning organs, just as fear blanches the face or hinders digestion. There is several times as much blood in the stomach when it is full of food as there is between meals, but we do not for this reason fancy that we have a pain after each meal. There is more blood in the generative organs during their functioning, but this means pain only when fear ties up the circulation and causes undue congestion. Fear acts further on the sturdy muscle of the womb, tying it up into just such knots as we feel in the esophagus when we say that we have a lump in the throat. It is safe to say that ninety-five cases of painful menstruation out of every hundred are caused by fear and by the expectation of pain. The cysts and tumors responsible for pain are so rare as to be fairly negligible, when compared with these other causes.

Dr. Clelia Duel Mosher of Stanford University has for many years carried on careful investigations among the students of the university. After describing in detail certain physical exercises which she has found of value, she continues:

But more important even than this is an alteration of the morbid attitude of women themselves toward this function; and almost equally essential is a fundamental change in the habit of mind on our part as physicians; for do we not tend to translate too much, the whole of a woman's life into terms of menstruation? If every young girl were taught that menstruation is not normally a "bad time" and that pain or incapacity at that period is as discreditable and unnecessary as bad breath due to decaying teeth, we might almost look for a revolution in the physical life of women.... In my experience the traditional treatment of rest in bed, directing the attention solely to the sex-zone of the body, and the accepted theory that it is an inevitable illness while at the same time the mind is without occupation, produces a morbid attitude and favors the development and exaggeration of whatever symptoms there may be.[56]

[Footnote 56: Clelia Duel Mosher: Health and the Woman Movement, pp. 25, 26, 19.]

=Pre-Menstrual Discomfort.= If it be objected that women often feel badly for a day or two before the period begins, before they know that it is due, and that this feeling of discomfort could not be caused by fear and expectation, it is easy to reply that the subconscious mind knows perfectly what is happening within the body. The emotion of fear, working within the subconscious, is able to translate all the varying bodily sensations into feelings of distress without any knowledge on the part of the conscious mind.

Sometimes before the period begins, a girl feels blue and upset for a day or two, a sign that the instinct is getting discouraged. The whole body is saying, "Get ready, get ready," but it has gotten ready many times before, and to no purpose. Unsatisfied striving brings discouragement. What reaches consciousness is a feeling of pessimism and a general dissatisfaction with life as a whole. If, instead of giving in to the blues or going to bed and predicting a pain, the girl finds other outlets for her energy, she finds that after all, her instinct may be satisfied in indirect ways and that she has strangely come into a new supply of vim.

=The Purpose of the Pain.= Although suggestion is behind all nervous symptoms, there is a deeper reason for the disturbance. When an unhealthy suggestion is seized and acted upon, it is because some unsatisfied part of the personality sees in it a chance for accomplishing its own ends. The pre-menstrual period is the blooming-time, the mating-time, the springtime of the organism. That means eminently a time for coming into notice, that one's charms may attract the desired complement. But if the rightfully insistent instinctive desires are held in check by unnatural repressions and misapplied social restrictions, the starved instinct can obtain expression only by a concealment of purpose. The disguise assumed is often one of indifference or positive distaste for the allurements of the other sex. But, as we know, an instinctive desire will not be denied. In this case, the misguided instinct which has been given the suggestion that menstruation means illness, fits this conception into the scheme of things and obtains notice in a roundabout way by the attention given to the invalid.

=The Treatment.= To find that the symptom has a purpose rather than a cause gives the indication for the treatment. Judicious neglect causes the symptom to cease by defeating its very purpose,--that of drawing attention to itself. The person who never mentions her discomfort, thinks about it as little as possible, and goes about her business as usual, is likely to find her trouble gone before she realizes it.[57]

[Footnote 57: Violent exercise at this time is unwise, but continuing one's usual activity helps the circulation and keeps the mind from centering on the affected part. The physiological congestion is unduly intensified by standing; therefore all employments should afford facilities for the woman to sit at least part of the time while continuing work.]

A little explanation gives the patient insight into the workings of her own mind, and usually causes the pain to disappear in short order. Astonished, indeed, and filled with gratitude have been some of my young-women patients who had all their lives been unable to plan any work or social engagements for the time of this functioning. Many of them were the worst kind of doubters when they were told that to go to bed and center their attention on the generative organs only made the muscles tighten up and the circulation congest. They could not conceive themselves up and around, pursuing their normal life during such a time. However, as they have found by experience that this point of view is not an optimistic dream, they have broken up the confidence-game which their subconscious had been playing on them, and have gone on their way rejoicing.

There was one young girl, a doctor's daughter, who suffered continuously from pain in the abdomen, and from back-pain which increased so greatly at the time of the menses that she was in the habit of going to bed for several days, to be waited on with solicitous care by her family. In an attempt to cure the trouble she had undergone an operation to suspend the uterus, but the pain had continued as before. When she came to me, I explained to her that there was no physical difficulty and that her trouble was wholly nervous. I made her play tennis every day and she had just finished a game when her period came on. She stayed up for luncheon, went for a walk in the afternoon, ate her dinner with the family, and behaved like other people. Her mother telephoned that evening and when I told her what her daughter had been doing, she gasped in astonishment. She had difficulty in believing that the new order was not miracle but simply the working out of natural law. Since that time her daughter has had no more trouble.

=The Ounce of Prevention.= If young girls had wiser counselors in their mothers and physicians, the misconception would never occur, and such an indirect outlet would not be needed; the organic sensations incident to puberty and the recurring menstrual period would have something of the significance of the annunciation to Mary, bringing wonder and a sense of well-being.

When your little daughter arrives at maturity, give her a joyous initiation into the noble order of women. She will welcome the new function as a badge of womanhood and as a harbinger of wonderful things to come.

A girl of fifteen came under my care to be helped out of a mood of increasing depression and uneasiness. Her glance was furtive, yet anxiously expectant. Tears came unbidden as she sat alone or fingered the keys of the piano. Tactful questioning elicited no response as to reasons for her unhappiness. Opportunities for giving confidence were not accepted. At a chance moment our talk drifted to the subject of menstruation. "Your periods are regular and easy; and do you know what they are for?" Then I painted for her a picture of the preparations that are made throughout the whole organism, for the germ-cell that comes each month and has in it all the possibilities of a new little life.

The result of this confidential talk may seem fanciful to any one but an eye-witness. We had only a week's association, but the depression ceased, the furtive look and deprecatory manner were replaced by a joyous buoyancy. In a few weeks the thin neck and awkward body rounded out into the symmetry which usually precedes the establishment of puberty, but which was delayed in this case until the unconscious conflict resolved itself.

=In the Large.= Looked at from any angle, this subject is an important one. There are involved not only the physical comfort and convenience of the sufferers themselves, but also the economic prospects of women as a whole. If women are to demand equal opportunity and equal pay, they must be able to do equal work without periodic times of illness. When employers of women tell us that they regularly have to hire extra help because some of their workers lose time each month, we realize how great is the aggregate of economic waste, a waste which would assuredly be justified if the health of the country's womanhood were really involved, but which is inefficient and unnecessary when caused merely by ignorant tradition. "Up to standard every day of every week," is a slogan quite within the range of possibility for all but the seriously ill. When reduced to their lowest terms, the inconveniences of this function are not great and are not too dear a price to pay for the possibilities of motherhood.

THE "CHANGE OF LIFE"

=Another Phantom Peril.= As the young girl is taught to fear the menstrual period, so the older woman is taught to dread the time when the periods shall cease. Despite the general enlightenment of this day and age, the menopause or "change of life" is all too frequently feared as a "critical period" in a woman's life, a time of distressing physical sensations and even of danger to mental balance.

As a matter of fact, the menopause is a physiological process which should be accomplished with as little mental and physical disturbance as accompanies the establishment of puberty. The same internal secretion is concerned in both. When the function of ovulation ceases the body has to find a new way to dispose of the internal secretion of the ovary. Its presence in the blood is the cause of the sudden dilatation of the blood-vessels that is known as the "hot flash."

The matter is altogether a problem of chemistry, with the necessity for a new adjustment among the glands of internal secretion. The body easily manages this if left to itself, but is greatly interfered with by the wrong suggestion and emotion. We have already seen how quickly emotion affects all secretions and how easily the adrenal and thyroid glands are influenced by fear. This is the root of the trouble in many cases of difficult "change." If an occasional body is not quite able to regulate the chemical readjustment, we may have to administer the glands of some other animal, but in the majority of cases, the body, unhampered by an extra burden of fear, is quite able to make its own adjustments. The hot flash passes in a moment, if not prolonged by emotion or if not converted into a habit by attention.

One source of trouble in the menopause is that it comes at a time in a woman's life when she is likely to have too much leisure. In no way can a woman so easily handicap her body at this time as by stopping work and being afraid. Those women who have to go on as usual find themselves past the change almost before they know it,--unless they consider themselves abused, and worry over the necessity for working through such a "critical time."

=Three Rules.= Here are a few pointers which have have been of help to a number of women:

1 Remember that this is a physiological process and therefore abundantly safeguarded by Nature. If you don't expect trouble you will not be likely to find it.

2 Remember that the sweating and flushing are made worse by notice.

3 Do everything in your power to keep from the public the knowledge that you are no longer a potential mother. If you are past forty, do not mop your face or gasp for breath or carry a fan to the theater! Shun attention and fear, and you will be surprised at the ease with which the "change" is effected.

=Nature's Last Chance.= While we are on the subject of the middle-aged woman, it may be well to mention a phenomenon sometimes noticed in the early forties. Often an "old maid" who has considered herself settled for life in her bachelor estate, suddenly takes to herself a husband. (I use the verb advisedly!) Mothers who have thought their child-bearing days long past sometimes find themselves pregnant. "The child of her old age" is not an uncommon occurrence. Unmarried women who have "kept straight" all their lives sometimes go down before temptation at this late time. There is a reason. It is as though Nature were making a last desperate attempt to produce another life before it is too late, speeding up all the internal secretions and flashing insistent messages throughout the whole organism.

It may help some woman who feels herself inexplicably impelled toward the male sex to know that she is not being "tempted by the devil" but merely driven by the insistent chemicals within her body. She is likely to rationalize and tell herself that it is too bad for a worth-while person like herself to leave no progeny behind her; or she may say, as one of my patients did when contemplating running away with another woman's husband,--that she could make that man so much happier than his wife did, and that she really owed it to him as well as to herself. When a woman knows what is the matter with her, it makes it easier to bide her time and wait for the demands of Nature to subside. Chemicals may not be so romantic as love, but neither are they so melodramatic!

OTHER TROUBLES

="Speaking of Operations."= Physicians are often called upon to diagnose some such vague symptom as pain in the abdomen, back and head; ache in the legs; constipation, or loss of appetite. Since the patient is very insistent that something shall be done, the physician may be driven to operate, even when he has an uneasy feeling that the trouble is "merely nervous." Sixty per cent. of the operations on women are necessitated by the results of gonorrheal infection. Next in frequency up to recent date, have been operations for nervous symptoms which could in no way be reached by the knife. Only too often a nerve-specialist hears the tale of an operation which was supposed to cure a certain pain but which left it worse rather than better. It is a pleasure to see some of these pains disappear under a little re-education, but one cannot help wishing that the re-education had come before the knife instead of after it.

A skilled surgeon can cut almost anything out of a person's body, but he cannot cut out an instinct. It sometimes takes great skill to determine whether the trouble is an organic affection or a functional disturbance caused by the misdirected instinct of reproduction. Often, however, the clinical pictures are so different as to leave no room for doubt, provided the diagnostician has his eyes open and is not over-persuaded by the importunity of the poor neurotic, who insists that the surgeon shall remove her appendix, her gall-bladder, her genital organs, and her tonsils, and who finally comes back that he may have a whack at the operation scar.

=The Bearing of Children.= A number of years ago I became acquainted with a charming young married woman who had all her life recoiled with fear from the phenomena of sex. She had been afraid of menstruation and of marriage, and had at this time almost a phobia for pregnancy and childbirth. Before long she came to me in terror, telling me that she had become pregnant. I explained to her that pregnancy is the time when most women are at their best, that the nausea which is often troublesome in the beginning is caused merely by a mixing of messages from the autonomic nerves, which refer new sensations in the womb to the more usual center of activity in the stomach; and that after the body has become accustomed to these sensations, most women experience a greater sense of well-being and peace than at any other time in life. We had a conversation or two on the subject and everything seemed to go well for a while.

As it happened, this young woman and her husband came to call on me one afternoon just before the baby was expected. During the visit she began to show signs of being in labor. Again she was in terror. Again I explained the phenomena of labor, telling her that the womb-contractions are caused by the presence in the blood of a chemical secretion (hormone) which continues its good work as long as there is a state of confidence, but which sometimes stops under fear or apprehension. I explained that these womb-efforts are a peristaltic movement, a contraction of the upper muscles and a letting go of the purse-string muscle at the mouth of the womb, and that fear only tends to tie up this purse-string muscle, making a difficult process out of one which was intended by Nature to be much more simple. She seemed to understand and to lose a good deal of her fright.

About six o'clock the couple went home on the street car from the upper end of Pasadena to the far end of Los Angeles. The next morning I had a jubilant telephone message from the happy father, announcing that the boy-baby had arrived at midnight and that, wonderful to relate, he had come without the mother's experiencing any pain whatever.

I give this account for what it is worth, without of course contending that labor could always be as easy as this. It happened that this girl was a normal, healthy woman and that there were no complications of any kind in the process of childbirth. A right attitude of mind could not have corrected any physical difficulty, but it did seem to help her let go of her fear, which would of itself have caused long and painful labor.

A patient once told me that when her first baby came, she happened to be out in the country where she had to call in a doctor whom she did not know. He was an uncouth sort of fellow who inspired fear rather than confidence. She soon found that labor stopped whenever he came into the room, and started again when he went out. She had the good sense to send him out and complete her labor with only the help of her mother. Unfortunate is the obstetrician who does not know how to inspire a feeling of confidence in his patients. Even childbirth may be mightily helped or hindered by the mother's state of mind.

SUMMARY

A woman's body has more stability than she knows. It is sometimes out of order, but it is more often misunderstood; usually it is an unobtrusive and satisfactory instrument, quite fit for its daily tasks. The average woman is really well put together. We hear about the ones who have difficulty, but not about the great majority who do not. We notice the few who are upset during the menopause, and forget all the others. To be comfortable and efficient most of the time is, after all, merely to be "like folks."

The special functions which Nature has been perfecting in a woman's body are as a rule, easily carried through unless complicated by false ideas or by fear.

If the woman who has no organic difficulty but who still finds herself handicapped by her body, will cease being either resigned to her languishing lot or envious of her stalwart brothers; if instead she will set out to learn how to be efficient as a woman, she will find that many of her ills are not the blunders of an inefficient Creator, but are home-made products, which quickly vanish in the light of understanding.

CHAPTER XIII

In which we lose our dread of night.

THAT INTERESTING INSOMNIA

THE FEAR OF STAYING AWAKE

To sleep or not to sleep! That is the question. In all the world there is nothing to equal it in importance,--to the man with insomnia. His days are mere interludes between troubled nights spent in restless tossing to and fro and feverish worry over the weary day to come. His mind filled with ideas about the disastrous effects of insomnia, he imagines himself fast sliding down hill toward the grave or the insane-asylum. It is true that his conversation very often politely begins something like this: "Good morning. Did you sleep well last night?" but if we fail to respond by an equally polite "and I hope you had a good night?" he seems restless until he has somehow disillusioned us by stating the exact number of hours and minutes during which he was able to lose himself in slumber.

We must not ridicule the man who doesn't sleep. We are all very much alike. If any one of us happens to lie awake for a night or two, he is likely to get into a panic, and if the spell should last a week, he begins looking up steamship agents and talking of voyages to Southern seas. The fact is that most people are dreadfully afraid of insomnia. Knowing the effects of a few nights of enforced wakefulness, and having had a little experience with the fagged feeling after a restless night, they believe themselves only logical when they fall into a panic over the prospect of persistent insomnia.

=Two Kinds of Wakefulness.= As a matter of fact, insomnia is a phantom peril. There is not the slightest danger from lying awake nights, provided one is not kept awake by some irritating physical stimulus. All fear of insomnia is based on ignorance of the difference between enforced wakefulness and deliberate wakefulness, or insomnia. The man who has acquired the habit may stay awake almost indefinitely without appreciable harm, but the one who is kept awake for a week by a pain, by a chemical poison from infection, or by the necessity for staying up on his job, may easily be in a state of exhaustion. Even in cases of prolonged pain or over-exertion, the body tends to maintain its equilibrium by hastening its rate of repair and by falling asleep before the danger point is reached. It is almost impossible to impair permanently the tissue of the brain except in the presence of a chemical irritant. In case of infection we often have to give medicine to neutralize the effect of the poison or to resort to narcotics which make the brain cells less susceptible to irritation. But nervous insomnia is another story.

A HARMLESS HABIT

=Long-Lived Insomniacs.= A man of my acquaintance once said in all seriousness and with evident alarm: "I am following in the footsteps of my mother. She lived to be seventy years old and she had insomnia all her life." If this man had been preaching a sermon on the harmlessness of chronic insomnia, he could not have chosen a better text, but he seemed just as much concerned about himself as if his mother had died from the effects of three months' wakefulness. People can live healthy lives during twenty or thirty years of insomnia because chronic insomnia is nothing more or less than a habit, and "habit spells ease." The brain cells are not irritated by either internal or external stimuli; there is no effort to keep awake; virtually no energy is expended,--except in restless tossing and worry. If the body is kept still and emotion eliminated, fatigue products are washed away and the reserves are filled in with perfect ease.

=Thinking in Circles.= Habit means automatic, subconscious activity, with the least expenditure of energy and the least amount of fatigue. We have already noted the ease with which heart and diaphragm muscles carry on their work from the beginning of life to its end. Anything relegated to the subconscious mind can be kept up almost indefinitely without tire, and to this subconscious type of activity belong the thoughts of a chronic insomniac. Despite all assertions to the contrary, his conscious mind is not really awake. If he is questioned about the happenings of the night, he is likely to have been unaware of the most audible noises. The thoughts that run through his brain are not new, constructive, energy-consuming thoughts, but the same old thoughts that have been going around in circles for days and weeks at a time.

It is true that a person sometimes chooses to wake up and do his constructive planning in the night. This kind of thought does bring fatigue, up to a certain point. After that the body hastens its rate of repair or automatically goes to sleep. Activity of this kind is always a matter of choice. He who really prefers sleep will shut the drawers containing the day's business and leave them shut until morning.

=Day-Dreaming at Night.= However, the man who makes a practice of staying awake rarely does much real thinking. He lets the thoughts run through his mind as they will, builds air-castles of things he would like to do and can't, or other kinds of air-castles about the disastrous effects of his insomnia on the day that is to come; he worries over his health, or his finances, and grieves over his sorrows. He is really indulging himself, thinking the thoughts he likes most to think, and these consume but little energy. Like a horse that knows the rounds, they can go jogging on indefinitely without guidance from the driver.

WHAT CAUSES THE FATIGUE

=Tossing and Fretting.= The thing that tires is not the insomnia but the emotion over the insomnia. If people who fail to sleep are perpetually fagged out, it is not from loss of sleep, but from worry and tossing. Often they spend a good deal of the night feeling sorry for themselves. They turn and toss, exclaiming with each turn: "Why don't I sleep? How badly I shall feel to-morrow! What a night! What a night!" Such a spree of emotionalism can hardly fail to tire, but it is not fair to blame the insomnia.

He who makes up his mind to it can rest almost as well without sleep as with it, provided he keeps his mind calm and his body relaxed. "Decent hygienic conditions" demand not necessarily eight hours of sleep but eight hours of quiet rest in bed. Tossing about drives away sleep and uses up energy. I make it a rule that my patients shall not turn over more than four times during the night. This is more important than that they should sleep. To be sure, I do not stay awake to enforce the rule, but most people catch the idea very quickly and before they know it they are sleeping.

HOW TO GO TO SLEEP

=Ceasing to Care.= The best way to learn to sleep is not to care whether you do or not. Nothing could be better than DuBois's advice: "Don't look for sleep; it flies away like a pigeon when one pursues it."[58] Attention to anything keeps the mind awake, and most of all, attention to sleep. More than one person has waked up to see whether or not he was going to sleep. We cannot, however, fool ourselves by merely pretending indifference. The only sensible way is to get the facts firmly fixed in our minds so that we actually realize that we do not need more sleep than our bodies take. As soon as it is realized that insomnia is really of no importance, it tends to disappear.

[Footnote 58: DuBois: Psychic Treatment of Nervous Disorders, p. 339.]

=Catching the Idea.= There came one day for consultation a very healthy-looking woman, a deaconess of the Lutheran Church. "Doctor," she said, "I came to get relief from insomnia. For twenty years I have not slept more than one or two hours a night." "Why do you want more?" I asked. "Why, isn't it very unhealthy not to sleep?" she exclaimed in astonishment. "Evidently not," I answered.

This woman had tried every doctor she could think of, including the splendid S. Weir Mitchell. Her insomnia had become a preoccupation with her, her chief thought in life. All I did was to explain to her that her body had been getting all the sleep it needed, and that neither body nor mind was in the least run down after twenty years of sleeplessness. "When you cease being interested in your insomnia, it will go away, although from a health standpoint it matters very little whether it does or not." We had two conversations on the subject, and a week later she came back to tell me that she was sleeping eight hours a night.

One woman had had insomnia for thirty years. After I had explained to her that her body had adjusted itself to this way of living and that she need not try to get more sleep, she snored so loud all night and every night that the rest of the family began to complain!

A certain banker proved very quick at catching the idea. He had been so troubled with insomnia and intense weakness that his doctors prescribed a six-months voyage in Southern waters. Knowing that my prescriptions involved a change in point of view rather than in scene, he came to me. Although he had been getting only about half an hour's sleep a night, he went to sleep in his chair the first evening, and then went upstairs and slept all night. He resumed his duties at the bank, walking a mile and a half the first day and three miles the second. During the months following, he reported, "No more insomnia."

=Keeping Account.= A bright young college graduate came to me for a number of ailments, chief among them being sleeplessness. She was also overcome by fatigue, having spent four months in bed. A four-mile walk in the canyon and a few other such outings soon dispelled the fatigue, but the insomnia proved more obstinate. After she had been with me for a week or two, I took her aside one day for a little talk. "Well?" I said as we sat down. Then she began: "Sunday night I was awake from half-past one to four, Monday from twelve to one, Tuesday from one to three, Wednesday from two to four, Thursday--" By this time she became aware of the quizzical expression on my face and began to be embarrassed. Then she stopped and laughed. "Well," she said, "I did not know that I was paying so much attention to my sleep." She was bright enough to see the point at once, gave up her preoccupation in the all-absorbing topic and promptly forgot to have any trouble with so natural a function as sleep.

=Making New Associations.= Examples like this show how natural is childlike slumber when once we take away the inhibitions of a hampering idea. Age-old habits like sleep are not lost, but they may easily be interfered with by a little too much attention. When a person who can scarcely keep his eyes open all the evening is instantly wide awake as soon as his head touches the pillow, we may be sure that a part of his trouble comes from the wrong associations which he has built up with the thought of night. When a dear little old lady told me of her constant state of apprehension about going to bed, I said to her: "When I go to my room, the darkness says sleep. When I take off my clothes, the very act says sleep. When I put my head on the pillow, the pillow says sleep." She liked that and found herself able to sleep all night. The next evening she wanted another "sleeping-potion" but as I did not want her to become dependent on anybody's suggestion, I put my mouth up close to her ear and whispered, "Abra ca dabra, dum, dum, dum." She laughed, but saw the point. After that she slept very well. She merely broke the habit by making a new kind of association with the thought of bed. Nature did the rest.

It seems hardly necessary to remark that drug-taking is the most inefficient way of handling the situation. Everybody knows that narcotics are harmful to the delicate cells of the brain and that the dose has to be continuously increased in cases of chronic insomnia. If a person realizes that the drug is far more harmful than the insomnia itself, he is weak indeed to yield to temptation for the sake of a few nights of sleep. As the cause of insomnia is psychic, so the only logical cure is a new idea and a new attitude of mind.

THE PURPOSE OF INSOMNIA

Like all nervous symptoms, insomnia is not an affliction but an indulgence. Somehow, and in ways unknown to the conscious mind, it brings a certain amount of satisfaction to a part of the personality. No matter how unpleasant it may be, no matter how much we consciously fear it, something inside chooses to stay awake.

Started, as a rule, through suggestion or imitation, insomnia is sometimes kept up as a means of making ourselves seem important,--to ourselves and to others. It at least provides an excuse for thinking and talking about ourselves, and furnishes a certain feeling of distinction. If something within us craves attention, even staying awake may not be too dear a price to pay for that attention. Strange to say, there are other times when the insomnia is chosen by the primitive subconscious mind with the idea of doing penance for supposed sins whose evil effects might possibly be avoided by this kind of expiation. Analysis shows that motives like this are not so uncommon as might be supposed. In other cases insomnia is chosen for the chance it gives for phantasy-building. A person denied the right kind of outlet for his instincts may so enjoy the day-dreaming habit that he prolongs it into the night, really preferring it to sleep. Such a state of affairs is not at all incompatible with an intense conscious desire to sleep and a real fear of insomnia. So strange may be the motives hidden away within the depths of the most prosaic individual!

SUMMARY

Nervous insomnia is something which a part of us makes use of and another part fears. It is a mistake on both sides. Although not in the least dangerous, the habit can hardly be considered a satisfactory form of amusement. Nature has provided a better way to spend the night, a way to which she speedily brings us when we choose to let her do it.

We do not have to ask for sleep as for a special boon which may be denied. We simply have to lie down in trust, expecting to be carried away like a child. If our expectation is not at once realized we can still trust, as with relaxed mind and body we lie in calm content, knowing that Nature is, minute by minute, restoring us for another day.

CHAPTER XIV

In which we raise our thresholds FEELING OUR FEELINGS

FINELY STRUNG VIOLINS

The young girl had been telling me about her symptoms. "You know, Doctor," she said. "I am a very sensitive person. In fact, I have always been told that I am like a finely strung violin." There was pride in every tone of her voice,--pride and satisfaction over possessing an organization so superior to the common clay of the average person. It was a typical remark, and showed clearly that this girl belonged among the nervous folk. For the nervous person is not only over-sensitive, but he accepts his condition with a secret and half-conscious pride as a token of superiority.

It seems that there are a good many kinds of sensitiveness. Whether it is a good or bad possession depends entirely on what kind of things a person is sensitive to. If he is quick to take in a situation, easily impressed with the needs of others, open-doored to beauty and to the appeal of the spiritual, keenly alive to the humorous, even when the joke is on himself and the situation uncomfortable, then surely he has a right to be glad of his sensitiveness. But too often the word means something else. It means feeling, intensely, physical sensations of which most people are unaware, or reacting emotionally to situations which call for no such response. It means, in short, feeling our feelings and liking to feel them. There seems to be nothing particularly praiseworthy or desirable about this kind of sensitiveness. If this is what it means to be a "finely-wrought violin," it might even be better to be a bass drum which can stand a few poundings without ruin to its constitution.

"But," says the sensitive person, "are we not born either violins or drums? Is not heredity rather than choice to blame? And what can a person do about it?" These questions are so closely bound up with the problems of nervous symptoms of indigestion, fatigue, a woman's ills, hysterical pains and sensations, and with all the problems of emotional control, that we shall do well to look more carefully into this question of sensibility, which is really the question of the relation of the individual to his environment.

SELECTING OUR SENSATIONS

=Reaction and Over-Reaction.= Every organism, if it is to live, must be normally sensitive to its environment. It must possess the power of response to stimuli. As the sea-anemone curls up at touch, and as the tiny baby blinks at the light, so must every living thing be able to sense and to react to the presence of a dangerous or a friendly force. Only by a certain degree of irritability can it survive in the struggle for existence. The five senses are simply different phases of the apparatus for receiving communications from the outside world. Other parts of the machinery catch the manifold messages continually pouring into the brain from within our bodies themselves. These communications cannot be stopped nor can we prevent their impress on the cells of the brain and spinal cord, but we do have a good deal to say as to which ones shall be brought into the focus of attention and receive enough notice to become real, conscious sensations.

=Paying Attention.= If a human being had to give conscious attention to every stimulus from the outer world and from his own body, to every signal which flashes itself along his sensory nerves to his brain, he would need a different kind of mind from his present efficient but limited apparatus. As it is, there is an admirable provision for taking care of the messages without overburdening consciousness. The stream of messages never stops, not even in sleep. But the conscious mind has its private secretary, the subconscious, to receive the messages and to answer them.

During any five minutes of a walk down a city street a man has hundreds of visual images flashed upon the retina of the eye. His eye sees every little line in the faces of the passers-by, every detail of their clothing, the decorations on the buildings, the street signs overhead, the articles in the shop-windows, the paving of the sidewalks, the curbings and tracks which he crosses, and scores of other objects to most of which the man himself is oblivious. His ear hears every sound within hearing distance,--the honk of every horn, the clang of every bell, the voices of the people and the shuffle of feet. Some part of his mind feels the press of his foot on the pavement, the rubbing of his heel on his stocking, the touch of his clothing all over his body, and all those so-called kinesthetic sensations,--sensations of motion and balance which keep him in equilibrium and on the move, to say nothing of the never-ending stream of messages from every cell of every muscle and tissue of his body.

Out of this constant rush of stimuli our man gives attention to only the smallest fraction. Whatever is interesting to him, that he sees and hears and feels. All other sensations he passes by as indifferent. Unless they come with extraordinary intensity, they do not get over into his consciousness at all.

="Listening-in" on the Subconscious.= The subconscious mind knows and needs to know what is happening in the farthermost cell of the body. It needs to know at any moment where the knees are, and the feet; otherwise the individual would fall in a heap whenever he forgot to watch his step. It needs to know just how much light is entering the eye, and how much blood is in the stomach. To this end it has a system of communication from every point in the body and this system is in constant operation. Its messages never cease. But these messages were never meant to be in the focus of attention. They are meant only for the subconscious mind and are generally so low-toned as to be easily ignored unless one falls into the habit of listening for them. Unless they are invested with a significance which does not belong to them, they will not emerge into consciousness as real sensations.

=Psychic Thresholds.= Boris Sidis has given us a word which has proved very useful in this connection. The limit of sensitivity of a cell--the degree of irritability--he calls the stimulus-threshold.[59] As the wind must come in gusts to drive the rain in over a high doorsill, so must any stimulus--an idea or a sensation--come with sufficient force to get over the obstructions at the doorway of consciousness. These psychic thresholds do not maintain a constant level. They are raised or lowered at will by a hidden and automatic machinery, which is dependent entirely on the ideas already in consciousness, by the interest bestowed upon the newcomer. The intensity of the stimuli cannot be controlled, but the interest we feel in them and the welcome given them are very largely a matter of choice.

[Footnote 59: Sidis: Foundations of Normal and Abnormal Psychology, Chap. XXX.]

Each organism has a wide field of choice as to which ideas and which physical stimuli it shall welcome and which it shall shut out. We may raise our thresholds, build up a bulwark of indifference to a whole class of excitations, shut our mental doors, and pull down the shades; or we may lower the thresholds so that the slightest flicker of an idea or the smallest pin-prick of a sensation finds ready access to the center of attention.

=Thresholds and Character.= There are certain thresholds made to shift frequently and easily. When one is hungry any food tastes good, for the threshold is low; but the food must be most tempting to be acceptable just after a hearty meal. On the other hand, a fairly constant threshold is maintained for many different kinds of stimuli. These stimuli are always bound together in groups, and make appeal depending upon the predominating interest. As anything pertaining to agriculture is noticed by a farmer, or any article of dress by a fashionable woman, so any stimulus coming from a "warm" group is welcomed, while any from a "cold" group is met by a high threshold. The kind of person one is depends on what kind of things are "warm" to him and what kind are "cold." The superman is one who has gained such conscious control of his psychic thresholds that he can raise and lower them at will in the interests of the social good.

=Thresholds and Sensations.= The importance of these principles is obvious. The next chapter will show more of their influence on ideas and emotions; but for the present we will consider their lessons in the sphere of the physical. Psychology speaks here in no uncertain terms to physiology. Whoever becomes fascinated by the processes of his own body is bound to magnify the sensations from those processes, until the most insignificant message from the subconscious becomes a distressing and alarming symptom. The person whose mental ear is strained to catch every little creaking of his internal machinery can always hear some kind of rumble. If he deliberately lowers his thresholds to the whole class of stimuli pertaining to himself, there is small wonder that they sweep over the boundaries into consciousness with irresistible force.

=The Motives for Sensitiveness.= Sensitiveness is largely a matter of choice, but what determines choice? Why is it that one person chooses altruism as the master threshold that determines the level of all the others, while another person who ought to be equally fine lowers his thresholds only to himself? What makes a person too interested in his own sensations and feelings? As usual there is a cause.

The real cause back of most cases of chronic sensitiveness is an abnormal desire for attention. Sometimes this love of attention arises from an under-developed instinct of self-assertion, or "inferiority complex." If there is a sense of inadequacy, a feeling of not being so important as other people, a person is quite likely to over-compensate by making himself seem important to himself and to others in the only way he knows. All unconsciously he develops an extreme sensitiveness which somehow heightens his self-regard by making him believe himself finely and delicately organized, and by securing the notice of his associates.

Or, again, the love of attention may be simply a sign of arrested development, a fixation of the Narcissistic period of childhood which loves to look at itself and make the world look. Or there may be lack of satisfaction of the normal adult love-life, a lack of the love and attention which the love-instinct naturally craves. If this instinct is not getting normal outlet, either directly through personal relationships or indirectly through a sublimated activity, what is more natural than that it should turn in on itself, dissociate its interest in other things and occupy itself with its own feelings, and at the same time secure the coveted attention through physical disability, with its necessity for special ministration?

In any case there is likely to develop a general overreaction to all outside stimulation, a hypersensitiveness to some particular kind of stimulus, or a chronic hysterical pain which somehow serves the personality in ways unknown to itself. No one "feels his feelings" unless, despite all discomfort, he really enjoys them. A hard statement to accept perhaps, but one that is repeatedly proved by a specialist in "nerves"!

DETERMINING CAUSES

=Accidental Association.= In many cases, the form which the sensitiveness takes is merely a matter of accident. Often it is based on some small physical disability, as when a slight tendency to take cold is magnified into an intense fear of fresh air.

Sometimes a past fleeting pain which has become associated with the stream of thought of an emotional moment--what Boris Sidis calls the moment-consciousness--is perpetuated in consciousness in place of the repressed emotion. "In the determination of the pathology of hysteria, the accidental moment plays a much greater part than is generally recognized; if a painful affect--emotion--originates while eating but is repressed, it may produce nausea and vomiting and continue for months as an hysterical symptom."[60]

[Footnote 60: Freud: Selected Papers, p. 2.]

One of Freud's patients, Miss Rosalie H----, found while taking singing-lessons that she often choked over notes of the middle register, although she took with ease notes higher and lower in the scale. It was revealed that this girl, who had a most unhappy home life, had, during a former period, often experienced this choking sensation from a painful emotion just before she went for her music lesson. Some of the left-over sensations had remained during the singing, and as the middle notes happen to involve the same muscles as does a lump in one's throat, she had often found herself choking over these notes. Later on, while living in a different city and in a wholly different environment, the physical sensations from her throat muscles, as they took these middle notes, brought back the associated sensations of choking,--without, however, uncovering the buried emotion.[61] Many a painful hysterical affliction is based on just such mechanisms as these. As Freud remarks, "The hysteric suffers mostly from reminiscences."[62]

[Footnote 61: Ibid, p. 43.]

[Footnote 62: Ibid, p. 5.]

=Subconscious Symbolism.= Sometimes, as we have seen, the form which a hypersensitiveness assumes is not determined by any physical sensation, either past or symbolism which acts out in the body the drama of the soul.

=Facing the Facts.= Whatever the motives and whatever the determining causes, hypersensibility is in any case a feeling of feelings which is not warranted by the present situation. Hypersensitiveness is never anything but a makeshift kind of satisfaction. Despite certain subconscious reasoning, it does not make one more important nor more beloved. Neither does it furnish a real expression for that great creative love-instinct whose outlet, if it is to bring satisfaction, must be a real outlet into the external world. An understanding of the motives is helpful only when it makes clear that they are short-sighted motives and that the real desires back of them may be satisfied in better ways.

SOME LOWERED THRESHOLDS

As the public appetite for specific cases appears to be insatiable, we will give from real life some examples of low thresholds which were raised through re-education. One hesitates to write down these examples because when they are on paper they sound like advertisements of patent medicines. However, there is no magic in any of these cures, but only the working out of definite laws which may be used by other sufferers, if they only know. Re-education through a knowledge of oneself and the laws at work really does remarkable things when it has a chance.

="Danger-Signals" without the Danger.= There was the man who had queer feelings all over his body, especially in his head and stomach, and who considered these sensations as danger-signals warning him to stop. This man had worked up from messenger boy to a position next to the president in one of the transcontinental railroad systems. On the appearance of these "danger-signals" he had tried to resign but had been given a year's leave of absence instead. Half the year had gone in rest-cure, but he was still afraid to eat or work, and believed himself "done for." After three weeks of re-education he saw that instead of having overdrawn his capital, he had in another sense overdrawn his sensations. He went away as fit as ever, finished his leave of absence doing hard labor on his farm, and then went back to even harder tasks, working for the Government in the administration of the railroads during the war. He is still at work.

=Enjoying Poor Health.= There was the woman who had been an invalid for twenty years, doing little else during all that time than to feel her own feelings. Because of the distressing sensations in her stomach, she had for a year taken nothing but liquid nourishment. She had queer feelings in her solar-plexus and indeed a general luxury of over-feeling. She could not leave her room nor have any visitors. She was the star invalid of the family, waited on by her two hard-working sisters who earned the living for them all.

Her sisters had inveigled her to my house under false pretenses, calling it a boarding-house and omitting to mention that I was a doctor, because "she guessed she knew more about her case than any doctor." For the first week I got in only one sentence a day,--just before I slipped out of the door after taking in her "liquid nourishment." But at the end of the week I announced that thereafter her meals would be served in the dining-room. When she found that there was to be no more liquid nourishment, she had to appear at the family table. After that it was only a short time before she was at home, cooking for her sisters. When she saw the role she had been unconsciously playing, she could hardly wish to go on with it.

=Feeling His Legs.= Mr. R. suffered from such severe and distressing pains in his legs that he believed himself on the verge of paralysis. He was also bothered by a chronic emotional state which made him look like a "weepy" woman. His eyes were always full of tears and his chin a-quiver, and he had, as he said, a perpetual lump in his throat. Under re-education both lump and paralysis disappeared completely and Mr. R. took his wife across the continent, driving his machine with his own hands--and feet.

=A Subconscious Association.= Mr. D.'s case admirably illustrates the return of symptoms through an unconscious association. He was a lawyer, prominent in public affairs of the Middle West, who had been my patient for several weeks and who had gone home cured of many striking disabilities. Before he came to me, he had given up his public work and was believed by all his associates to be afflicted with softening of the brain, and "out of the game" for good. From being one of the ablest men of his State, he had fallen into such a condition that he could neither read a letter nor write one. He could not stand the least sunshine on his head, and to walk half a mile was an impossibility. He was completely "down and out" and expected to be an invalid for the rest of his life.

But these symptoms had one by one disappeared during his five-weeks stay with me. He had done good stiff work in the garden, carried a heavy sack of grapefruit a mile in the hot sun, and was generally his old self again. Now he was back in the harness, hard at work as of old. Suddenly, as he sat reading in his home one evening, all his old symptoms swept over him,--the pains in his head and legs, the pounding of the heart, the "all-gone" sensations as though he were going to die on the spot. He became almost completely dissociated, but through it all he clung to the idea which he had learned,--namely that this experience was not really physical as it seemed but was the result of some idea, and would pass. He did not tell any one of the attack, ignored it as much as possible, and waited. In a few minutes he was himself again. Then he looked for the cause and realized that the article he was reading was one he had read several months previous, when suffering most severely from the whole train of symptoms. When the familiar words had again gone into his mind, they had pressed the button for the whole physiological experience which had once before been associated with them. This is the same mechanism as that involved in Prince's case, Miss Beauchamp, who became completely dissociated at one time when a breeze swept across her face. When Dr. Prince looked for the cause, he found that once before she had experienced certain distressing emotions while a breeze was fanning her cheek. The recurrence of the physical stimulation had been sufficient to bring back in its entirety the former emotional complex.

=Another Kind of Association.= One of my women patients illustrates another kind of association-mechanism, based not on proximity in time but proximity of position in the body. This woman had complained for years of "bladder trouble" although no physical examination had been able to reveal any organic difficulty. She referred to a constant distress in the region of the bladder and was never without a certain red blanket which she wrapped around her every time she sat down. During psycho-analysis she recounted an experience of years before which she had never mentioned to anybody. During a professional consultation her physician, a married man, had suddenly seized her and exclaimed, "I love you! I love you!" In spite of herself, the woman felt a certain appeal, followed by a great sense of guilt. In the conflict between the physiological reflex and her moral repugnance, she had shunted out of consciousness the real sex-sensation and had replaced it with a sensation which had become associated in her subconscious mind with the original temptation. Since the nerves from the genital region and from the bladder connect with the same segment of the spinal cord, she had unconsciously chosen to mix her messages, and to cling to the substitute sensation without being in the least Conscious of the cause. As soon as she had described the scene to me and had discerned its connection with her symptoms, the bladder trouble disappeared.

=Afraid of the Cold.= Patients who are sensitive to cold are very numerous. Mr. G.--he of the prunes and bran biscuits--was so afraid of a draft that he could detect the air current if a window was opened a few inches anywhere in a two-story house. He always wore two suits of underwear, but despite his precautions he had a swollen red throat much of the time. His prescription was a cold bath every morning, a source of delight to the other men patients, who made him stay in the water while they counted five. He was required to dress and live like other folks and of course his sensitiveness and his sore throat disappeared.

Dr. B----, when he came to me, was the most wrapped-up man I had ever met. He had on two suits of underwear, a sweater, a vest and suit coat, an overcoat, a bear-skin coat and a Jaeger scarf--all in Pasadena in May!

Besides this fear of cold, he was suffering from a hypersensitiveness of several other varieties. So sensitive was his skin that he had his clothes all made several sizes too big for him so that they would not make pressure. He was so aware of the muscles of the neck that he believed himself unable to hold up his head, and either propped it with his hands or leaned it against the back of a chair.

He had been working on the eighth edition of his book, a scientific treatise of nation-wide importance, but his eyes were so sensitive that he could not possibly use them and had to keep them shaded from the glare. He was so conscious of the messages of fatigue that he was unable to walk at all, and he suffered from the usual trouble with constipation. All these symptoms of course belonged together and were the direct result of a wrong state of mind. When he had changed his mind, he took off his extra clothes, walked a mile and a half at the first try, gave up his constipation, and went back to work. Later on I had a letter from him saying that his favorite seat was an overturned nail-keg in the garden and that he was thinking of sawing the backs off his chairs.

Miss Y---- had worn cotton in her ears for a year or two because she had once had an inflammation of the middle ear, and believed the membrane still sensitive to cold. There was Miss E----, whose underwear always reached to her throat and wrists and who spent her time following the sun; and Dr. I----, who never forgot her heavy sweater or her shawl over her knees, even in front of the fire. The procession of "cold ones" is almost endless, but always they find that their sensitiveness is of their own making and that it disappears when they choose to ignore it.

=Fear of Light.= Fear of cold is no more common than fear of light. Nervous folk with half-shut eyes are very frequent indeed. From one woman I took at least seven pairs of dark glasses before she learned that her eye was made for light. A good example is furnished by a woman who was not a patient of mine at all, but merely the sister of a patient. After my patient had been cured of a number of distressing symptoms--pain in the spine, sore heels, a severe nervous cough, indigestion and other typical complaints,--she began to scheme to get her sister to come to me.

This sister, the wife of a minister in the Middle West, had a constant pain in her eyes, compelling her to hold them half-shut all the time. When she was approached about coming to me, she said indignantly, "If that doctor thinks that my trouble is nervous, she is much mistaken," and then proceeded to get well. Once the subconscious mind gets the idea that its game is recognized, it is very apt to give it up, and it can do this without loss of time if it really wants to.

=Pain at the Base of the Brain.= Of all nervous pains, that in the back of the neck is by all odds the most common. It is rare indeed to find a nervous patient without this complaint, and among supposedly well folk it is only too frequent. Indeed, it almost seems that in some quarters such a pain stands as a badge of the fervor and zeal of one's work.

But work is never responsible for this sense of discomfort. Only an over-sensitiveness to feelings or a false emotionalism can produce a pain of this kind, unless it should happen to be caused by some poison circulating in the blood. The trouble is not with the nerves or with the spine, despite the fad about misplaced vertebr? When a doctor examines a sensitive spine, marking the sore spots with a blue pencil, and a few minutes later repeats the process, he finds almost invariably that the spots have shifted. They are not true physical pains and they rarely remain long in the same place.

Pain in the spine and neck is an example of exaggerated sensibility or over-awareness. Since all messages from every part of trunk and limb must go through the spinal cord, and since very many of them enter the cord in the region of the neck and shoulder blades, it is only natural that an over-feeling of these messages should be especially noticed in this zone.

Sometimes a false emotionalism adds to the discomfort by tensing the whole muscular system and making the messages more intense. When a social worker or a business man gets tense over his work or ties himself into knots over a committee meeting, he not only foolishly wastes his energy but makes his nerves carry messages that are more urgent than usual. Then if he is on the look-out for sensations, he all the more easily becomes aware of the central station in the spine where the messages are received. By centering his attention on this station and tightening up his back-muscles, he increases this over-awareness and easily gets himself into the clutch of a vicious habit.

Sometimes a tenseness of the body is the result, not of a false attitude toward one's work, but of a lack of satisfaction in other directions. If the love-force is not getting what it wants, it may keep the body in a state of tension, with all the undesirable results of such tension. The person who keeps himself tense, whether because of his work or because of tension in other directions, has not really learned how to throw himself into his job and to forget himself, his emotions, and his body.

=Various Pains.= Tender spots may appear in almost any part of the body. There was the girl with the sore scalp, who was frequently so sensitive that she could not bear to have a single hair touched at its farthermost end, and who could not think of brushing her hair at such a time. There was the man whose wrists and ankles were so painful that the slightest touch was excruciating; the woman with the false sciatica; the man with the so-called appendicitis pains; and the man with the false neuritis, who always wore jersey coats several sizes too large. Each one of these false pains was removed by the process of re-education.

=Low Thresholds to Fatigue.= Mr. H. was habitually so overcome by fatigue that he could not make himself carry through the slightest piece of work, even when necessity demanded it. On Sunday night, when there was no one else to milk the cow, he had had to stop in the middle of the process and go into the house to lie down. To carry the milk was impossible, so low were his thresholds to the slightest message of fatigue. It turned out that things were not going right in the reproductive life. His threshold was low in this direction, and it carried down with it all other thresholds. After a general revaluation of values, he found himself able to keep his thresholds at the normal level.

A fine, efficient missionary from the Orient had been so overcome with fatigue that he was forced to give up all work and return to this country. He had been with me for a while and was again ready to go to work. He came one day with a radiant face to bid me good-by. "Why are you so joyous?" I asked. "Because," he answered, "before I came home I was so fatigued that it used me up completely just to see the native servants pack our luggage. Now we are taking back twice as much, and I not only packed it all myself but made the boxes with my own hands. No more fatigue for me!"

A charming young girl who in many ways was an inspiration to all her associates fell into the habit of over-feeling her fatigue. "You know, Doctor," she said, "that I give out too much of myself; everybody tells me so." That was just the trouble. Everybody had told her so, and the suggestion had worked. It did not take her long to learn that in scattering abroad she was enriching herself, and that her "giving out" was not exhausting to her but rather the truest kind of self-expression. It is only when a "giving out" is accompanied by a "looking in" that it can ever deplete. The "See how much I am giving," and "How tired I shall be," attitude could hardly fail to exhaust, but a real self-expression and the fulfilment of a real desire to give are never anything else than exhilarating. There is something wrong with the minister who is used up after his Sunday sermons. If his message and not himself is his real concern, he will have only a normal amount of fatigue, accompanied by a general sense of accomplishment and well-being, after he has fed his flock. To be sure, I have never been a minister, but I have had a goodly number among my patients and I speak from a fairly close acquaintance with their problems.

=Stopping Our Ears.= Roosters seem to be a perpetual source of annoyance to the folk whose thresholds are not under proper control. But as roosters seem to be necessary to an egg-eating nation, it seems simpler to change the threshold than to abolish the roosters. There was one woman who complained especially about being disturbed by early-morning Chanticleers. I explained that the crowing called for no action on her part, and that therefore she should not allow it to come into consciousness. "Do you mean," she said, "that I could keep from hearing them?" As it happened, she was sitting under the clock, which had just struck seven. "Did you hear the clock strike?" I asked. "No," she said; "did it strike?"

This poor little woman, who suffered from a very painful back and other distressing symptoms, had been married at sixteen to a rou?of forty; and, without experiencing any of the psychic feelings of sex, had been immediately plunged into the physical sex-relations. Since sex is psycho-physical and since any attempt to separate the two elements is both desecrating and unsatisfactory; it is not surprising that misery, and finally divorce, had been her portion. Another equally unpleasant experience had followed, and the poor woman in the strain and disappointment of her love-life, and in the lowering of the thresholds pertaining to this thwarted instinct, had unconsciously lowered the thresholds to all physical stimuli, until she was no longer master of herself in any line. When she saw the reason for her exaggerated reactions, she was able to gain control of herself, and to find outlet in other ways.

Too many persons fall into the way of being disturbed by noises which are no concern of theirs. As nurses learn to sleep through all sounds but the call of their own patients, so any one may learn to ignore all sounds but those which he needs to hear. Connection with the outside world can be severed by a mental attitude in much the same way as this is accomplished by the physical effect of an anaesthetic. Then the usual noises, those which the subconscious recognizes as without significance, will be without power to disturb. The well-known New York publisher who spent his last days on his private yacht, on which everything was rubber-heeled and velvet-cushioned, thought that he couldn't stand noises; but how much more fun he would have had, if some one had only told him about thresholds!

SUMMARY

There are two kinds of people in the world,--masters and puppets. There is the man in control of his thresholds, at leisure from himself and master of circumstance, free to use his energy in fruitful ways; and there is the over-sensitive soul, wondering where the barometer stands and whether people are going to be quiet, feeling his feelings and worrying because no one else feels them, forever wasting his energy in exaggerated reactions to normal situations.

This "ticklish" person is not better equipped than his neighbor, but more poorly equipped. True adjustment to the environment requires the faculty of putting out from consciousness all stimuli that do not require conscious attention. The nervous person is lacking in this faculty, but he usually fails to realize that this lack places him in the class of defectives. A paralyzed man is a cripple because he cannot run with the crowd; a nervous individual is a cripple, but only because he thinks that to run with the crowd lacks distinction. Something depends on the accident of birth, but far more depends on his own choice. Understanding, judicious neglect of symptoms, whole-souled absorption in other interests, and a good look in the mirror, are sure to put him back in the running with a wholesome delight in being once more "like folks."

CHAPTER XV

In which we learn discrimination CHOOSING OUR EMOTIONS

LIKING THE TASTE

It was a summer evening by the seaside, and a group of us were sitting on the porch, having a sort of heart-to-heart talk about psychology,--which means, of course, that we were talking about ourselves. One by one the different members of the family spoke out the questions that had been troubling them, or brought up their various problems of character or of health. At length a splendid Red Cross nurse who had won medals for distinguished service in the early days of the war, broke out with the question: "Doctor, how can I get rid of my terrible temper? Sometimes it is very bad, and always it has been one of the trials of my life." She spoke earnestly and sincerely, but this was my answer: "You like your temper. Something in you enjoys it, else you would give it up." Her face was a study in astonishment. "I don't like it," she stammered; "always after I have had an outburst of anger I am in the depths of remorse. Many a time I have cried my eyes out over this very thing." "And you like that, too," I answered. "You are having an emotional spree, indulging yourself first in one kind of emotion and then in another. If you really hated it as much as you say you do, you would never allow yourself the indulgence, much less speak of it afterward." Her astonishment was still further increased when several of the group said they, too, had sensed her satisfaction with her moods.

Hard as it is to believe, we do choose our emotions. We like emotion as we do salt in our food, and too often we choose it because something in us likes the savor, and not because it leads to the character or the conduct that we know to be good.

THE POWER OF CHOICE

Whether we believe it or not, and whether we like it or not, the fact remains that we ourselves decide which of all the possible emotions we shall choose, or we decide not to press the button for any emotion at all.

To a very large extent man, if he knows how and really wishes, may select the emotion which is suitable in that it leads to the right conduct, has a beneficial effect on the body, adapts him to his social environment, and makes him the kind of man he wants to be.

=The Test of Feeling.= The psychologist to-day has a sure test of character. He says in substance: "Tell me what you feel and I will tell you what you are. Tell me what things you love, what things you fear, and what makes you angry and I will describe with a fair degree of accuracy your character, your conduct, and a good deal about the state of your physical health."

Since this test of emotion is fundamentally sound, it is not surprising that the nervous man is in a state of distress. Indigestion, fatigue, over-sensibility, sound like problems in physiology, but we cannot go far in the discussion of any of them without coming face to face with the emotions as the real factors in the case. When we turn to the mental characteristics of nervous folk, we even more quickly find ourselves in the midst of an emotional disturbance. Worried, fearful, anxious, self-pitying, excitable, or melancholy, the nervous person proves that whatever else a neurosis may be, it is, in essence, a riot of the emotions.

There is small wonder that a riot at the heart of the empire should lead to insurrection in every province of the personality. It is only for the purpose of discussion that we can separate feeling from thinking and doing. Every thought and every act has in it something of all three elements. An emotion is not an isolated phenomenon; it is bound up on the one hand with ideas and on the other with bodily states and conduct. Whoever runs amuck in his emotions runs amuck in his whole being. The nervous invalid with his exhausted and sensitive body, his upset mind and irrational conduct is a living illustration of the central place of the emotions in the realm of the personality.

But it is not the nervous person only who needs a better understanding of his emotional life. The well man also gets angry for childish reasons; he is prejudiced and envious, unhappy and suspicious for the very same reason as is the nervous man. Since the working-capital of energy is limited to a definite amount, the control of the emotions becomes a central problem in any life,-- a deciding factor in the output and the outcome, as well as in comfort and happiness by the way.

Nothing is harder for the average man to believe than this fact that he really has the power to choose his emotions. He has been dissatisfied with himself in his past reactions, and yet he has not known how to change them. His anger or his depression has appeared so undesirable to his best judgment and to his conscious reason that it has seemed to be not a part of himself at all but an invasion from without which has swept over him without his consent and quite beyond control.

A HOUSE DIVIDED AGAINST ITSELF

Most of the confusion comes from the fact that we know only a part of ourselves. What we do not consciously enjoy we believe we do not enjoy at all. What we do not consciously choose we believe to be beyond our power of choice,--the work of the evil one, or the natural depravity of human nature, perhaps; but certainly not anything of our choosing.

The point is that a human being is so constituted that he can, without knowing it, entertain at the same time two diametrically opposite desires. The average person is not so unified as he believes, but is, in fact, "a house divided against itself."

The words of the apostle Paul express for most of us the truth about ourselves: "For what I would, that I do not; but what I hate that I do." What Paul calls the law of his members warring against the law of his mind is simply what we call to-day the instinctive desires coming into conflict with our conscious ideal.

=Hidden Desires.= Although we choose our emotions, we choose in many cases in response to a buried part of ourselves of which we are wholly unaware, or only half-aware. When we do not like what we have chosen, it is because the conscious part of us is out of harmony with another part and that part is doing the choosing. If the emotions which we choose are not those that the whole of us--or at least the conscious--would desire, it is because we are choosing in response to hidden desires, and giving satisfaction to cravings which we have not recognized. Repeated indulgence of such desires is responsible for the emotional habits which we are too likely to consider an inevitable part of our personality, inherited from ancestors who are not on hand to defend themselves. When we form the habit of being afraid of things that other people do not fear, or of being irritated or depressed, or of giving way to fits of temper, it is because these habit-reactions satisfy the inner cravings that in the circumstances can get satisfaction in no better way.

These hidden desires are of several different kinds, when squarely looked at. Some of the cravings are found to be childish, and so out of keeping with our real characters that we could not possibly hold on to them as conscious desires. Others turn out to be so natural and so inevitable that we wonder how we could ever have imagined that they ought to be repressed. Still others, legitimate in themselves, but denied because of outer circumstances, are found to be easily satisfied in indirect ways which bear no resemblance to their old unfortunate forms of outlet.

WHEN KNOWLEDGE HELPS

The way to get rid of an undesirable emotion is not by working at the emotion itself, but by realizing that this is merely an offshoot of a deeper root, hidden below the surface. The great point is to recognize this deeper root.

=Childish Anger.= It helps to know that uncalled-for anger is a defense reaction--a sort of camouflage or smoke cloud which we throw out to hide from ourselves and others the fact that we are being worsted in an argument, or being shown up in an undesirable light. Better than any amount of weeping over a hot temper is an understanding of the fact that when we fly into unseemly rage we are usually giving indulgence to a childhood desire to run away from unpleasant facts and to cover up our own faults.

=Enjoying the Blues.= It helps to know that the easiest way to fight the blues is by realizing that they are a deliberate, if unconscious, attempt to gain the pity of ourselves and others. There seems to be in undeveloped human nature something that really enjoys being pitied, and if we cannot get the commiseration of other people, we can, without much trouble, work up a case of self-pity. Most of us would have to acknowledge that we seldom find tears in our eyes except when our own woes are under consideration. "Whatever else the blues accomplish, they certainly afford us a chance to submerge ourselves in a sea of self-engrossment."[63]

[Footnote 63: Putnam: Human Motives.]

=The Chip on the Shoulder.= It helps to know that irritability and over-sensitiveness are usually the result of tension from unsatisfied desires which must find some kind of outlet. If a person is secretly restive under the fact that he cannot have the kind of clothes he wants, cannot shine in society, or secure a college education or a large fortune,--all of which minister to our insistent and rarely satisfied instinct of self-assertion,--or if he is secretly yearning for the satisfaction of the marriage relation, or for the sense of completion in parenthood; then the tension from these unsatisfied desires shows itself in a hundred little everyday instances of lack of self-control. These mystify him and his friends, but they are understandable when the whole truth is known.

=Anxiety and Fear.= Nowhere is understanding more valuable than when we approach the subject of anxiety and fear. Whenever a person falls into a state of abnormal fear, his friends and his physician spend a good deal of time in attempting to prove to him that there is no cause for apprehension, and in exhorting him to use his reason and give up his fear. But how can a person help himself when he is fighting in the dark? How can he free himself when the thing he thinks he fears is merely a symbol of what he really fears? The woman who was afraid she would choke her child had been several months in the hands of Christian Scientists, and had earnestly tried to replace fear with courage. But in the circumstances, and without further knowledge, this was as impossible as it is for a man to lift himself by his own boot-straps. She had no point of contact with her real fear, as the man has no leverage contact with the earth from which he wishes to lift himself.

To be sure there are many cases in which an assumed cheerfulness and courage do have a mighty effect on the inner man. The forces of the personality are not set, but plastic, and are constantly acting and interacting upon one another. Surface habits do influence the forces below the surface. William James's advice, "Square your shoulders, speak in a major key, smile, and turn a compliment," is good for most occasions, but sometimes even a little understanding of the cause is far more effective.

It helps to know that persistent anxiety, lacking obvious cause, is found to be the anxiety of the thwarted instinct of reproduction. When the sex-instinct is repeatedly stimulated and then checked it sets in motion some of the same glands that are activated in fear. What comes up into consciousness is therefore very naturally a fear or dread of impending disaster, very like the poignant anxiety that one feels when stepping up in the dark to a step that is not there.

Simultaneous with the fear lest these repressed desires should not be satisfied, there is an intense fear lest they should. The more insistent the repressed desire, and the more it seems likely to break through into consciousness, the keener the anguish of the ethical impulses. Abnormal fear, however it may seem to be externalized, always implies at the bottom a fear of something within. There is no truth which is harder to believe on first hearing but which grows more compelling with further knowledge, than this truth that an exaggerated fear always implies a desire which somehow offends the total personality. When we observe the various distressing phobias, such as the common fear of contamination, a woman's fear to undress at night, a fear that the gas was not turned off, or that one's clothing is out of order; fear lest the exact truth has not been told, or that the uttermost farthing of one's obligations has not been met,--then we may know that there is something in the fear situation which either directly or symbolically refers to some hidden desire; a desire which the individual would not for the world acknowledge to himself, but which is too keen to be altogether repressed.

The close connection between fear and desire is often shown in the unfounded fear of having committed a crime. Both doctors and lawyers in their professional work occasionally come upon individuals who believe that they have committed some heinous crime of which they are really innocent, and who insist upon their guilt despite all evidence to the contrary. A quiet, gentle youth who at the age of twenty was under my medical care, is still not sure in his own whether he, at twelve years of age, was the burglar who broke into the village store and killed the owner. It is difficult for the normally self-satisfied individual to understand the appeal of heroics to a person whose starved instinct of self-assertion makes him choose to be known as a villain rather than not to be known at all.

=Breaking the Spell.= When once we bring up into consciousness these hidden desires that manifest themselves in such troublesome ways, we find that we have robbed them of much of their power over our lives. Sometimes, it is true, a detailed and thorough exploration by psycho-analysis is necessary, but in many cases it is sufficient just to know that there are underlying causes. To know these things is far from excusing ourselves because of them. Even though emotions are determined by forces that are deep in the subconscious, we may still choose in opposition to those forces, if we but know that we can do so. The fact that some of the roots of our bad habits reach down into the subconscious is no excuse for not digging them up. As Dr. Putnam says, "It is the whole of us that acts, and we are as responsible for the supervision of the unseen as for the obvious factors that are at work. The moon may be only half illumined and half visible, but the invisible half goes on, none the less, exerting its full share of influence on the motion of the tides and earth."[64]

[Footnote 64: Putnam: _Freud's Psychoanalytic Method and Its Evolution_, p. 34.]

THE HIGHEST KIND OF CHOICE

There is no easier way to enliven any conversation than by dropping the remark that a human being always does what he wants to do. Simple as the statement seems, it is quite enough to quicken the dullest table-talk and loosen the most reticent tongue.

"I don't do what I want to do," says the college student. "I want to play tennis every afternoon; but what I do is to sit in a stuffy room and study."

"I don't do what I want to do," says the mother of a family. "At night I want to sit down and read the latest magazine, but what I do is to darn stockings by the hour."

Nevertheless we shall see that, even in cases like these, each of us is acting in accordance with his strongest desire. There may be--there often is--a bitter conflict, but in the end the desire that is really stronger always conquers and works itself out into action.

It is possible to imagine a situation in which a man would be physically unable to do what he wanted to do. Bound by physical cords, held by prison walls, or weakened by illness, he might be actually unable to carry out his desires. But apart from physical restraint, it is hard to imagine a situation in real life in which a person does not actually do what he wants to do; that is, what in the circumstances he wants to do. This is simply saying in another way that we act in accordance with the emotion which is at the moment strongest.

=Will Is Choice.= Just here we can imagine an earnest protest: "But why do you ignore the human will? Why do you try to make man the creature of feeling? A high-grade man does--not what he wants to do but what he thinks he ought to do. In any person worthy of the adjective 'civilized' it is conscience, not desire, which is the motive power of his life."

It is true: in the better kind of man the will is of central importance; but what is "will"? Let us imagine a raw soldier in the trenches just before a charge into No-Man's Land. He is afraid, but the word of command comes, and instantly he is a new creature. His fear drops away and, energized by the lust of battle, he rushes forward, obviously driven by the stronger emotion. He goes ahead because he really wants to, and we say that he does not have to use his will.

Imagine another soldier in the same situation; with him fear seems uppermost. His knees shake and his legs want to carry him in the wrong direction, but he still goes forward. And he goes forward, not so much because there is no other possibility as because, in the circumstances, he really wants to. All his life, and especially during his military training, he has been filled with ideals of loyalty and courage. More than he fears the guns of the enemy or of his firing-squad does he fear the loss of his own self-respect and the respect of his comrades. Greater than his "will to live" is his desire to play the man. There is conflict, and the desire which seems at the moment weaker is given the victory because it is reinforced by that other permanent desire to be a worthy man, brave, and dependable in a crisis. He goes forward, because in the circumstances, he really wants to, but in this case we say that he had to use his will.

Is it not apparent that will itself is choice,--the selection by the whole personality of the emotion and the action which best fit into its ideals? Will is choice by the part of us which has ideals. McDougall points out that will is the reinforcement of the weaker desire by the master desire to be a certain kind of a character.[65]

[Footnote 65: "The essential mark of volition is that the personality as a whole, or the central feature or nucleus of the personality, the man himself, is thrown upon the side of the weaker motive."--McDougall: Introduction to Social Psychology, p. 240.]

Each human being as he goes through life acquires a number of moral ideals and sentiments which he adopts as his own. They become linked with the instinct of self-assertion, which henceforth acts as the motive power behind them, and attempts to drive from the field any emotion which happens to conflict.

Men, like the lower animals, are ruled by desire, but, as G.A. Coe says, "Men mold themselves. They form desires not merely to have this or that object, but to be this or that kind of a man."[66]

[Footnote 66: Coe: Psychology of Religion.]

If a man be worthy of the name, he is not swayed by the emotion which happens for the moment to be strongest. He has the power to reinforce and make dominant those impulses which fit into the ideal he has built for himself. In other words, he has the power to choose between his desires, and this power depends largely upon the ideals which he has incorporated into his life by the complexes and sentiments which compose his personality.

Ideas and Ideals. If emotion is the heart of humanity, ideas are its head. In our emphasis on emotion, we must not forget that as emotion controls action, so ideas control emotion. But ideas, of themselves, are not enough. Everybody has seen weaklings who were full of pious platitudes. Ideas do control life, but only when linked up with some strong emotion. No moral sentiment is strong enough to withstand an intense instinctive desire. If ideas are to be dynamic factors in a life, they must become ideals and be really desired. They must be backed up by the impulse of self-assertion, incorporated with the sentiment of self-regard, and so made a permanent part of the central personality.

Parents and teachers who try to "break a child's will" and to punish every evidence of independence and self-assertion little know that they are undermining the foundations of morality itself, and doing their utmost to leave the child at the mercy of his chance whims and emotions. There can be no strength of character without self-regard, and self-regard is built on the instinctive desire of self-assertion.

=Education and Religion.= It is easy to see how important education is in this process of giving the right content to the self-regarding sentiment. The child trained to regard "temper" as a disgrace, self-pity as a vice, over-sensitiveness as a sign of selfishness, and all forms of exaggerated emotionalism as a token of weakness, has acquired a powerful weapon against temptation in later life. Indulgence in any of these forms of gratification he will regard as unworthy and out of keeping with his personality.

It is easy, too, to see how central a place a vital religious faith has in enriching and ennobling the ego-ideal, and in giving it driving-power. A force which makes a high ideal seem both imperative and possible of achievement could hardly fail to be a deciding factor. Every student of human nature knows in how many countless lives the Christian religion has made all the difference between mere good intentions and the power to realize those intentions; how many times it has furnished the motive power which nothing else seemed able to supply. Moral sentiments which have been merely sentiments become, through the magic of a new faith, incorporated into conscience and endowed with new power.

Just here lies the value of any great love, or any intense devotion to a cause. As Royce says: "To have a conscience, then, is to have a cause; to unify your life by means of an ideal determined by this cause, and to compare this ideal and the life."[67]

[Footnote 67: Royce: Philosophy of Loyalty, p. 175.]

=Avoiding the Strain.= It seems that a human being is to a large extent controlled by will, and that will is in itself the highest kind of choice. But too often will is crippled because it does not speak for the whole personality. Knowledge helps a person to relate conscience with hitherto hidden parts of himself, to assert his will, and to choose only those emotions and outlets which the connected-up, the unified personality wants. Sometimes, indeed, a little knowledge makes the exercise of the will power unnecessary. Using will power is, after all, likely to be a strenuous business. It implies the presence of conflict, and the strain of defeating the desire which has to be denied.[68] Why struggle to subdue emotional bad habits when a little insight dispels the desire back of them, and makes them melt away as if by magic? For example, why use our will to keep down fear or anger when a little understanding dissipates these emotions without effort?

[Footnote 68: Freud: Introduction to Psychoanalysis, p. 42.]

Whatever we do with difficulty we are not doing well. When it requires effort to do our duty this means that a great part of us does not want to do it. When we get rid of our hidden resistances we work with ease. As a strong wind, applied in the right way, drives the ship without effort, just so the forces in our lives, if they are adjusted to one another, will without strain or stress easily and naturally work together to carry us in the direction we have chosen. When we get rid of blind conflicts, even the business of ruling our spirits becomes feasible.

SUMMARY

=Various "Sprees."= The human animal has a constitutional dislike for dullness and will seize upon almost any device which promises to lift him out of what he considers the monotony of daily grind. An elaborate essay might be written on the means which human beings have taken to create the sense of aliveness which they so much crave. Some of them--we call them savages-- have found satisfactory certain wild orgies in primitive war-dances; others-- we shall soon call them "out of date"--have found simpler a bottle of whisky or a glass of champagne; still others find a cold shower more invigorating, or a brisk walk or a good stiff job which sets them aglow with the sense of accomplishment. But there are always those who, for one reason or another, find most satisfactory of all a chronic emotional tippling, or a good old-fashioned emotional spree. Persons who would be shocked at the idea of whisky or champagne allow themselves this other kind of indulgence without in the least knowing why.

Nor is the connection between alcoholism and emotionalism so far-fetched as it seems. Psycho-analytic investigations have repeatedly revealed the fact that both are indulged in because they remove inhibitions, give vent to repressed desires, and bring a sense of life and power which has somehow been lost in the normal living. Both kinds of spree are followed by the inevitable "morning after" with its proverbial headache, remorse, and vows of repentance but despite all this, both are clung to because the satisfaction they bring is too deep to be easily relinquished.

Whenever an emotion quite out of keeping with conscious desire is allowed to become habitual, we may know that it is being chosen by a part of the personality which needs to be uncovered and squarely faced. Nervous symptoms and exaggerated emotionalism are alike evidence of the fact that the wrong part of us is doing the choosing and that the will needs to be enlightened on what is taking place in the outer edge of its domain. In the choice between emotionalism and equanimity, the selection of the former can only be in response to unrecognized desire.

A nervous person is invariably an emotional person, and as a rule lays the blame for his condition upon past experiences. But experience is what happens to us plus the way we take it. We cannot always ward off the blow, but we can decide upon our reaction. "Even if the conduct of others has been the cause of our emotion, it is really we ourselves who have created it by the way in which we have reacted."[69]

[Footnote 69: DuBois: Psychic Treatment of Nervous Disorders, p. 155.]

One ship drives east, another drives west, While the self-same breezes blow; 'Tis the set of the sail, and not the gale That bids them where to go. Like the winds of the sea are the ways of fate, As we journey along through life; 'Tis the set of the soul that decides the goal, And not the calm or the strife. REBECCA R. WILLIAMS.

CHAPTER XVI

In which we find new use for our steam FINDING VENT IN SUBLIMATION

THE RE-DIRECTION OF ENERGY

A child pent up on a rainy day is a troublesome child. His energy keeps piling up, but there is no opportunity for him to expend it. The nervous person is just such a pent-up child. A portion of his personality is developing steam which goes astray in its search for vent; this portion is found to be the psychic side of his sex-life. Something has blocked the satisfactory achievement of instinctive ends and turned his interest in on himself.

Perhaps he does not come into complete psychic satisfaction of his love-life because his wife is out of sympathy or is held back by her own childish repressions. Perhaps his love-instinct is baffled by finding itself thwarted in its purpose of creating children, restrained by the social ban and the desire for a luxurious standard of living. Perhaps he is jealous of his chief, or of an older relative whose business stride he cannot equal.

Jung has pointed out how frequently introversion or turning in of the life-force is brought about by the painfulness of present reality and by the lack of the power of adaptation to things as they are. But this lack always has its roots in childhood. The woman who is shocked at the thought of sex is the little girl who reacted too strongly to early impressions. The man of forty who is disgruntled because he is not made manager of a business created by others is the little boy who was jealous of his father and wanted to usurp his place of power. The man who suffers from a sense of inferiority because his friend has a handsomer or more intellectual wife is the same little boy who strove with his father for possession of the mother, the most desired object in his childish environment. The measure of escape from these childish attitudes means the measure of success in life.

Fortunately for society, the average person achieves this success. The normal person in his childhood learned how to switch the energy of his primitive desires into channels approved by society. Stored away in his subconscious, this acquired faculty carries him without conscious effort through all the necessary adjustments in maturity. The nervous person, less well equipped in childhood, may fortunately acquire the faculty in all its completeness, although at the cost of genuine effort and patient self-study.

=Sublimation the Key Word.= In the prevention and in the cure of nervous disorders there is one factor of central importance, and that factor is sublimation--or the freeing of sex-energy for socially useful, non-sexual ends. To sublimate is to find vent for oneself and to serve society as well; for sublimation opens up new channels for pent-up energy, utilizing all the surplus of the sex-instinct in substitute activities. When the dynamic of this impulse is turned outward, not inward, it proves to be one of man's greatest possessions, a valuable contribution of energy to creative activities and personal relationships of every kind.

=The Failure to Sublimate.= A neurosis is nonconstructive use of one's surplus steam. The trouble with a nervous person is that his love-force is turned in on himself instead of out into the world of reality. This is what his friends mean when they say that he is self-absorbed; and this is what the psychologists mean when they say that a neurotic is introverted. A person, in so far as he is nervous, does not see other people at all--that is, he does not see them as real persons, but only as auditors who may be made to listen to the tale of his woes. His own problems loom so large that he becomes especially afflicted with what Cabot calls "the sin of impersonality"; or to use President King's words, he lacks that "reverence for personality" which enables one to see people vividly as real persons and not as street-car conductors or servants or merely as members of one's family. To be sure, many a so-called normal individual is afflicted with this same kind of blindness; here as elsewhere the neurotic simply exaggerates. Engrossed in his own mental conflicts and physical symptoms, he is likely to find his interest withdrawing more and more from other people and centering upon himself.

=Sublimation and Religion.= We do not need psychology to tell us that engrossment in self is a disastrous condition. When the psycho-analyst says that the life-force must be turned out, not in, he is approaching from a new angle the truth as it is found in the gospel,--"Thou shalt love the Lord thy God with all thy heart," and "thy neighbor as thyself." Religion provides the love-object in the Creator; altruism provides it in the "neighbor." Christianity and psychology agree that as soon as love ceases to be an outgoing force, just so soon does the individual become an incomplete and disrupted personality.[70]

[Footnote 70: For emphasis on religion as a means to sublimation, see Freud, Putnam, Pfister, James, and DuBois.]

=Carlyle's Doctrine of Work.= "Produce! produce! produce!" Life for a social being involves not only rich personal relationships, but absorbing, creative work. No nervous person is cured until he is willing to take and to keep a "man-size job." A good piece of work is not only the sign of a cure; it is the final step without which no cure is complete.

=Along Nature's Lines.= If the psychologist is asked what kind of task this is to be, he answers that each person must decide for himself his own life-work. An individual may not know why, but he does know that there are certain things which he most likes to do. Sublimation is more readily accomplished if his energy is directed toward self-chosen interests. Parents or teachers or physicians who try to force another person into any definite plan of action are making a grievous blunder. Help may be given toward self-knowledge and the understanding of general principles, but advice should never be specific.

Taken in the large, it is found that men and women choose different ways of sublimation. Man and woman differ in the psychic components of the sex-life even as they differ in the physical. Sublimation to be successful must follow the lines laid down by nature. The urge of the average man is toward construction, domination, mastery. The urge of the average woman is toward mothering, protection, nurture. The masculine characteristics find ready sublimation in a career; the man builds bridges, digs canals, harnesses mountain streams, conquers pests, overcomes gravity, brings the ends of the earth together by "wireless" or by rail; he provides for the weak and the helpless--his own progeny--or, incarnated in the body of a Hoover, he gives life to the children of the world.

In woman, the dominant force is the nurturing instinct. Child and man of her own come first, but when these are lacking, to paraphrase Kipling, in default of closer ties, she is wedded to convictions; Heaven help him who denies! Only as a career opens up full vent for this nurturing instinct, will it provide satisfactory substitute in sublimation. Its natural trend can be seen in the recent tidal wave of social legislation--for prohibition, child-labor laws, sanitation, recognition and control of venereal disease, acknowledgment of paternity to the illegitimate child.

Since the women of the day, in numbers up to the million, have been compelled to sacrifice both man and unformed babe to the grim Juggernaut of war, this nurturing urge may press hard against many of the social and business barriers now impeding its flow. But if society understands and readjusts these barriers, making it possible for its citizens--women as well as men--to approximate the natural instinctive bent, it will not only save itself much unrest but will also go far toward preventing the spread of nervous invalidism.

SUMMARY

That which a nervous invalid most needs is a redirection of energy. Since, in spite of appearances, there is never any real lack of energy, no time is needed for the making of strength, and a cure can take place just as soon as the inner forces allow the energy to flow out in the right direction. Sometimes, indeed, an outer change may start the inner process. Often the "work cure" does cure; occasionally the sudden necessity to earn one's living or to mother a little child frees the life-force from its old preoccupation and forces it into other channels. In most cases, however, the nervous invalid is suffering not from lack of opportunities for outside interest but from an inner inability to meet the opportunities which present themselves. The great change that has to be made is not in external conditions and habits but in the hidden corners of the mind; a change that can be accomplished only by self-knowledge and re-education.

But if self-knowledge is the first step in any cure, so self-giving must be the final step. Sooner or later in the life of every nervous invalid there comes a time when nothing will serve to unify his disorganized forces but steady and unswerving responsibility for a good stiff piece of work. Happy for him that this is so and that he is living in a day when science no longer tells him to fold his hands and wait.

GLOSSARY

Autonomic nervous system: The vegetative nervous system which controls vital functions,--as digestion, respiration, circulation.

Censor: A hypothetical faculty of the fore-conscious mind which resists the emergence into consciousness of questionable desires.

Common path: In physiology, the final route over which response is made to physical stimulation; similarly in psychology, the one outlet for the finally dominant impulse.

Compensation: Exaggerated manifestation of one character-trend as a defense against its opposite which is painfully repressed; relief in substitute symptom formation.

Complex: A group of ideas held together by emotion (usually referring to a group which is wholly or in part unconscious).

Compulsion: A persistent compelling impulse to perform some seemingly unreasonable (but really substitute or symbolic) act, or to hold some irrational fear or idea; an emotional force which has been separated from the original idea.

Conflict: (Special) Struggle between instincts (unconscious).

Conversion: (Special) The process by which a repressed mental complex expresses itself through a physical symptom.

Displacement: 1. Transposition of an emotion from its original idea to one more acceptable to the personality. 2. The shifting of emphasis, in dreams, from essential to less significant elements.

Dissociation: 1. The state of being shut out from taking active part (applied to a group of ideas), as in normal forgetfulness. 2. (Abnormal) An exaggerated degree of separation of groups of ideas, with loss to the personality of the forces or memories which these groups contain, as in double personality.

Fixation: Establishment in childhood of over-strong habit-reactions.

Free Association: A device for uncovering buried complexes by letting the mind wander without conscious direction.

Homo-sexual: The quality of being more attracted by an individual of the same sex (abnormal) than by one of the opposite sex (hetero-sexual, normal).

Hysteria: That form of functional nervous disorder which manifests itself in physical symptoms; an attempt to dramatize unconscious repressed desires.

Inhibition: Restraint (Special) limitation of function, physical or ideational, due to unconscious emotional attitudes.

Libido: Life-force, 閘 an vital, or (restricted) the energy of the sex-instinct.

Neurosis: Used loosely for psycho-neurosis or nervous disorder.

Obsession: A compulsive idea inaccessible to reason.

Oedipus Complex: Over-strong bond between mother and son, or (more loosely) between father and daughter.

Over-determined: Used of an impulse made over-strong by lack of discharge, with accumulation of emotional tension from added factors.

Phobia: A persistent, unreasoning fear of some object or situation.

Psycho-neurosis: "A perversion of normal (psychic) reactions," (Prince); a general term for functional dissociation of the personality, resulting in: psychasthenia--disturbed ideation; neurasthenia--disturbed emotions; hysteria--disturbed motor or sensory activity.

Psychotherapy: Treatment by psychic or mental measures.

Rationalization: The process of substituting a plausible, false explanation for a repressed, unconscious desire.

Repression: Expulsion from consciousness of a pain-provoking mental process.

Resistance: The force which impedes the return of a repressed complex to consciousness.

Subconscious: That part of the mind of which one is unaware; the storehouse of memories ancestral and personal.

Sublimation: The act of freeing sex-energy from definitely sexual aims; utilization of sex-energy for nonsexual ends.

Suggestion: The process by which any idea, true or false, takes hold of one; the idea may enter the mind consciously or unconsciously, through reason or through impulse.

Symbol: An object or an attitude which stands for an ides or a quality; (Special) that which stands for or represents some unconscious mental process.

Threshold (door-sill): A figure which represents the level of the barrier erected by the mind against the perception of an idea or sensation.

Transference: Unconscious identification of a present personal relationship with an earlier one, with conveyance of the earlier emotional attitudes (hostile or affectionate) to the present relationship.

BIBLIOGRAPHY

BOOKS ON THE GENERAL LAWS OF BODY AND MIND

Cannon, Walter B: Bodily Changes in Pain, Hunger, Fear and Rage.

Crile, George W.: The Origin and Nature of the Emotions.

Coe, George Albert: The Psychology of Religion.

Hudson, Thomas Jay: The Law of Psychic Phenomena.

Janet, Pierre: The Major Symptoms of Hysteria; The Mental State of Hystericals.

James, William: Psychology; Talks to Teachers on Psychology; Varieties of Religious Experience.

Jastrow, Joseph: The Subconscious.

Kempf, Edward J.: The Tonus of Autonomic Segments in Psychopathology.

Long, Constance: Psychology of Fantasy.

McDougall, William: Social Psychology.

Mosher, Clelia Duel: Health and the Woman Movement.

Phillips, D. E.: Elementary Psychology.

Prince, Morton: The Unconscious; The Dissociation of a Personality; My Life as a Dissociated Personality.

Sherrington, Charles L.: The Integrative Action of the Nervous System.

Sidis, Boris: The Foundations of Normal and Abnormal Psychology; Psychopathological Researches.

Tansley, A. G.: The New Psychology.

Thomson, William Hanna: Brain and Personality.

White, William A.: Principles of Mental Hygiene; The Mental Hygiene of

Childhood.

Proceedings of the International Conference of Women Physicians. (National Board, Y.W.C.A., 600 Lexington Avenue, New York City.)

BOOKS ON MENTAL HYGIENE

Brown, Charles R.: Faith and Health.

Bruce, H. Addington: Scientific Mental Healing.

Cabot, Richard: What Men Live By; Social Service and the Art of Healing.

DuBois, Paul: The Psychic Treatment of Nervous Disorders.

Huckel, Oliver: Mental Medicine.

James, William: Vital Reserves.

Prince, Morton, and others: Psychotherapeutics.

Sadler, William S.: The Physiology of Faith and Fear.

Worcester, Elwood } McComb, Samuel } Religion and Medicine. Coriat, Isador H. }

BOOKS ON PSYCHO-ANALYSIS

Brill, A. A.: Fundamentals of Psychoanalysis.

Emerson, L. E.: Nervousness.

Freud, Sigmund: The Interpretation of Dreams; The Psychopathology of Everyday Life; Wit and the Unconscious; Selected Papers and Sexual Theory; A General Introduction to Psychoanalysis.

Frink, H. W.: Morbid Fears and Compulsions.

Hitschmann, E.: Freud's Theories of the Neuroses.

Holt, E. B.: The Freudian Wish.

Jung, Carl G.: The Psychology of the Unconscious; Analytical Psychology.

Jones, Ernest: Psycho-analysis; Treatment of the Neuroses, Including Psychoneuroses--in Modern Treatment of Nervous and Mental Diseases--White and Jelliffe.

Pfister, Oskar: The Psychoanalytic Method.

Putnam, James Jackson: Addresses on Psychoanalysis--Human Motives.

Tridon, Andr? Psychoanalysis.

White, William A.: The Mechanisms of Character Formation.

JOURNALS DEVOTED TO THE SUBJECT OF NERVOUS DISORDERS

Journal of Abnormal Psychology, published in Boston.

Psychoanalytic Review, published in Washington, D.C.

International Journal of Psychoanalysis, published in London.